Taste and See
that the Lord is good
~ Psalm 34:8

40th Anniversary

A Collection of Recipes by
Lord of Love Lutheran Church
10405 Fort St.
Omaha, NE 68104
www.lord-of-love.org

Printed in the U.S.A. by

MORRIS PRESS
COOKBOOKS
P.O. Box 2110 • Kearney, NE 68848
800-445-6621 • www.morriscookbooks.com

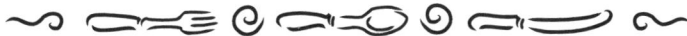

Lord of Love Lutheran Church

Celebrating 40 Years of Ministry!

At the 1970 annual meeting of Our Savior's Lutheran Church, Omaha, Nebraska, the congregation voted to establish a mission church at a new location at 104th and Fort Street.

The ground-breaking ceremony took place on August 23, 1971 for a church yet without a name. The Luther League youth suggested "Lord of Love" from the popular Christian song *Pass it On*. The first worship service of Lord of Love Lutheran Church occurred at the new location on June 11, 1972.

Since that time numerous pastors, staff, members, and volunteers have contributed to the ministry and mission of Lord of Love.

With a heart for mission and service, a love of worship and music, we also engage in a weekly meal at the Lord's table. We hear the words of invitation, "Taste and See that the Lord is Good" inviting us to participate in the meal that unites us as Christian people in thankfulness for what God has done for us.

Throughout the year, Lord of Love also invites members and friends to share in potluck meals and times of fellowship. This cookbook contains recipes for many of the wonderful meals that have graced the tables of the Fellowship Hall and those around our family table. We are blessed by the hands that prepare the food and the people who share it. They now share their recipes with us.

May the meals prepared from this cookbook provide memorable opportunities of fellowship for your family and friends as you "Taste and See that the Lord is Good."

Peace, Pastor Brad E. Meyer

Cookbook Committee Members

Dawn Burton	Ruth Manning
Julie Concannon	Dayla Miller
Shari Garder	Lynette Nore
Debra Gillespie	Pauline Shaffer
Amy Kragnes	Nancy Shinrock

Table Prayers

1. We thank you, dear God, for the food set before us,
   For all of our loved ones sitting beside us,
   We thank you, dear God, for being above us,
   Around us, below us, beside us to guide us. Amen.

2. Thank you for the food we eat,
   Thank you for the world so sweet,
   Thank you for the birds that sing,
   Thank you God for everything.

3. The Lord is good to me
   and so I thank the Lord
   for giving me the things I need
   the sun and the rain and the apple seed.
   The Lord is good to me. Amen!

4. God is great, God is good.
   Let us thank him for our food.
   By his hands, we all are fed.
   Give us, Lord, our daily bread. Amen.

5. Thanks for food that helps me grow,
   For family and friends I know,
   Thank you for the world I see,
   Thank you, God, for loving me. Amen.

6. Come Lord Jesus, be our guest,
   and let these gifts to us be blest. Amen.

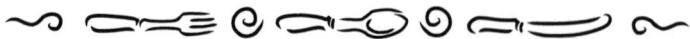

Table of Contents

Appetizers And Beverages 1

Breads And Rolls 23

Breakfast And Brunch 39

Cooking For A Crowd 55

Grandma's / Mom's Recipes 67

Healthy Eating 93

Holiday Favorites 107

Main Dishes And Meats 127

Salads & Soups 185

Slow Cooker Cooking 229

Sweets And Treats 241

Vegetables & Side Dishes 291

Index 309

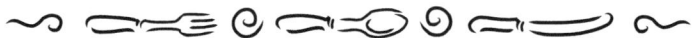

Appetizers & Beverages

Helpful Hints

- Add flavor to tea by dissolving old-fashioned lemon drops or hard mint candies in it. They melt quickly and keep the tea brisk.

- Make your own spiced tea or cider. Place orange peels, whole cloves, and cinnamon sticks in a 6-inch square piece of cheesecloth. Gather the corners and tie with a string. Steep in hot cider or tea for 10 minutes; steep longer if you want a stronger flavor.

- Always chill juices or sodas before adding them to beverage recipes.

- Calorie-free club soda adds sparkle to iced fruit juices and reduces calories per portion.

- To cool your punch, float an ice ring made from the punch rather than using ice cubes. It appears more decorative, prevents diluting, and does not melt as quickly.

- Place fresh or dried mint in the bottom of a cup of hot chocolate for a cool and refreshing taste.

- When making fresh lemonade or orange juice, one lemon yields about ¼ cup juice, while one orange yields about ⅓ cup juice.

- Never boil coffee; it brings out acids and causes a bitter taste. Store ground coffee in the refrigerator or freezer to keep it fresh.

- Always use cold water for electric drip coffee makers. Use 1–2 tablespoons ground coffee for each cup of water.

- How many appetizers should you prepare? Allow 4–6 appetizers per guest if a meal quickly follows. If a late meal is planned, allow 6–8 appetizers per guest. If no meal follows, allow 8–10 pieces per guest.

- If serving appetizers buffet-style or seating is limited, consider no-mess finger foods that don't require utensils to eat.

- Think "outside the bowl." Choose brightly-colored bowls to set off dips or get creative with hollowed-out loaves of bread, bell peppers, heads of cabbage, or winter squash.

- Cheeses should be served at room temperature—approximately 70°.

- To keep appetizers hot, make sure you have enough oven space and warming plates to maintain their temperature.

- To keep appetizers cold, set bowls on top of ice or rotate bowls of dips from the fridge every hour or as needed.

APPETIZERS AND BEVERAGES

APPETIZERS

❦ 8 LAYER NACHO DIP ❦
Lisa Rieff

1 lb. ground beef, cooked and drained
1 can refried beans, heated
Guacamole
Shredded lettuce
Sour cream
Shredded Cheddar cheese
1 - 2 tomatoes, chopped
Sliced black olives

Sprinkle hamburger on a serving plate. Pour beans on top and spread. Cover with guacamole, lettuce, sour cream (drop by dollops and spread), cheese, tomatoes, and olives. Serve with tortilla chips.

❦ ARTICHOKE DIP ❦
Heidi Meyer

2 cans artichoke hearts, drained
1 c. mayonnaise
1 c. Parmesan cheese

Shred artichokes with a fork. Blend in mayonnaise and cheese. Bake 20 minutes at 350°. Serve with crackers.

❦ BACON WRAPPED WATER CHESTNUTS ❦
Shawn Lorenzen

4 cans whole water chestnuts, drained
Soy sauce
Sugar
2 lbs. bacon
1 c. brown sugar
1 c. ketchup

Soak water chestnuts in soy sauce for at least 20 minutes. Drain, reserve some soy sauce. Roll the chestnuts in white sugar and wrap in uncooked bacon; secure with a toothpick. Place close together in a 9 x 11-inch

(continued)

1 ❦

cake pan. Bake at 350° for 30 minutes and pour off grease. Combine brown sugar, ketchup, and reserved soy sauce. Pour over pan and bake for an additional 30 minutes.

❦ BANG BANG SHRIMP ❦
Laura Armitage

4 - 5 tsp. chili garlic sauce, such as Sriracha sauce	1 tsp. salt
½ c. mayonnaise	½ tsp. ground black pepper
1 tsp. granulated sugar	¼ tsp. onion powder
1 tsp. rice vinegar	¼ tsp. garlic powder
1 egg, beaten	¼ tsp. dried basil
1 c. milk	1 lb. med. shrimp, peeled and deveined
½ c. all-purpose flour	8 - 12 c. vegetable oil for frying
½ c. panko breadcrumbs	

Combine mayonnaise, chili garlic sauce, granulated sugar, and rice vinegar in a small bowl; cover and set aside. Combine beaten egg with milk in a shallow bowl; set aside. Combine flour, panko, salt, black pepper, onion powder, garlic powder, and basil in another shallow bowl; set aside. Bread the shrimp by first coating each with the breading mixture (flour, panko, etc.). Dip breaded shrimp into the egg and milk mixture, then back in the breading. Arrange the coated shrimp on a plate and chill in fridge for at least 20 minutes. This step helps breading stick to the shrimp while frying. Heat oil in deep fryer to 350°. Use amount of oil required by your fryer. When oil is hot, fry shrimp 2 to 3 minutes or until golden brown. Drain on rack or paper towels. When all shrimp has been fried, drop the shrimp into a large bowl. Spoon about ¼ cup of sauce mixture (mayo, chili sauce, etc.) over shrimp and stir gently to coat.

❦ BLACK BEAN AND CORN SALSA ❦
Lisa Rieff

2 (16 oz.) cans black beans, rinsed and drained	¼ c. minced green onion
1 (16 oz.) can corn, drained	¼ c. minced red onion
½ c. chopped cilantro	1½ tsp. ground cumin
6 T. fresh lime juice	Salt and pepper to taste
6 T. vegetable oil	½ c. chopped tomato
	1 - 2 avocados

(continued)

Mix all ingredients except the tomato and avocado in a large mixing bowl. Season to taste with salt and pepper. Cover and refrigerate until cold (can be done a day in advance). Before serving, mix in tomato and the avocado cut into chunks.

❦ BUFFALO CHICKEN DIP ❦
Lisa Rieff

16 oz. cream cheese
2 c. shredded Cheddar cheese
1¼ c. Frank's hot sauce

3 chicken breasts, cooked and shredded

Mix all ingredients and put in Pyrex dish. Bake at 350° for 25-30 minutes. You can also cook it in a small crockpot for a couple hours. Serve with Ritz crackers, celery sticks or tortilla chips.

❦ BUFFALO CHICKEN DIP ❦
Shawn Lorenzen
Cheyrle Badtke

2 (8 oz.) pkgs. cream cheese, softened
1 c. ranch dressing
¾ c. red hot sauce (more or less depending on your preference)

10 oz. canned chicken
1 c. shredded Cheddar cheese

Beat cream cheese, ranch dressing, and hot sauce. Fold in shredded chicken. Spread mixture into sprayed pie plate. Bake at 350° for 15 minutes. Add Cheddar cheese on top and bake an additional 10-15 minutes. Serve with tortilla chips or corn chips. Note: Cheryle cooks and shreds 10 oz. of chicken. She uses only ½ c. shredded Cheddar cheese and mixes it in with the cream cheese mixture rather than spreading it on top.

❦ BUFFALO WING DIP ❦
Debra Gillespie

1 c. ranch dressing
1 c. Frank's buffalo wing
  sauce
1 c. Mexican blend shredded
  cheese, divided

3 lg. cans chicken
8 oz. cream cheese, softened

Mix all ingredients together until well blended, reserving ⅓ c. of shredded cheese for topping. Pour ingredients into a 9 x 13-inch pan. Top with remaining cheese. Bake at 350° for 25 to 30 minutes. Serve with Tostito chips.

❦ CHAMPP'S SEASONED SOUR CREAM ❦
Julie Concannon

2 c. light mayonnaise
18 oz. light sour cream
⅛ c. bottled lemon juice
⅛ c. thinly sliced green onions
⅛ c. dried parsley
½ T. garlic powder
1⅛ tsp. paprika

1⅛ tsp. onion powder
1⅛ tsp. Worcestershire sauce
½ tsp. celery salt
½ tsp. dried dill weed
½ tsp. cayenne pepper
¼ tsp. curry powder

Mix mayonnaise and sour cream in a large bowl. Add remaining ingredients in order, mixing well after each addition. Refrigerate overnight to blend flavors. This makes a large quantity, I usually prepare a half batch and serve with waffle fries. This is my lighter version. The original recipe calls for regular mayonnaise and regular sour cream.

❦ CHEESE BALL ❦
Lisa Rieff

12 oz. cream cheese
1 c. shredded Cheddar cheese
1 tsp. curry
½ tsp. cayenne pepper

Chopped pecans
Chutney or strawberry jam
Chopped scallions

(continued)

121822-12

Mix cream cheese, Cheddar cheese, curry and cayenne pepper until well blended. Form into a flat circle. Sprinkle pecans on top and sides and pat in so they don't fall off. Just before serving, pour chutney or jam on top and so it runs down the sides. Top with scallions. Serve with baguette slices and crackers.

❦ CHICKEN ENCHILADA DIP ❦
Dayla Miller

8 oz. cream cheese
1 c. mayonnaise
8 oz. Cheddar cheese

1 lb. shredded chicken
1 sm. can green chilies or Rotel

Mix the above together in casserole dish. Bake at 350° for 30 minutes (or prepare in microwave or crock pot). I have put some chopped green onion in this as well.

❦ CHICKEN ROLL UPS ❦
Cheyrle Badtke

1 c. Miracle Whip (may add a little more if mixture is dry)
¼ c. honey mustard
1½ - 2 c. chicken, cooked and cubed

1 c. celery, diced
¼ c. onion, diced
1½ - 2 c. shredded Cheddar cheese
Tortillas, burrito size

Mix all ingredients well and spread on tortilla shells. Roll tortillas and slice into 1-inch pieces. Variations: use turkey or tuna instead of chicken.

❦ CILANTRO DIP ❦
Dave Egr

1 (12 oz.) cream cheese
1 (12 oz.) Jalapeño Cheez-Whiz
1 bunch cilantro
3 bunches green onions

1 green bell pepper
3 med. diced tomatoes
Shredded Cheddar cheese
"Big Scoop" Fritos

Spread cream cheese over a plate. Spread Jalapeño Cheez-Whiz over cream cheese. Cut up cilantro and spread over Cheez-Whiz. Dice up

(continued)

green onions and spread over. Dice up green pepper and spread over. Dice up tomatoes and spread over. Spread Cheddar cheese over the top. Serve with "Big Scoop" Fritos.

❦ COCKTAIL SMOKIES ❦
Lisa Rieff

2 pkgs. Hillshire Farm Lil'
  Smokies
2 c. ketchup

¾ c. brown sugar
¾ c. bourbon
½ c. water

Combine all ingredients and warm in saucepan or small crockpot.

❦ CUCUMBER SALSA ❦
Susan Lueders

4 cucumbers, peeled and finely
  diced
3 fresh tomatoes, finely diced
1 sm. red onion, finely diced

⅔ c. vinegar
1 T. sugar
2 pkgs. ranch seasoning mix

Combine all ingredients, cover and chill. Serve with tortilla chips.

❦ FESTIVE CRANBERRY BRIE ❦
Ruth Manning

2 c. fresh or frozen
  cranberries
¾ c. water
½ c. granulated sugar
¼ c. packed brown sugar
½ tsp. cinnamon
½ tsp. ground ginger

⅛ tsp. ground cloves
⅛ tsp. ground allspice
1 med. Granny Smith apple,
  peeled, cored and chopped
¼ c. golden raisins
2 (8 oz.) rounds Brie cheese

Rinse cranberries in cold water; drain. In small saucepan, combine water and sugars. Bring to boiling, stirring to dissolve sugar. Boil rapidly for 5 minutes. Stir in cranberries and spices. Return to boiling, reduce heat. Simmer, uncovered, for 5 minutes, stirring occasionally. Stir in apple and raisins. Simmer, uncovered, 5 minutes more or until desired consistency. Cool to room temperature. Place the rounds of Brie in a baking dish or an oven-safe serving dish. Bake, uncovered,

(continued)

at 350° for 15 minutes or until cheese is warm and slightly softened. To serve, spoon cranberry mixture over warmed Brie. Serve with crackers. Makes 16 appetizer servings.

❦ FIESTA BAKED CHEESE DIP ❦
Julie Concannon

2 pkgs. (8 oz. each) cream
   cheese, softened
1 pkg. (8 oz.) Mexican style
   shredded four cheese,
   divided

1 can (4 oz.) chopped green
   chilies
1¼ c. sour cream, divided
¼ - ½ tsp. ground red pepper

Beat cream cheese in large mixing bowl with electric mixer on medium speed until softened. Reserve ¼ cup shredded cheese for garnish. Add remaining shredded cheese, chilies, ½ cup of the sour cream and ground red pepper to cream cheese; mix well. Spoon into 10-inch pie plate or quiche dish. Bake at 350° for 20 minutes or until lightly browned around edge. Spread remaining ¾ cup sour cream over baked cheese spread. Sprinkle with reserved ¼ cup shredded cheese. Serve with tortilla chips. 32 (2-tablespoon) servings.

❦ GRAMMA RUTH'S FRUIT PIZZA ❦
Shawn Lorenzen

Crust:

½ c. powdered sugar
¾ c. butter

1½ c. sugar

Mix crust ingredients, pat onto cookie sheet. Bake at 350° for 15-20 minutes or until golden brown. Cool.

Topping:

½ c. sugar
8 oz. cream cheese
1 tsp. vanilla

Fruit of your choice (whatever
   is in season)

Mix sugar, cream cheese and vanilla. Spread topping onto crust. Arrange fruit over topping.

❦ GREEK HUMMUS DIP ❦
Lisa Rieff

1 container original flavor hummus	Finely chopped red onion
Kalamata olives, pitted and chopped	Chopped tomatoes
Feta cheese	Cucumber, seeded and finely chopped
	Chopped mint

Layer half the hummus on a plate. Sprinkle generously with olives, feta, onion, tomatoes and cucumber. Repeat a second time with more hummus and then the toppings. Sprinkle mint on the top. Serve with pita chips, carrots, celery, red pepper strips, and fresh pea pods.

❦ HERBED CREAM CHEESE SPREAD ❦
Randi VenHuizen

1 T. chopped walnuts	2 oz. blue cheese
1 T. chopped chives	8 oz. cream cheese
1 T. chopped parsley	French bread

Chop walnuts, chives and parsley briefly in a food processor. Toss together with crumbled blue cheese and mix well. Process cream cheese until creamy; add blue cheese and walnut mixture. Blend until thoroughly combined but DO NOT OVERMIX. Serve with French bread

❦ HOT CORN DIP ❦
Amy Kragnes

1 (15 oz.) can white corn, drained	1 (8 oz.) pkg. cream cheese, diced and softened
1 (15 oz.) can yellow corn, drained	½ tsp. chili powder
1 (10 oz.) can diced tomatoes with green chili peppers, drained	½ tsp. garlic powder
	Chopped fresh cilantro to taste

Preheat oven to 350°. In medium baking dish, mix all ingredients. Bake 30 minutes, or until hot and bubbly. Serve with tortilla chips. Add cumin or cayenne pepper to taste if you want it a little hotter.

121822-12

❦ JANEEN'S DIP ❦
Kathy Christiansen
Janeen Pearson

½ c. sour cream
½ c. mayonnaise
⅓ c. picante sauce
¼ tsp. black pepper

⅓ tsp. garlic powder
3 c. shredded Cheddar cheese
¼ c. seeded and chopped
jalapeño pepper

In a large bowl stir together sour cream, mayonnaise, picante sauce, black pepper and garlic powder. Stir in cheese and jalapeño pepper. Cover and chill at least 2 hours. Serve with tortilla chips or carrot and celery sticks.

❦ MARDI GRAS DIP ❦
Debra Gillespie

Mayonnaise
Sharp Cheddar cheese, finely
grated
Chopped green onion

Chopped pecans
Hot pepper jelly
Tostito Scoops

Combine equal portions of the mayonnaise, Cheddar, green onion and pecans. Cover and refrigerate overnight. Spread dip in a shallow serving dish and spread a thin layer of the hot pepper jelly over the cheese dip. Serve with Tostito Scoops. This is an easy but very tasty dip. Enjoy!

❦ MEXICAN DIP ❦
Deb Lund and Michelle Martin

3 lg. tomatoes, cored, peeled if
desired, and chopped
1 can chopped black olives
4 green onions, chopped
(including some green parts)
1 can chopped chilies or 1 - 2
fresh jalapeños, chopped

3 T. olive oil
2 T. vinegar
Garlic powder or salt
Pepper
Cilantro
Tabasco sauce, if desired

Chop ingredients and place in glass bowl. Add oil, vinegar, and seasonings and stir gently. Serve with chips or crackers or use as salsa. Keeps in refrigerator up to a week.

❦ MOM'S APPLE DIP ❦
Randi VenHuizen

8 oz. cream cheese
¾ c. brown sugar
¼ c. granulated sugar

1 tsp. vanilla
Red and green apples

Blend cream cheese, sugars and vanilla together. Serve with sliced red and green apples.

❦ MOM'S CHEESE BALL ❦
Randi VenHuizen

2 (8 oz.) cream cheese,
softened
8 oz. can crushed pineapple,
drained very well

½ c. chopped green pepper
3 T. chopped onion
1 tsp. seasoned salt
¾ c. chopped nuts

Mix all ingredients together except nuts. Chill over night. Form into ball and roll in chopped nuts. Serve with crackers.

❦ MOM'S OLIVE DIP ❦
Rose Roberts

½ c. ripe black olives, chopped
1 (4 oz.) can mushrooms,
drained
1 c. Cheddar cheese

1 c. mayonnaise
½ c. green olives, chopped
1 c. Monterey Jack cheese
1 c. green onions, chopped

Combine all ingredients in a baking dish and bake at 350° for 8-10 minutes.

❦ NACHO APPETIZER ❦
Randi VenHuizen

8 oz. cream cheese
1 can Hormel chili (no beans)

1 pkg. grated Mexican cheese
Tortilla chips

In a square 8 x 8-inch casserole dish, spread the cream cheese. Pour chili over cream cheese. Cover with grated cheese. Lightly cover with plastic wrap. Microwave for approximately 6 minutes. Serve with tortilla chips.

121822-12

❦ OYSTER CRACKER APPETIZERS ❦
Randi VenHuizen
Paula Foster

2 boxes oyster crackers
2 pkgs. Hidden Valley dry
  dressing mix

12 oz. bottle Orville
  Redenbacher's popcorn oil
1 T. dry dill

Mix all of the ingredients together. Stir every half hour. In 2 or 3 hours, the oil will be absorbed. I usually put the appetizers back in the oyster cracker boxes. They can then be frozen until ready to be used.

❦ PEACH SALSA ❦
Deb Lund

2 - 3 peaches, peeled and
  chopped into very small
  pieces
2 - 3 tomatoes, cored, peeled
  and chopped fine
3 - 4 green onions, chopped
  fine, using some green
1 - 2 jalapeños or 1 can
  chopped green chilies

1 - 2 tsp. lime juice
1 tsp. sugar
Garlic powder to taste or may
  use garlic salt
1 T. chopped cilantro
Black pepper to taste
½ tsp. salt (unless garlic salt is
  used)

Place all ingredients in a bowl and mix together gently. Serve with tortilla chips or with Mexican dishes.

❦ PIGS IN A BLANKET ❦
Lisa Rieff

½ c. melted butter
½ c. chopped pecans
3 T. honey

3 T. brown sugar
1 can crescent rolls
½ pkg. Lil' Smokies

Mix butter, nuts, honey and brown sugar. Put in bottom of pan. Cut the crescent rolls into 3 pieces each to make 24 pieces. Wrap smokies with crescent rolls and place on top of mixture in pan. Bake at 400° for 15-20 minutes.

❦ POT STICKERS ❦
Marilyn Thomsen

3 c. Napa cabbage, chopped fine	1½ tsp. fresh ginger, grated
¾ tsp. salt	3 egg whites
¾ lb. ground pork	6 green onions, white and green parts, minced
4 tsp. soy sauce	Won ton wrappers
⅛ tsp. pepper	2 tsp. oil
1 clove garlic, minced	½ c. water

Place cabbage in colander and sprinkle with salt. Let stand for 20 minutes and drain. Mix ground pork, soy sauce, pepper, garlic, ginger, egg whites, onion, and cabbage. Chill covered for ½ to 8 hours. Put 1 T. of meat mixture in center of won ton wrapper. Wet edge of won ton wrapper and close securely. At this point, the pot stickers can be frozen in a single layer and when frozen solid, placed in a sealed plastic bag. To cook, place 2 tsp. oil in frying pan, add single layer of pot stickers. Cook on medium heat for 5 minutes. Add ½ cup water and turn heat to low. Cover and cook for 10 minutes (all water should be absorbed). Uncover and increase heat to medium high for 3-4 minutes. Serve with your favorite sauce, like sweet and sour.

❦ PROSCIUTTO ARTICHOKE APPETIZERS ❦
Ruth Manning

¼ c. pine nuts	1¼ c. whipping cream
7 oz. prosciutto, thin slices	8 oz. Gorgonzola cheese, crumbled
14 oz. (2 cans) artichoke hearts	Optional: Parmesan cheese

Preheat oven to 350°. Place pine nuts on a piece of aluminum foil and place all in the oven. Bake pine nuts until golden brown (watch carefully). Cut prosciutto slices into quarters. Drain artichokes and pat dry with a paper towel. Cut into quarters. Wrap one quarter of a prosciutto slice around each artichoke. Arrange all in one layer in a 9 x 13-inch baking dish. Pour whipping cream over the layer of artichokes. Sprinkle with Gorgonzola cheese. Sprinkle pine nuts over the top and place in the oven. Bake for 25 minutes or until bubbly and golden brown. Optional: Sprinkle with Parmesan cheese before serving. Serve warm with baguette slices.

121822-12

❦ PUMPKIN APPLE DIP ❦
Laura Armitage

15 oz. can pumpkin
2 (8 oz.) pkgs. cream cheese
1 tsp. cinnamon

1 tsp. nutmeg
2 c. powdered sugar

Mix all ingredients until smooth. Serve with apple slices or other fruit.

❦ PUMPKIN FLUFF DIP ❦
Christie Klos

1 (5 oz.) pkg. instant vanilla
  pudding mix
1 (15 oz.) can solid pack
  pumpkin

1 tsp. pumpkin pie spice
1 (16 oz.) container frozen
  whipped topping, thawed

In a bowl mix vanilla pudding mix, pumpkin, and pumpkin spice. Fold in whipped topping. Chill in refrigerator. Serve with graham crackers and fruit.

❦ RANCH PRETZELS ❦
Lisa Meyer

1 stick butter, melted
1 T. Worcestershire sauce
1 oz. pkg. Hidden Valley
  Ranch dressing mix

1 lb. bag pretzels

Mix butter, Worcestershire sauce and dressing mix. Pour over pretzels in roaster pan. Bake at 300° for 15 minutes. Stir every 5 minutes so it doesn't burn.

❦ REUBEN DIP ❦
Connie Walther

¾ lb. corned beef
15 oz. can sauerkraut

¾ c. Thousand Island dressing
1 lb. Swiss cheese, grated

Combine all ingredients, cook until heated through in Dutch oven. Can transfer to crock pot on low to keep warm while serving. Serve with party rye bread or crackers.

❦ ROASTED RED PEPPER DIP ❦
Debra Gillespie

1 pkg. ranch dressing
1 (8 oz.) cream cheese, softened

½ lg. jar Dunbar's roasted red peppers in olive oil and garlic, drained

Using food processor, mix dressing, cream cheese and ½ jar of peppers. Place dip in small serving dish and serve with sliced French baguette bread.

❦ ROTEL SALSA ❦
Pat Brewer

1 can Rotel sauce
1 can white shoe peg corn
1 can black beans, rinsed and drained

1½ c. salsa

Mix all ingredients and place in bowl. Refrigerate.

❦ SALSA ❦
Lisa Meyer

4 - 5 Roma tomatoes
1 can corn, drained
1 can black beans, drained
2 - 3 green onions, chopped

½ tsp. crushed red pepper
½ bottle ranch dressing (or to taste)

Cut off ends of Roma tomatoes and squeeze juice out. Cut up tomatoes. Add with above ingredients. Let sit in refrigerator overnight. May need to add more dressing after it has been refrigerated overnight. Serve with tortilla chips.

❦ SANTA FE CHEESECAKE ❦
Connie Walther

2 (8 oz.) pkgs. cream cheese, softened
2 c. shredded Cheddar cheese
1 can green chilies, drained

1 pkg. taco seasoning
1 c. sour cream
Salsa of choice

(continued)

121822-12

Mix the cream cheese, Cheddar, chilies and taco seasoning and pour into a sprayed springform pan. Bake at 350° for 40 minutes. When done, set for 10 minutes. Spread top with sour cream. Put back in oven for 5 minutes. Cool on rack, loosen around pan. Remove sides of pan. Chill for 3-4 hours. Top with salsa, and serve with taco chips.

❦ SAUSAGE CHEESE BALLS ❦
Harry Naasz

1 lb. sausage   2 c. Bisquick
2 c. grated cheese

Mix well. Shape into balls and bake at 350° until brown and cooked through.

❦ SAUSAGE CHEESE DIP ❦
Karen Anderson

1 lb. ground beef   1 can cream mushroom soup
1 lb. pork sausage   1 tsp. garlic powder
1 onion, chopped
1 (7½ oz.) can hot jalapeño
   relish

Cook beef, sausage and onion. Drain well. Add remaining ingredients and stir over low heat until melted. Serve with corn chips.

❦ SAUSAGE STUFFED MUSHROOMS ❦
Kathy Christiansen

1 lb. ground pork sausage   2 (8 oz.) pkgs. fresh whole
1 (8 oz.) pkg. cream cheese   mushrooms
   (See Note)   3 - 4 T. sliced green onions

Note: Instead of 8 oz. cream cheese, you can use 4 oz. cream cheese and ¼ cup crumbled blue cheese. Preheat oven to 350°. Spray a 9 x 13-inch baking dish with non-stick spray. Clean mushrooms, finely dice stems and save caps for stuffing. Arrange mushroom caps hollow side up in baking dish. Cook pork sausage over medium heat until no longer pink, adding in the finely diced mushroom stems toward the
(continued)

end of the cooking time. In a medium bowl, combine the cream cheese (or cream cheese and blue cheese crumbles), green onion and the cooked sausage/stem mixture. Generously fill the mushroom caps. Bake in preheated oven for 30 minutes or until lightly browned. These can be frozen and baked when needed for a quick appetizer.

❦ SEASONED OYSTER CRACKERS ❦
Dayla Miller

3 pkgs. oyster crackers
1 c. cooking oil
1 pkg. Hidden Valley dry mix

1 T. garlic salt
1 tsp. onion salt

Combine all ingredients in large bowl or paper bag, enjoy.

❦ SHOEPEG CORN DIP ❦
Marjorie Keiser

1 c. sour cream
½ c. mayonnaise
12 oz. can shoepeg corn (small white kernels), drained

4 oz. grated Cheddar cheese
¼ c. grated Parmesan cheese
1 T. grated onion

Mix all ingredients thoroughly and chill several hours to blend flavors. Serve with chips, crackers, etc.

❦ SHRIMP IN GARLIC SAKE SAUCE ❦
Lisa Rieff

2 servings brown rice
1 tsp. olive oil
1 garlic clove, minced
1 tsp. minced onion
8 oz. raw shrimp, peeled and deveined

½ c. Sake
3 T. butter
1 T. soy sauce
1 tsp. chopped parsley

Prepare brown rice according to package directions. Meanwhile, heat oil in medium frying pan over medium heat. Stir in garlic and onion. Add shrimp and Sake. Stir often until shrimp are opaque, about 2-3 minutes. Add butter, soy sauce, and parsley. Stir until butter is melted.

(continued)

121822-12

Put rice in 4 small bowls. Evenly distribute shrimp and sauce over the rice. 4 servings.

❦ SOUTHWESTERN CHICKEN DIP ❦
Connie Walther

1 lb. light Velveeta
1 (6 oz.) pkg. southwestern
  chicken strips
1 (10 oz.) can diced tomatoes
  with green chilies, lime,
  cilantro

1 tsp. cumin
¼ c. chopped green onions

Mix ingredients and microwave on medium heat 6-7 minutes, stirring periodically to melt cheese. Serve with tortilla chips.

❦ SPINACH ARTICHOKE BREAD ❦
Cheyrle Badtke

1 loaf baguette bread
4 oz. cream cheese
1 container spinach artichoke
  dip

Mozzarella cheese

Slice bread on a slant and spread each piece with cream cheese, then spread each piece with spinach artichoke dip. Top with mozzarella cheese. Bake at 350° until cheese is melted and bread is golden brown.

❦ SPINACH DIP ❦
Lisa Rieff

1 pkg. frozen spinach
1 pkg. imitation crab meat
8 oz. mayonnaise

8 oz. sour cream
1 pkg. ranch seasoning mix

Cook spinach and drain really well squeezing all the juice from it. Finely chop crab meat with chopper or food processor. Mix the mayonnaise and sour cream with the ranch seasoning. Add crab and spinach. Chill. Can be served in a bread bowl with bread slices, crackers and tortilla chips.

❦ STUFFED CRESCENT ROLLS ❦
Deb Schuchard

1½ lbs. hamburger
1 sm. can green chilies

1 pkg. cream cheese, softened
2 pkgs. crescent rolls

Brown hamburger, drain. Mix green chilies and cream cheese into hamburger. Unroll crescent rolls and spoon hamburger mixture into wide end. Roll up and bake at 350° for 15 to 20 minutes until crescents are done.

❦ TOMATO AND BASIL BRUSCHETTA ❦
Heidi Meyer

2 cloves garlic, chopped
2¼ tsp. balsamic vinegar
½ tsp. kosher salt
¼ tsp. fresh cracked pepper
2 T. chopped fresh basil
3 T. olive oil

6 roma tomatoes, diced
8 slices Italian bread, cut about 1-inch thick
2 cloves garlic, peeled
2 T. grated Parmigiano-Reggiano cheese

Whisk together chopped garlic, vinegar, salt, pepper, and basil. When combined slowly drizzle in oil. Add tomatoes and let sit for 20 minutes at room temperature. Toast the bread under a broiler. When the bread is toasted rub each piece, on one side, with the whole garlic pieces. Place the bread on a cookie sheet and top with tomato mixture. Sprinkle on cheese and broil until melted. Serve immediately.

❦ TOMATO AND BASIL SQUARES ❦
Judy Egr

1 pkg. (10 oz.) refrigerated pizza crust
2 c. shredded mozzarella cheese, divided
1 clove garlic

4 plum tomatoes, thinly sliced
1 oz. shredded Parmesan cheese
2 tsp. dried basil
⅔ c. real mayonnaise

Preheat oven to 375°. Roll dough into a rectangle shape. Sprinkle with 1 cup of mozzarella cheese. Press garlic over cheese. Arrange sliced tomatoes over cheese. Mix rest of mozzarella cheese, Parmesan cheese, basil and mayonnaise and spread over tomatoes. Bake 15-20 minutes.

121822-12

❦ TORTILLA WRAPS ❦
Lisa Meyer

2 (8 oz.) pkgs. cream cheese, softened
2 T. chopped black olives
1½ T. chopped onion
1½ T. chopped jalapeños
1 pkg. flour tortillas
Salsa

Mix all ingredients except tortillas and salsa. Spread mixture on tortillas. Let set about 1 minute to soften. Roll the tortilla and put plastic wrap around it. Refrigerate overnight and slice the next day. Serve with salsa.

BEVERAGES

❦ CHAI ❦
Deb Lund

2 c. water
2 individual tea bags (green and/or black tea)
1 cinnamon stick
6 cardamom seeds, crushed or ¼ tsp. ground cardamom
1 - 3 whole cloves
4 - 5 whole all spice
¼ tsp. ground ginger
2½ c. milk
¼ - ⅓ c. sugar or sugar substitute

Combine water, tea, and spices in a saucepan and bring to a boil. Reduce heat and simmer for 5 minutes. Stir in milk and heat for a minute or so. Strain and discard spices. Stir in sugar and serve in mugs or cups, garnishing with whipped cream, cinnamon, and a cinnamon stick, if desired. Serves 4. I usually make this with 4 cups water, then add powdered milk, which works fine, too.

❦ CRANBERRY PUNCH ❦
Ruth Manning

2 qt. cranberry juice cocktail (e.g., cranapple, cran-raspberry etc.)
1 (12 oz.) can frozen orange juice concentrate, thawed
1 (12 oz.) frozen pink lemonade concentrate, thawed
1 qt. chilled gingerale

(continued)

Combine cranberry juice cocktail, orange juice and pink lemonade concentrates. Pour over ice or ice ring in a bowl. Stir in ginger ale when ready to serve. 25-30 punch cup servings.

❦ FACE BOOK FRIENDS ROOT BEER FLOAT NIGHT ❦
Doug Aden

Computer	Chairs
Internet Access	Serving table
Face Book Account	16 oz. cups
Face Book Friends	12 oz. cups
Root beer	Plastic spoons
Ice Cream	Straws
Patio	

Pick a day for the root beer night. Should be a warm evening. Send an email to all Face Book Friends inviting them to the Face Book Friends Root Beer Float Night. You might ask them if they have a favorite brand of root beer. Create an event on Face Book. Buy the root beer (might include a guest's favorite if it is not too expensive), ice cream, cups, spoons and straws. On the day of Root Beer Float Night, set up chairs and serving table on the patio. As guests arrive, put two scoops of ice cream in each cup and show them where the root beer is. They can pour their own. If the guests want seconds, they can make it.

❦ HOT BUTTERED RUM ❦
Paula Foster

2 c. brown sugar	6 whole cloves
½ c. butter	½ tsp. nutmeg
Pinch salt	2 qt. hot water
3 cinnamon sticks	3 c. rum

Put all ingredients into the crock pot, stir well. Cover and cook on high for 2 hours, then turn to low and cook 3 to 10 hours. Serve in warm mugs. Makes 15 to 20 servings.

 121822-12

❦ MOJITO ❦
Deb Lund

Fresh mint leaves
1 T. sugar
3 T. lime juice

1½ oz. light rum
Club soda or lemon lime soda
Crushed ice

In tall beverage glass, crush several large mint leaves with a muddler or spoon to coat the inside of glass. Add the sugar and lime juice, and stir thoroughly. Top with crushed ice. Add rum and mix. Top off with chilled club soda or lemon lime soda. Serve using a sprig of fresh mint as a garnish.

❦ MULLED CIDER PUNCH ❦
Ruth Manning

2 ¼ c. sugar
4 c. water
1 stick cinnamon
6 whole allspice berries

6 whole cloves
4 c. pineapple juice
2 c. lemon juice
2 qt. apple cider

Combine sugar and water and boil five minutes. Remove from heat; add spices. Cover and let stand to blend flavors. Strain. Just before serving combine spiced syrup, pineapple juice, lemon juice and cider and heat to the boiling point. Remove from heat and serve at once. Makes about one gallon of punch, about 45 punch cup servings.

❦ ORANGE JUBILEE ❦
Lisa Rieff

6 oz. can frozen orange juice
1 c. milk
1 c. water

¼ c. sugar
1 tsp. vanilla
10 ice cubes

Combine all ingredients in a blender and process until ice cubes are crushed. Serves 4-5 small glasses. Easy to double for a larger group. Great for your special breakfast, brunch or shower.

❦ TROPICAL PUNCH ❦
Ruth Manning

1 (46 oz.) can red Hawaiian
fruit punch
1 (6 oz.) can frozen lemonade
concentrate
1 (6 oz.) can frozen orange
juice concentrate

1 (6 oz.) can frozen grape juice
concentrate
1 (2 liter) bottle of ginger ale,
chilled

Combine Hawaiian fruit punch, lemonade, orange and grape juice
concentrates, and water called for with the concentrates. Pour over ice
in a large punch bowl. Resting bottle on rim of punch bowl, carefully
pour in ginger ale. Makes 30 to 35 servings.

❦ WASSAIL ❦
Paula Foster

2 qt. apple juice or cider
1 pt. cranberry juice
1 tsp. bitters
2 cinnamon sticks

1 tsp. whole allspice
1 sm. orange studded with
whole cloves
1 c. rum optional

Put all ingredients into the crock pot, cover and cook on high for 1
hour, then on low for 4 to 8 hours. Serve warm from crock pot, about
12 cups.

Breads & Rolls

Helpful Hints

- When baking bread, a small dish of water in the oven will keep the crust from getting too hard or brown.

- Use shortening, not margarine or oil, to grease pans when baking bread. Margarine and oil absorb more readily into the dough.

- To make self-rising flour, mix 4 cups flour, 2 teaspoons salt, and 2 tablespoons baking powder. Store in a tightly covered container.

- One scant tablespoon of bulk yeast is equal to one packet of yeast.

- Hot water kills yeast. One way to test for the correct temperature is to pour the water over your wrist. If you cannot feel hot or cold, the temperature is just right.

- When in doubt, always sift flour before measuring.

- Use bread flour for baking heavier breads, such as mixed grain, pizza doughs, bagels, etc.

- When baking in a glass pan, reduce the oven temperature by 25°.

- When baking bread, you can achieve a finer texture if you use milk. Water makes a coarser bread.

- Fill an empty salt shaker with flour to quickly and easily dust a bread pan or work surface.

- For successful quick breads, do not overmix the dough. Mix only until combined. An overmixed batter creates tough and rubbery muffins, biscuits, and quick breads.

- Muffins can be eaten warm. Most other quick breads taste better the next day. Nut breads are better if stored 24 hours before serving.

- Nuts, shelled or unshelled, keep best and longest when stored in the freezer. Unshelled nuts crack more easily when frozen. Nuts can be used directly from the freezer.

- Enhance the flavor of nuts, such as almonds, walnuts, and pecans, by toasting them before using in recipes. Place nuts on a baking sheet and bake at 300° for 5–8 minutes or until slightly browned.

- Overripe bananas can be frozen until it's time to bake. Store them unpeeled in a plastic bag.

- The freshness of eggs can be tested by placing them in a large bowl of cold water; if they float, do not use them.

BREADS AND ROLLS

❧ APRICOT-ORANGE CREAM SCONES ❧
Shirley Schuchard

2 c. all-purpose flour	½ c. chopped dried apricots
3 T. sugar	½ c. white vanilla baking chips
3 tsp. baking powder	1⅓ c. whipping cream
½ tsp. salt	1 c. powdered sugar
2 tsp. grated orange peel	2 - 3 T. orange juice

Heat oven to 400°. Lightly grease cookie sheet. In large bowl, sift flour, sugar, baking powder and salt. Add orange peel. Stir in apricots and baking chips. Add whipping cream all at once, stir just until dry ingredients are moistened. On floured board, knead 6-7 times until smooth. Divide dough in half. Pat each half into 6-inch round. Cut each round into 6 wedges. Place 2-inches apart on cookie sheet. Bake 10-13 minutes until brown. Mix orange juice and powdered sugar. Drizzle over scones. Serve warm. I have made these with cran-blueberries and coconut and white chocolate. Use your imagination.

❧ BLACK FOREST BREAD ❧
Connie Walther
Cooking Light

1¾ c. flour	¾ c. low-fat buttermilk
½ c. cocoa	⅔ c. sugar (or substitute
1 tsp. baking soda	equivalent)
½ tsp. salt	⅓ c. honey
½ c. dried cranberries	2 T. vegetable oil
(cranraisins work too)	2 tsp. vanilla
1 T. hot water	1 lg. egg
2 tsp. instant coffee granules	Cooking spray

Combine first 4 ingredients. Stir in cranberries, make a well in center of mixture. Combine water and coffee granules; add milk, sugar, honey, oil, vanilla, and egg. Stir well with whisk. Add to flour mixture, stir until just moist. Spoon batter into 8 x 4-inch cooking sprayed loaf pan. Bake at 350° for 50 minutes, or until tooth pick comes out clean. Cool 10 minutes and remove from pan.

❦ BLUEBERRY CRUMBLE COFFEE CAKE ❦
Debra Gillespie

1 c. sugar	2 tsp. baking powder
½ c. Crisco shortening	½ tsp. salt
2 eggs	½ c. milk
2 c. flour	2 c. blueberries

Cream together sugar and Crisco, then add eggs and mix well. Thoroughly combine flour, baking powder, salt, and milk with the the creamed mixture. Gently fold in blueberries last. Pour batter into slightly greased 9 x 13-inch cake pan.

Topping:

½ c. brown sugar	⅓ c. flour
¼ c. butter	½ tsp. cinnamon

Combine brown sugar, butter, flour and cinnamon. Sprinkle topping over cake batter. Bake 45-50 minutes at 350°. Serve warm.

❦ BLUEBERRY-BANANA BREAD ❦
Julie Concannon

1¼ c. sugar	½ c. buttermilk
½ c. butter or margarine, softened	1 tsp. vanilla
2 lg. eggs	2½ c. all-purpose flour
1½ c. mashed very ripe bananas (about 3 med.)	1 tsp. baking soda
	1 tsp. salt
	1 c. fresh or frozen blueberries

Move oven rack to low position so that tops of pans will be in center of oven. Heat oven to 350°. Grease bottoms only of two 8 x 4-inch loaf pans or one 9 x 5-inch loaf pan with shortening or spray with cooking spray. In large bowl, stir sugar and butter until well mixed. Stir in eggs until well mixed. Stir in bananas, buttermilk and vanilla; beat with spoon until smooth. Stir in flour, baking soda and salt just until moistened. Gently stir in blueberries. Divide batter evenly between 8-inch pans or pour into 9-inch pan. Bake 8-inch loaves about 1 hour, 9-inch loaf about 1 hour 15 minutes, or until toothpick inserted in center comes out clean. Cool 10 minutes in pans on wire rack. Loosen sides of loaves from pans; remove from pans and place top side up on

(continued)

wire rack. Cool completely, about 2 hours, before slicing. Wrap tightly and store at room temperature up to 4 days, or refrigerate up to 10 days. 1-2 loaves.

❦ BREAD MACHINE CINNAMON ROLLS ❦
Julie Concannon

Rolls:

1 c. milk	¾ tsp. salt
¼ c. sugar	3½ c. all-purpose flour
2 T. butter	1 pkg. (2 - 3 tsp.) quick rising
1 lg. egg, beaten	yeast

Measure roll ingredients into baking pan in order given for your machine (for my machine it is as listed above). Insert baking pan securely into baking unit, close lid. Select "dough" setting. Push start button. When complete, remove dough from pan, pull out kneading blade. Cover dough, let rest for 15 minutes.

Filling:

⅓ c. butter, softened	½ c. raisins or chopped pecans
¾ c. brown sugar	(if desired)
2 tsp. cinnamon	

On lightly floured surface, roll dough in to a 14 x 18-inch rectangle. Spread surface with ⅓ cup softened butter, leaving a 1-inch border along each of the long edges. Sprinkle surface with a mixture of ¾ cup packed brown sugar and 2 teaspoons cinnamon (add ½ cup chopped pecans or raisins, if desired). Lightly moisten both long edges with water. Starting with 18-inch side, roll dough "jelly roll" style, pinch seam to seal. With seam side down and using a serrated knife, cut into 18 one inch pieces. Place in two buttered 8 x 8 or 9 x 9-inch baking pans. Cover lightly with plastic wrap and a towel; allow to rise in a warm place until doubled, about 40 minutes. Bake at 375° for 10 to 15 minutes or longer (check rolls every few minutes and cover loosely with foil if becoming too brown, rolls should spring back when lightly touched). Makes 18 cinnamon rolls. The original recipe calls for 12 rolls from the recipe but I get 18 nice size rolls.

(continued)

Sweet Glaze:

1½ c. powdered sugar
2½ T. milk or light cream

2 T. melted butter
Drop or two vanilla extract

Mix powdered sugar, milk, butter and vanilla. Drizzle glaze over warm cinnamon rolls or let each person put glaze on as desired. In our family some like the glaze, some don't, so I let everyone glaze their own if they want.

❦ CHERRY CHEESE DANISH ❦
(from Lucky Leaf)
Connie Walther

2 (8 oz.) tubes of crescent dough
1 (8 oz.) softened cream cheese
1 c. plus 1 T. sugar, divided
1 tsp. vanilla

1 (21 oz.) premium cherry pie filling
½ c. sliced almonds
1 T. melted butter

Preheat oven to 350°. Press 1 pkg. of dough into bottom of ungreased 9 x 13-inch pan. Mix together cream cheese, 1 c. sugar, and vanilla. Spread mixture over dough, add pie filling. Lay 2nd pkg. of dough on top. Mix 1 T. sugar, almonds and butter then spread over dough. Bake 30 minutes, until golden brown.

❦ COCONUT PECAN RING ❦
Ruth Manning

2 (8 oz.) pkgs. refrigerated butterflake rolls (24 rolls)
⅔ c. granulated sugar
½ tsp. cinnamon
¼ c. milk
¼ c. flaked coconut

¼ c. chopped pecans
½ c. sifted powdered sugar
1 T. milk
¼ tsp. vanilla
2 T. chopped pecans

Separate refrigerated dough into rolls. Combine the granulated sugar and the cinnamon; dip each roll in the ¼ c. milk; then in cinnamon-sugar mixture, turning to coat all sides. Place half the rolls, slightly overlapping, in the bottom of a 6½ c. ring mold. Sprinkle with coconut and ¼ c. chopped pecans. Add remaining rolls, forming a second layer of overlapping rolls. Bake at 350° for 25 to 30 minutes, until golden

(continued)

brown. Loosen with tip of spatula; turn out onto serving plate. Drizzle with vanilla nut glaze: combine powdered sugar, 1 T. milk and vanilla and blend well. Sprinkle with the 2 T. chopped pecans. Makes 8 to 10 servings.

28-19
Quilting

❦ CRANBERRY ORANGE BREAD ❦
Karen Armitage
Jean Kellogg

2 c. flour, sifted	1 c. cranberries, coarsely cut
¾ c. sugar	½ c. walnuts, chopped
1½ tsp. baking powder	1 egg, beaten
½ tsp. baking soda	¾ c. orange juice
1 tsp. salt	3 T. oil
1 tsp. cinnamon	

Whisk together flour, sugar, baking powder, baking soda, salt and cinnamon. Stir in cranberries and walnuts. Combine egg, orange juice and oil; add to dry ingredients, stirring just until moistened. Bake at 350° in greased pans. 1 (9½ x 5-inch) pan, 50 minutes or 2 (7½ x 3½-inch) pans, 30-35 minutes.

❦ DUMPLINGS "FOR SUNDAY" ❦
Harry Naasz

⅓ c. butter, softened	½ tsp. baking powder
1 egg	1 qt. meat broth
2 c. flour	

Cream together butter and egg. Stir in flour and baking powder. Cut dough into pieces and drop pieces into boiling broth. Cover and boil for 20 minutes. DO NOT LIFT lid during the boiling process.

❦ EASY GOOEY CARAMEL ROLLS ❦
Matt Garder

⅓ c. melted butter	4 cans buttermilk biscuits
⅓ c. maple syrup	Chopped pecans or walnuts
¾ c. brown sugar	(optional)

(continued)

Melt butter, maple syrup, and brown sugar together. Stir. Use a greased bundt pan. Pour ½ of the melted ingredients into bottom of the pan. Place biscuits (standing up) around the circle of the pan. If you like pecans or walnuts, put them in here. Pour remainder of the melted ingredients over the biscuits. Bake at 350° for 45 minutes or until brown and beginning to pull apart. Place on plate.

❦ EASY WHEAT BREAD IN A BAG ❦
Rose Roberts

Mix in heavy duty plastic bag:

½ c. all-purpose flour
1 pkg. yeast

½ c. warm water
2 T. sugar

Work bag with fingers until completely blended. Close bag and let rest for 15 minutes.

Add:

2 c. whole wheat flour
¾ c. warm water
1 T. vegetable oil

1 tsp. salt
1½ c. all-purpose flour

Mix well. Slowly add enough all purpose flour to make a stiff dough. Turn out onto floured surface and knead 5-6 minutes. Add more flour if sticky. Cover with plastic bag and let rest for 10 minutes. Shape and put into greased loaf pan. Cover and let rise 45-60 minutes. Bake 30-35 minutes in 400° oven. Remove from pan and cool.

❦ FROZEN BREAD CARAMEL ROLLS ❦
Kathy Christiansen
Marilyn Mattheis

2 loaves frozen bread dough
½ c. butter
1 c. brown sugar
1 lg. pkg vanilla pudding
  (NOT INSTANT)

2 T. milk
1 tsp. cinnamon

(continued)

Thaw bread but do not let it rise (it is easier to cut up with a sharp knife or kitchen shears if it is still slightly frozen). Spray bottom of 9 x 13-inch pan with cooking spray. Cut up one loaf of bread into small pieces and place in greased pan. Melt butter in saucepan. Add brown sugar, pudding, milk and cinnamon and beat until smooth. Pour this mixture over the first layer of bread dough. Tear or cut up second loaf and scatter on top. Let rise 2½ to 3½ hours, or until double, and then bake 30 minutes at 375°. OR - You can prepare dough late in the evening, cover it with a piece of plastic wrap sprayed with non-stick cooking spray and let it rise overnight on kitchen counter to bake first thing in the morning.

❦ FRY BREAD ❦
Harry Naasz

5 lbs. flour
2 T. baking powder
1 tsp. salt
1 T. sugar

1 pkg. yeast (if desired)
2½ qt. water or more if
  needed

Mix together; knead a little bit. Roll dough out to about ½-inch thick and cut into desired pieces. Fry in hot oil, shortening or lard. Delicious with honey. See the movie Smoke Signals to see the value of fry bread!

❦ HERB CHEESE BEER BREAD ❦
Connie Walther

2½ c. flour
2 T. sugar
1½ tsp. baking soda
1 T. baking powder
1 tsp. salt

1½ tsp. dried sage
12 oz. beer
1 c. finely grated Cheddar
  cheese

Combine all ingredients and bake in a greased and floured pan at 375° for 50-55 minutes. Cool 10 minutes and turn out to finish cooling.

❦ KOLACHES FROM THE BREAD MACHINE ❦
Julie Concannon

1¼ c. warm water
½ c. butter, softened
1 egg
1 egg yolk
⅓ c. milk powder
¼ c. instant mashed potato flakes
¼ c. white sugar

1 tsp. salt
3⅞ c. bread flour
2 tsp. active dry yeast
Apricot, cherry, blueberry pie filling or fillings of your choice
¼ c. butter, melted

Place water, softened butter, egg, egg yolk, milk powder, potato flakes, sugar, salt, flour and yeast in the pan of the bread machine in the order recommended by the manufacturer. Select Dough cycle; press start. Check dough after 5 minutes of mixing, adding 1-2 tablespoons of water if necessary. When the cycle is complete, spoon out dough with tablespoon and roll into walnut sized balls. Place 2-inches apart on a lightly greased cookie sheet. Cover and let rise until doubled, about 1 hour. Flatten balls slightly with the palm of your hand and make a depression in center with your thumb. Fill each with 1 tablespoon of filling. Cover and let rise for about 30 minutes. Meanwhile preheat oven to 375°. Bake in preheated oven for 13 to 15 minutes, until lightly browned. Remove from oven and brush with melted butter. Cool on wire rack. 24 servings.

❦ LITTLE TEXAS CORN BREAD ❦
Julie Concannon

1 c. cornmeal
1 c. shredded Cheddar cheese
1 T. baking powder
2 eggs
1 can (8½ oz.) cream-style corn

1 c. sour cream
½ c. vegetable oil
1 can (4 oz.) chopped green chilies, drained

In a large bowl, combine the cornmeal, cheese and baking powder. In another bowl, combine the eggs, corn, sour cream, oil and chilies. Stir into dry ingredients just until moistened. Pour into a greased 8-inch square baking pan. Bake at 400° for 30-35 minutes or until a toothpick comes out clean. Serve warm. Refrigerate leftovers. 8 servings.

❦ MOM'S BRAN MUFFINS ❦
Shawn Lorenzen

4 eggs	5 c. flour
1 c. Mazola oil	3 c. sugar
1 qt. buttermilk	5 tsp. soda
1 box (15oz.) Raisin Bran	2 tsp. salt

Beat eggs, oil and buttermilk. Set aside. In a big bowl, mix all dry ingredients. Pour wet over dry and mix well. Fill muffin cups ½ full. Bake at 400° for 15-20 minutes.

❦ MONKEY BREAD ❦
(Sticky Buns)
Randi VenHuizen

Non stick butter spray	1 cube butter
4 cans refrigerator biscuits	2 T. water
Sugar and cinnamon in Ziploc	1 c. sugar
bag	2 tsp. cinnamon

Spray bundt pan with non stick butter spray. Cut the refrigerator biscuits into fourths. Put pieces in plastic Ziploc bag that is filled with sugar/cinnamon mixture. Shake to cover all pieces. Put coated pieces in bundt pan. In small saucepan, melt butter and combine with water, 1 c. sugar and 2 tsp. cinnamon. Cook until sugar dissolves. Pour over biscuit pieces. At this point, you can cover with aluminum foil and put in refrigerator until ready to bake. Bake at 350° for 30 minutes or until golden brown. Cool upright for ten minutes. Invert carefully onto plate as glaze will ooze down sides. Serve warm.

❦ MY FAVORITE ROLLS ❦
Deb Lund

1 pkg. active dry yeast
⅓ c. warm water with 1 tsp.
   sugar
½ c. mashed potatoes (no
   seasoning added)
(May use instant potato flakes
   and water to make ½ c.
   mashed potatoes)
¼ c. canola oil

1 c. warm milk (or powdered
   milk and water to make 1 c.)
¼ c. sugar
1 tsp. salt
3½ c. or more unbleached
   flour, divided
1 egg
1 c. whole wheat flour
2 T. milled flax seed

Stir yeast into warm sugar water, and let proof several minutes. Add mashed potatoes (or water and instant potato flakes); oil, warm milk, sugar, and salt. Stir in 2 cups flour and egg. Beat well by hand or with mixer for several minutes. Add whole wheat flour and flaxseed, and stir well. Gradually add in enough flour to make a soft dough that leaves the sides of the bowl. Turn onto floured board and knead until smooth and elastic, adding a bit of flour, if necessary. Place in greased bowl, and cover with towel. Let rise 1 to 1½ hours. Punch down dough, then shape into dinner rolls; or roll out and add butter and cinnamon sugar to make cinnamon or caramel rolls. Let rise about an hour, then bake at 375° about 20 minutes or until done. Makes 18-30 rolls, depending on size. I often double this recipe. May refrigerate dough for a day or two after kneading, but cover well. Then shape into desired rolls, let rise, and bake at 375° until done.

❦ ORANGE ROLLS ❦
Shirley Schuchard
From Ron Paul Cook Book

Dough:

1 pkg. yeast
¼ c. very warm water
¼ c. sugar
1 tsp. salt
2 eggs

½ c. sour cream
6 T. melted butter
3½ c. all-purpose flour,
   divided

Dissolve the yeast in water, let stand 5 minutes. In mixer combine yeast, sugar, salt, eggs, sour cream and melted butter. Gradually add

(continued)

only 2 cups of the flour. Knead remaining flour into dough. Let rise in a warm place until dough doubles, about 2 hours. Knead dough on well floured surface about 15 minutes.

Filling:

¾ c. sugar	2 T. melted butter, divided
2 T. grated orange rind	

Roll half the dough out into a 12-inch circle. Brush it with 1 tablespoon melted butter and sprinkle with half of filling mixture (¾ cup sugar mixed with 2 tablespoons orange rind). Cut into 12 wedges (triangles). Roll up starting with wide end. Repeat with remaining dough. Place point side down in 3 rows in a greased 9 x 13-inch pan. Cover and let rise, or refrigerate overnight. Bake dough at 350° for 20-25 minutes.

Glaze:

¾ c. sugar	½ c. butter
½ c. sour cream	
2 T. fresh squeezed orange juice	

Combine glaze ingredients in a small saucepan and boil for 3 minutes. Pour glaze over rolls when out of oven.

❦ PIZZA DOUGH ❦
Marilyn Thomsen

2 - 2½ c. flour	1 tsp. salt
1 pkg. quick-rise yeast (2¼ tsp.)	1 T. olive oil
1 tsp. sugar	¾ c. water heated to 120 - 130°

Put 2 cups flour, yeast, sugar and salt in bowl of food processor. Pulse a couple times to mix well. Add olive oil to hot water. With processor running, add water/oil to bowl. The dough should form a ball and roll around the bowl. Check the dough and if it is too wet, add ¼ cup more flour. If still to wet, add another ¼ cup flour. (I've never had to add more flour, so I'm guessing that 2 cups is just what is needed in Nebraska.) Place dough in oiled bowl, turning so top is oiled too. Cover and let stand for 30 minutes while you assemble what you want for pizza sauce and toppings. Put a thin coat of oil on counter surface and rolling pin. Roll out dough to desired thickness. The recipe will make

(continued)

2 small thin crust pizzas. Add your favorite pizza sauce and toppings to within 1-inch of the edge of the dough. Bake in 400° oven until crust and cheese are golden brown.

❧ PLACHENDA/BLADGINDA/ PLATCHINTA ❧
Harry Naasz

Dough:

4 c. flour
1½ c. lard
1 tsp. salt

2 tsp. baking powder
½ c. water

Mix all ingredients for dough and make pastry into small round balls.

Filling:

1 qt. cooked pumpkin
½ c. sugar
½ tsp. salt

Pinch of pepper
Cinnamon, nutmeg, ginger as
    desired

Roll out individual pastry balls and put one tablespoon filling on one side and bring other side over (like a turnover) and press together with fork. Place on cookie sheet and bake about 20-30 minutes at 375°. If you see smoke, it's been too long!

❧ SCONES ❧
Ruth Manning

2 c. flour
1½ T. baking powder
¼ c. sugar
½ tsp. salt
1 stick butter, room
    temperature

½ c. plus 1 T. either milk,
    cream, half and half or
    buttermilk

Preheat oven to 425°. Put flour, baking powder, sugar and salt in a large bowl. Blend with a whisk. Cut butter into chunks and add to flour. Mix with electric mixer until crumbly. Add milk and mix briefly with mixer until milk is mixed in. Move dough to a sheet of waxed paper. Pat dough into a ½-inch circle. Place dough on ungreased baking

(continued)

121822-12

sheet and use a plain table knife to cut into 8 slices. Bake for about 12 minutes or until light golden brown. Transfer to a wire rack to cool before serving. Separate sections and serve with butter, lemon curd or jam/jelly. Variations: Orange Currant Scones - add grated peel of 1 large orange, 1 tsp. orange extract and ⅓ c. currants; Cranberry Scones - add ⅔ c. dried cranberries, 1 tsp. orange zest; Cinnamon Sugar Scones - add 1 tsp. cinnamon, ½ c. cinnamon chips, and sprinkle with cinnamon mixed with 2 tsp. sugar before baking. Make your own blends using dried blueberries with lemon zest, cherries or cherry baking chips with almond flavoring, chocolate chips, etc. May divide dough in half and make smaller scones.

❦ SNICKERDOODLE BREAD ❦
Laura Armitage

Bread:

1 c. butter, softened	¾ c. sour cream
2 c. sugar	2½ c. all-purpose flour
½ tsp. salt	1 tsp. baking powder
2 tsp. cinnamon	1 pkg. Hershey's cinnamon
3 eggs	chips
1 tsp. vanilla	

Cream butter, sugar, salt, and cinnamon until fluffy. Add eggs and mix well. Add vanilla and sour cream, mix well. Mix flour and baking powder in a separate bowl. Add to wet ingredients and mix until all combined. Add cinnamon chips and stir into batter. Spoon batter into 4 greased and floured mini loaf pans until about ⅔ full.

Topping:

3 T. sugar	3 tsp. cinnamon

Mix sugar and cinnamon, sprinkle over batter in loaf pans. Bake at 350° for 35-38 minutes. Let cool before removing from pan.

❦ SOMETHING DIFFERENT SWEET ROLLS ❦
Shirley Schuchard

1 pkg. yellow cake mix
  WITHOUT pudding
2 pkgs. yeast
2 T. sugar
5 c. flour
2½ c. hot water

1 T. butter
4 T. white corn syrup
2 tsp. cinnamon
4 T. brown sugar
¾ c. nuts

In large bowl, mix cake mix, yeast, sugar and flour. Stir in water slowly. Cover and let rise 1 hour. Roll dough on floured board to 12 x 14-inches. Roll up jelly roll fashion and cut 1½-inches thick. Place in baking pan. Let rise ½ hour. Combine butter, corn syrup, cinnamon and brown sugar; heat until melted. Pour over rolls and sprinkle with nuts. Bake at 350° for 25 minutes.

❦ STAY-SOFT CARAMEL ROLL SYRUP ❦
Deb Lund

½ c. margarine or butter
2 c. brown sugar
4 T. white corn syrup

4 T. milk
½ tsp. vanilla
Scant 1 T. vinegar

Melt margarine or butter in microwave in a 4 cup microwave safe glass bowl or measuring cup. Stir in sugar, syrup, and milk. Cook on high and bring to a boil. Stir, then boil one minute. Add vanilla and stir. Stir in vinegar. Pour into bottoms of two 10 x 14-inch pans for caramel rolls. There is no taste of vinegar after baking. The caramel topping stays soft. However, if using refrigerator dough, let dough rise in fridge, then add caramel syrup right before baking. Make ½ the recipe for one pan of rolls.

121822-12

❦ SWEET CORN BREAD MUFFINS ❦
Heidi Meyer

2 eggs, beaten
1 c. milk
2 c. Bisquick

¾ c. sugar
½ tsp. baking soda
5 heaping T. yellow cornmeal

Beat eggs in a bowl and add milk. Fold in Bisquick, sugar, baking soda, and cornmeal. Fill muffin cups with mixture. Bake at 350° approximately 15-20 minutes.

❦ ZUCCHINI BREAD ❦
Randi VenHuizen

3 eggs
1 c. oil
2 c. sugar
2 c. peeled and grated zucchini
2 tsp. vanilla
3 c. flour

¼ tsp. baking soda
¼ tsp. baking powder
1 tsp. salt
3 tsp. cinnamon
½ c. nuts (optional)

Beat eggs until light and foamy. Add oil, sugar, zucchini and vanilla. Mix lightly but well. Mix flour, soda, baking powder, salt and cinnamon in bowl. Add flour mixture to first mixture and blend. Add nuts if using. Bake in 2 greased 9 x 5-inch loaf pans at 325 ° for one hour or longer until tooth pick comes out clean.

❦ ZUCCHINI BREAD ❦
Lisa Rieff

3 c. flour
1 tsp. salt
1 tsp. baking soda
1 tsp. baking powder
3 tsp. cinnamon
3 eggs

1 c. vegetable oil
2 ¼ c. sugar
3 tsp. vanilla
2 c. grated zucchini
1 c. chopped walnuts

Grease and flour two 8 x 4-inch bread pans. Sift together the flour, salt, baking soda, baking powder, and the cinnamon. In a large bowl, beat together the eggs, vegetable oil, sugar and vanilla. Add the flour mixture to the large bowl and mix well. Stir in the zucchini and nuts. Bake at 325° for 40-60 minutes. Cool in pan 20 minutes before removing.

Breakfast & Brunch

Helpful Hints

- Never overcook foods that are to be frozen. Foods will finish cooking when reheated. Don't refreeze cooked, thawed foods.

- When freezing foods, label each container with its contents and the date it was put into the freezer. Always use frozen, cooked foods within 1–2 months.

- To avoid teary eyes when cutting onions, cut them under cold running water or briefly place them in the freezer before cutting.

- Fresh lemon juice will remove onion scent from hands.

- To get the most juice out of fresh lemons, bring them to room temperature and roll them under your palm against the kitchen counter before cutting and squeezing.

- Add raw rice to the salt shaker to keep the salt free flowing.

- Transfer jelly and salad dressings to small plastic squeeze bottles – no more messy, sticky jars!

- Ice cubes will help sharpen garbage disposal blades.

- Separate stuck-together glasses by filling the inside glass with cold water and setting both in hot water.

- Clean CorningWare® by filling it with water and dropping in two denture cleaning tablets. Let stand for 30–45 minutes.

- Always spray your grill with nonstick cooking spray before grilling to avoid sticking.

- To make a simple polish for copper bottom cookware, mix equal parts of flour and salt with vinegar to create a paste.

- Purchase a new coffee grinder and mark it "spices." It can be used to grind most spices; however, cinnamon bark, nutmeg, and others must be broken up a little first. Clean the grinder after each use.

- In a large shaker, combine 6 parts salt and 1 part pepper for quick and easy seasoning.

- Save your store-bought bread bags and ties—they make perfect storage bags for homemade bread.

- Next time you need a quick ice pack, grab a bag of frozen peas or other vegetables out of the freezer.

BREAKFAST AND BRUNCH

❦ APPLE CINNAMON FRENCH TOAST ❦
Valerie Florea

¾ c. butter, melted
1 c. brown sugar
1 tsp. ground cinnamon
1 or 2 (21-oz.) cans apple pie
   filling

15 slices white bread
6 eggs
1½ c. milk
1 tsp. vanilla extract
½ c. maple syrup

Grease a 9 x 13-inch baking pan. In a small bowl, stir together the melted butter, brown sugar and cinnamon. Spread the sugar mixture into the bottom of the prepared pan. Spread the apple pie filling evenly over the sugar mixture. Layer the bread slices on top of the filling, pressing down as you go. In a medium bowl, beat the eggs with the milk and vanilla. Slowly pour this mixture over the bread, making sure that it is completely absorbed. Cover the pan with aluminum foil and refrigerate overnight. In the morning, preheat oven to 350°. Place covered pan into the oven and bake for 75 minutes. When done remove from oven and turn on broiler. Remove foil and drizzle maple syrup on top of the egg topping; broil for 2 minutes or until the syrup begins to caramelize. Remove from the oven and let stand for 10 minutes, then cut into squares. Invert the pan onto a serving tray or baking sheet so the apple filling is on top. Serve hot.

❦ BAKED EGG BRUNCH ❦
Shari Garder

¼ c. chopped onion
¼ c. chopped green pepper
5 T. butter, divided
12 eggs, beaten
2 c. diced ham or cooked
   sausage or cooked venison

4½ oz. can mushrooms
2 T. flour
1 tsp. chicken bouillon
½ c. milk
2 oz. shredded Swiss cheese
¼ c. grated Parmesan cheese

Cook onion and pepper in 3 T. butter. Add eggs and ham; cook until firm but moist. Stir in mushrooms. In separate pan melt 2 T. butter. Whisk in flour and bouillon. Add milk; stir until thick. Add cheeses;

(continued)

stir until melted. Fold sauce into egg mixture. Pour into greased 9 x 13-inch pan.

Topping:

2 c. soft bread crumbs
¼ c. grated Parmesan cheese
¼ c. melted butter or
   margarine

2 T. chopped parsley

Mix together and sprinkle on egg mixture. Bake at 350° for 25-30 minutes. This can be made ahead and refrigerated or frozen, but do not put on topping until ready to bake.

❦ BANANA PANCAKES ❦
Marilyn Thomsen

⅓ c. flour
½ tsp. baking powder
1 egg, lightly beaten

½ tsp. vanilla
1 ripe banana, mashed

Combine flour and baking powder. Combine egg, vanilla and banana and add to dry ingredients. Pour batter onto hot griddle coated with cooking spray. Turn when bubbles form on top. Cook until second side is golden brown. Serve with syrup as desired. Makes two pancakes.

❦ BREAKFAST BAKE ❦
Julie Concannon

1 can (8 oz.) refrigerated
   crescent dinner rolls
1 pkg. (8 oz.) smoked ham,
   chopped
6 eggs

½ c. milk
½ tsp. pepper
1 c. shredded Cheddar cheese
1 c. shredded mozzarella
   cheese

Heat oven to 350°. Unroll dough in 13 x 9-inch baking dish; press to cover bottom of dish, firmly pressing perforations and seams together to seal. Top with ham. Whisk eggs, milk and pepper until well blended; pour over ham. Top with cheeses. Bake 25 minutes or until center is set. 8 servings.

121822-12

❧ BREAKFAST CASSEROLE ❧
Paula Foster

1 lb. pork sausage
10 eggs, beaten
3 c. milk (whole, 2%, 1% or skim)
2 tsp. dry mustard
1 tsp. salt
6 c. cubed bread or use stuffing mix, divided
½ tsp. pepper, divided
2 c. shredded Cheddar cheese, divided
½ c. diced green pepper (optional), divided
½ c. diced onion, divided

Preheat oven to 325°. Brown sausage until no longer pink and then drain off grease. In large mixing bowl, combine eggs, milk, mustard and salt. Stir well. Put 3 cups of bread cubes in a buttered, or use cooking spray, 9 x 13-inch baking pan. Sprinkle ½ of the pepper, 1 cup of cheese, ¼ cup of green pepper and onion and ½ of the cooked sausage over the bread cubes. Repeat the layer using remaining bread, pepper, cheese, sausage, green pepper and onion. Pour the egg mixture over the casserole. Bake uncovered for 60 minutes or until the eggs are set. If the top starts to get too brown, cover with foil. Serves 6.

❧ BREAKFAST HOT DISH ❧
Julie Concannon
From my Aunt Carol Montgomery

2½ c. herb croutons
2 c. shredded sharp Cheddar cheese
2 lbs. ground sausage
4 eggs
¾ tsp. dry mustard
2½ c. milk
1 can cream of mushroom soup
1 sm. can mushrooms

Place croutons in two greased 8 x 8 x 2-inch pans, top with cheese. Cook sausage in skillet until brown; drain on paper toweling. Place sausage over cheese in pans. Beat eggs; mix with mustard, milk, mushroom soup and mushrooms. Pour over sausage in pans. May be refrigerated overnight before baking, if desired. Bake in preheated 300° oven for 1½ hours. 12-18 servings.

❦ BREAKFAST PIE ❦
Lisa Rieff

5 eggs
2½ c. frozen shredded hash
  browns
½ c. cottage cheese
⅓ c. milk

1 green onion, sliced
1 tsp. salt
⅛ tsp. pepper
8 slices bacon, cooked crispy

Grease bottom of 9-inch pie plate. Beat eggs until foamy. Stir in hash browns, cottage cheese, milk, green onion, salt and pepper. Crumble bacon over the top. Cover and refrigerate overnight. Bake uncovered at 325° for 50-60 minutes or until knife comes out clean.

❦ BREAKFAST PIZZA ❦
Karen Anderson

1 pizza crust (pre-made or
  refrigerated variety)
1 sm. jar cheese spread
6 - 8 eggs, scrambled
½ lb. seasoned sausage,
  browned

6 - 8 slices bacon, browned
  and crumbled
Shaved ham
2 c. shredded Cheddar cheese

Prepare all ingredients before making crust. Prepare crust according to box/package. Bake crust 5 minutes before adding toppings. Cover crust with cheese spread to taste. Top with scrambled eggs, sausage, bacon, ham and Cheddar cheese. Bake for remaining time (10-12 minutes).

❦ BROCCOLI, EGG AND HAM BAKE ❦
Susan Lueders

2 (10 oz.) pkgs. cut broccoli in
  cheese sauce
12 slices white bread, divided
2 c. cubed cooked ham
1 c. shredded Cheddar cheese
6 beaten eggs

3 c. milk
2 T. minced onion
½ tsp. salt
¼ tsp. pepper
1½ c. shredded Cheddar
  cheese

(continued)

121822-12

Cook broccoli as package directs. Line a greased 9 x 13-inch cake pan with 6 slices of bread. Cover the bread with the following layers; broccoli, ham and cheese. Repeat, starting with bread. Combine eggs, milk, onion, salt, pepper and cheese. Pour over broccoli mixture. Bake uncovered at 325° for 1 hour. Let stand 10 minutes and serve. Note: To prepare the night before serving: Save the remaining 1½ cups of cheese. Combine all other ingredients, cover and refrigerate overnight. In the morning, sprinkle with cheese and then bake.

❦ BRUNCH FRUIT SALAD ❦
Ruth Manning

1 (20 oz.) can pineapple chunks	1 Golden Delicious apple, sliced
2 lg. firm bananas, cut into ¼-inch chunks	1 Red Delicious apple, sliced
1 c. green grapes	½ c. sugar
1 (15 oz.) can mandarin oranges, drained	2 T. cornstarch
	⅓ c. orange juice
	1 T. lemon juice

Drain pineapple, reserving juice. Combine the pineapple, bananas, grapes, oranges and apples in a large bowl and set aside. In a saucepan, combine sugar and cornstarch. Add the orange juice, lemon juice and reserved pineapple juice. Stir until smooth. Bring to a boil; reduce heat. Cook and stir for 2 minutes. Pour over fruit; mix gently. Cover and refrigerate until ready to serve. Serves 6.

❦ BRUNCH PIZZA ❦
Julie Concannon
Pampered Chef

Crust:

1 pkg. (24 oz.) frozen shredded hash brown patties, thawed and broken apart	1 egg
	Salt and pepper to taste

Preheat oven to 400°. Place parchment paper on 15-inch baking stone. Combine potatoes and 1 egg in batter bowl. Spread potatoes on baking stone in 14-inch circle. Pat down, season with salt and pepper. Bake for 20 minutes.

(continued)

Egg Topping:

7 eggs
½ c. milk
1½ c. shredded Cheddar
cheese
Optional ingredients: Chopped
onions, chopped green
peppers,

sliced mushrooms, cooked and
crumbled bacon, chopped
ham, etc.

Whisk eggs and milk in batter bowl. Place in microwave and cook on high for 3 minutes. Stir. Cook for an additional 3 minutes. Stir. Spread cooked eggs evenly over baked potato crust. Top with optional ingredients. Sprinkle with cheese and bake an additional 10 minutes. Cut into wedges with pizza cutter. 10-12 servings.

❦ CASSY'S QUICHE ❦
Barb Haskins

1 pie crust (I use pre-made
frozen crusts)
½ lb. or less meat (hamburger,
ham, or chicken, all cooked)
Green peppers, broccoli,
onion, etc. to taste
½ c. mayonnaise (not salad
dressing)

½ c. milk
3 eggs
1 T. corn starch
Salt and pepper to taste
1½ c. shredded Cheddar
cheese

Bake pie crust for 5 to 7 minutes. Remove from oven. Prepare meat and any vegetables you are using. In a mixing bowl, mix together the mayonnaise, milk, eggs, cornstarch, salt and pepper. Beat until well blended. Add prepared meat, veggies and cheese. Stir and pour into partially baked pie crust. Bake at 350° for 35 to 40 minutes or until knife comes out clean. Serves 4 to 5.

121822-12

❦ CREME BRULEE FRENCH TOAST ❦
Lisa Rieff

½ c. butter
1 c. brown sugar
2 T. corn syrup
6 - 8 slices Texas bread
5 eggs

1½ c. half and half
1 tsp. vanilla
1 tsp. Grand Marnier
¼ tsp. salt

Melt butter in small saucepan over medium heat. Add brown sugar and corn syrup, stirring until sugar dissolves. Pour into 9 x 13-inch pan and spread evenly. Remove crust from bread. Cut bread to fit and cover entire surface of pan. Whisk together eggs, half and half, vanilla, Grand Marnier and salt. Pour over bread. Cover and refrigerate overnight. Remove and bring to room temperature (about 30-45 minutes). Bake at 350° for 35-40 minutes until puffy and golden.

❦ CROISSANT STUFFED FRENCH TOAST ❦
Randi VenHuizen
Debra Gillespie
Ruth Manning

Nonstick cooking spray
4 croissants, split
8 oz. softened cream cheese
2 eggs, lightly beaten

½ c. milk
½ tsp. ground cinnamon
Powdered sugar
Maple syrup, warmed

Preheat oven to 375°. Line a shallow baking pan with foil. Coat the foil with cooking spray. Set aside. Spread cut sides of croissants with cream cheese. Place cut sides back together. In a shallow dish, beat together the eggs, milk and cinnamon with a fork. Dip each filled croissant in the egg mixture for 30 seconds turning once. Place in prepared baking pan. Bake about 15 minutes or until browned and heated through. Sprinkle with powdered sugar. Serve warm with warm maple syrup. Makes 4 servings.

❦ EGG CASSEROLE ❦
Matt Garder

10 slices English muffin loaf bread	¾ c. milk
2 lbs. sausage	Chopped onion (optional)
2 c. shredded Colby cheese, divided	Salt and pepper to taste
12 lg. eggs	1 family size can cream of mushroom soup

Use 9 x 13-inch pan, spray with cooking spray. Cut or tear bread into small pieces and cover bottom of pan. Brown sausage, drain and place on top of bread. Lightly sprinkle some of the cheese over the warm sausage. In a bowl, blend eggs, milk, onion, salt, and pepper. Pour egg mixture over sausage. Cover with tin foil and refrigerate over night. Just before baking, mix mushroom soup with a splash of milk (to make spreading consistency). Pour over eggs. Lastly, cover with remainder of cheese. Bake at 350° for 45-50 minutes; uncovered. Contents should be solid, not jiggly, and slightly brown on top.

❦ FESTIVE FILLED FRENCH TOAST ❦
Ruth Manning

8 slices Vienna or Italian bread, 1½-inches thick	4 lg. eggs
6 oz. cream cheese, softened	1 c. half and half
2 T. sugar	½ c. milk
10 oz. jar marmalade or preserves (your choice of flavor)	1 tsp. vanilla
	½ tsp. cinnamon, ground
	Dash of ground nutmeg

Using a serrated knife, carefully cut a horizontal pocket in the middle of each bread slice, cutting only ¾-inch into slice, leaving a flap. Set aside. Mix the cream cheese with sugar. Mix well. Add marmalade or preserves, and mix well. Divide cream cheese mixture evenly among the pockets of the bread slices, and close flap. Place in 9 x 13-inch glass baking dish. Combine eggs, half and half, milk, vanilla, cinnamon and nutmeg and beat well. Pour half of the egg mixture over the bread, allowing a minute or two for the mixture to be absorbed. Turn slices over. Pour the remaining egg mixture over the bread slices to coat

(continued)

evenly. Cover and refrigerate over night. Remove from refrigerator 30 minutes before baking. Preheat oven to 425°. Butter a baking sheet and place soaked bread slices onto the sheet. Bake for about 7 minutes. Turn bread slices over and bake an additional 8 minutes more or until golden brown.

❦ FRENCH TOAST CASSEROLE WITH MAPLE SYRUP ❦
Shari Garder

1 loaf French bread cut into 20, 1-inch slices	**2 T. sugar**
8 lg. eggs	**1 tsp. vanilla**
2 c. half and half	**¼ tsp. cinnamon**
1 c. milk	**¼ tsp. ground nutmeg**

Arrange bread slices in a generously buttered 9 x 13-inch baking dish in 2 rows, seriously overlapping the slices. In a large bowl, combine the eggs, half and half, milk, sugar, vanilla, cinnamon, and nutmeg whisking until blended but not too bubbly. Pour the mixture over the bread slices, making sure all are covered evenly with the milk-egg mixture. Spoon some of the mixture in between the slices. Cover with foil and refrigerate overnight.

Praline Topping:

½ lb. (2 sticks) butter, melted	**2 T. light corn syrup**
1 c. packed light brown sugar	**½ tsp. cinnamon**
1 c. chopped pecans	**½ tsp. ground nutmeg**

In the morning, preheat oven to 350°. While preheating, prepare the praline topping. Combine all ingredients in a medium bowl and blend well. Spread praline topping evenly over the bread and bake for 40 minutes, until puffed and lightly golden. Can serve with maple syrup if desired.

❦ FROZEN FRUIT CUPS ❦
Lisa Meyer

3 c. water
3 c. sugar
16 oz. can crushed pineapple
  with juice
3 (11 oz.) cans mandarin
  oranges with juice

3 T. real lemon juice
3 sliced bananas
2 (10 oz.) pkgs. frozen
  strawberries
2 (16 oz.) bags frozen
  raspberries

Boil water and sugar. Then mix boiled mixture with all other ingredients. Pour into 8 oz. plastic cups and freeze. Makes approximately 24 cups.

❦ HAM & CHEESE OMELET BREAD ❦
Karen Anderson

6 eggs, beaten until foamy
¾ c. milk
½ c. flour
2½ tsp. baking powder
½ tsp. salt
1 c. Monterey Jack cheese,
  cubed

1 c. Swiss cheese, cubed
1 c. sharp Cheddar cheese,
  cubed
1 c. cooked ham, cubed
6 slices bacon, fried and
  crumbled

Mix eggs, milk, flour, baking powder and salt. Add cheeses, ham and bacon to egg mixture. Pour into 1 greased and floured loaf pan. Bake at 350° for 50-60 minutes or until golden brown and dry in center when tested. Vary the bread by adding green peppers, onions, etc.

❦ HAM AND EGG STUFF ❦
Judy Egr

3 c. cubed, cooked ham or
  cooked bacon
3 c. bread (broken up)
½ lb. Cheddar cheese
4 T. flour
1 T. prepared mustard

3 T. melted butter
3 c. milk
4 eggs, beaten
Salt and pepper to taste
Onion and green pepper,
  chopped (optional)

(continued)

Layer ⅓ ham, bread and cheese and repeat the layers 3 times. Mix flour, mustard and butter. Add milk, eggs, salt and pepper and optional ingredients if using. Pour over ham, bread and cheese. Refrigerate overnight. Bake at 350° for 1 hour in a greased 13 x 9-inch pan.

❦ HASHBROWN BREAKFAST CASSEROLE ❦
Kathy Christiansen
Marilyn Mattheis

1 stick butter, melted
Bag of frozen hashbrowns
10 - 12 eggs
1 c. milk
1 can of cream of mushroom soup (or cream of chicken or celery)

½ c. sour cream
2 c. shredded cheese
Breakfast meat of choice (cooked sausage, diced ham, diced cooked bacon)

Pour ¾ of melted butter into 9 x 13-inch pan. Reserve 1 cup of hashbrowns. Pour remaining hashbrowns over butter. In a large bowl, beat eggs. Add in milk, soup and sour cream and mix well. Stir in cheese and breakfast meat. Sprinkle reserved hash browns over the top and drizzle with remaining butter. Cover and bake at 350° for 1¼ hours. Remove foil last 30 minutes to brown up the top. You can make this the night before, cover with foil and refrigerate. Remove from fridge about 30 minutes before baking. Bake as above.

❦ IMPOSSIBLE BACON QUICHE ❦
Julie Concannon

12 slices bacon, cooked and crumbled
1 c. shredded Swiss cheese
⅓ c. chopped onion
2 c. milk

1 c. Bisquick
4 eggs
¼ tsp. salt
⅛ tsp. pepper

Preheat oven to 400°. Lightly grease a 10-inch pie plate. Sprinkle bacon, cheese and onion in pie plate. Beat milk, Bisquick, eggs, salt and pepper in medium bowl with electric mixer until smooth. Pour into pie plate. Bake for 35 minutes. Let stand 5 minutes before serving. 6-8 servings.

❦ OMELETTE IN A BAG ❦
Jackie Combes

Freezer bags (1 pt. size)
2 eggs
2 T. milk

Your choice of other
ingredients: cheese, ham,
vegetables, etc.

For each person, place two large eggs in a freezer bag. Add milk. Squish eggs and milk to mix. Add additional ingredients. Mix together. Squeeze all air from the bag, seal. Place bags in large pot of boiling water. Cook about 15 minutes. Check omelette for doneness before serving.

❦ OVEN BAKED EGG CASSEROLE ❦
Randi VenHuizen
Brad VenHuizen

9 slices white bread with
crusts removed
1 lb. grated Cheddar cheese
1 lb. cooked bacon, chopped
6 eggs

1 tsp. dry mustard
1 tsp. onion salt
Salt and pepper to taste
2 c. milk
2 c. half and half

Cut bread into cubes. Layer bread, cheese and bacon in greased 9 x 13-inch pan. Mix remaining ingredients together. Pour over bread mixture. Cover tightly and refrigerate overnight. Uncover and bake for approximately one hour in 350° oven.

❦ OVERNIGHT EGG CASSEROLE ❦
Julie Concannon

4 c. frozen shredded hash
brown potatoes, thawed
1 c. cubed fully cooked ham
1 can (4 oz.) chopped green
chilies
½ c. shredded Monterey Jack
cheese

½ c. shredded Cheddar cheese
6 eggs
1 can (12 oz.) evaporated milk
¼ tsp. pepper
Salsa, optional

In a greased 8-inch square baking dish, layer the hash browns, ham, chilies and cheeses. In a large bowl, whisk the eggs, milk and pepper; pour over the cheese. Cover and refrigerate overnight. Remove from

(continued)

the refrigerator 30 minutes before baking. Bake, uncovered, at 350°
for 1 hour or until a knife inserted near the center comes out clean.
Let stand for 5-10 minutes. Serve with salsa if desired. 9 servings.

❦ PEACH FRENCH TOAST ❦
Karen Armitage

1 c. packed brown sugar	5 eggs
½ c. butter or margarine	1½ c. milk
2 T. water	1 T. vanilla
1 can (29 oz.) sliced peaches,	Ground cinnamon
drained	Syrup
12 slices day-old French bread	
(¾-inch thick)	

In a saucepan, bring brown sugar, butter and water to a boil. Reduce
heat and simmer for 10 minutes, stirring frequently. Pour into a greased
9 x 13-inch baking dish. Top with peaches. Arrange bread over peaches.
In a bowl, whisk eggs, milk and vanilla; slowly pour over the bread.
Cover and refrigerate for 8 hours or overnight. Remove from the
refrigerator 30 minutes before baking. Sprinkle with cinnamon. Cover
and bake at 350° for 20 minutes. Uncover and bake 25-30 minutes
longer or until the bread is golden brown. Serve with a spoon, drizzling
syrup over the French toast. Yield: 6-8 servings.

❦ QUICHE ❦
Shari Garder

6 eggs	1 c. browned bacon, ham or
1 c. half and half	imitation crab
1¼ tsp. seasonings-lemon	1 c. Swiss or mozzarella cheese
pepper, cayenne red pepper,	1 deep dish pie crust
pepper, dillweed	

Whisk eggs, add half and half, and seasonings. Stir in meat and cheese.
Pour into pie crust. Bake at 375° for 50 minutes. Knife inserted in
center should come out clean. You can make ahead and freeze in
ziplock bags. To reheat thaw in refrigerator overnight. Heat in 350°
oven for 30 minutes or you can reheat frozen for 60 minutes.

❦ SAUSAGE PIE ❦
Dayla Miller

1 pkg. skinless pork sausage
3 c. frozen hashbrowns
½ c. chopped green onion
2 T. milk
½ tsp. salt
¼ tsp. pepper

1 (8 oz.) pkg. cream cheese, softened
¾ c. Bisquick
⅓ c. milk
2 eggs

Cook sausage until light brown, drain. Grease pie plate, spread potatoes in pie plate. Mix green onion, 2 T. milk, salt, pepper and cream cheese; spread over the potatoes and arrange sausage over top. Beat baking mix, ⅓ cup milk and eggs with wire whisk or hand beater until smooth and pour mixture around sausages. Bake in 400° oven, uncovered, until edge is light brown and center is set, 25-30 minutes.

❦ STUFFIN' EGG MUFFIN ❦
Julie Concannon

1 pkg. (6 oz.) Stove Top stuffing mix for chicken (and ingredients to prepare)

12 sm. eggs
3 T. real bacon bits
½ c. shredded Colby and Monterey Jack cheese

Heat oven to 400°. Prepare stuffing as directed on package, omitting the stand time. Press ¼ cup stuffing onto bottom and up side of each of 12 muffin cups sprayed with cooking spray, forming ¼-inch rim around top of cup. Add 1 egg to each cup. Top with bacon and cheese. Bake 20 minutes or until yolks are set. Let stand 5 minutes before serving. 6 servings (2 "muffins" each).

❦ WAKE UP BREAKFAST CASSEROLE ❦
Rose Roberts
Janet Guthrie

8 frozen hash brown patties
2 c. shredded Cheddar cheese
2 c. fully cooked, cubed ham
7 eggs

1 c. milk
½ tsp. salt
½ tsp. ground mustard

(continued)

121822-12

Place hash brown patties in a single layer in a greased 9 x 13-inch pan. Sprinkle with cheese and ham. In a bowl, beat eggs, milk, salt and mustard. Pour over ham. Cover and bake at 350° for 1 hour. Uncover and bake for 15 minutes longer or until edges are golden brown and knife inserted near the center comes out clean.

Recipe Favorites

Cooking for a Crowd

Helpful Hints

- If the soup is not intended as the main course, count on 1 quart to serve 6. As the main dish, plan on 1 quart to serve 2.

- After cooking vegetables, pour any water and leftover vegetable pieces into a freezer container. When full, add tomato juice and seasoning to create a money-saving "free soup."

- Instant potatoes help thicken soups and stews.

- A leaf of lettuce dropped in a pot of soup absorbs grease from the top – remove the lettuce and serve. You can also make soup the day before, chill, and scrape off the hardened fat that rises to the top.

- To cut down on odors when cooking cabbage or cauliflower, add a little vinegar to the water and don't overcook.

- Three large stalks of celery, chopped and added to about two cups of beans (navy, brown, pinto, etc.), make the dish easier to digest.

- Fresh is best, but to reduce time in the kitchen, use canned or frozen broths or bouillon bases. Canned or frozen vegetables, such as peas, green beans, and corn, also work well.

- Ideally, cold soups should be served in chilled bowls.

- Perk up soggy lettuce by spritzing it with a mixture of lemon juice and cold water.

- You can easily remove egg shells from hard-boiled eggs if you quickly rinse the eggs in cold water after they are boiled. Add a drop of food coloring to help distinguish cooked eggs from raw ones.

- Your fruit salads will look better when you use an egg slicer to make perfect slices of strawberries, kiwis, or bananas.

- The ratio for a vinaigrette is typically 3 parts oil to 1 part vinegar.

- For salads, cook pasta al dente (slightly chewy to the bite). This allows the pasta to absorb some of the dressing and not become mushy.

- Fresh vegetables require little seasoning or cooking. If the vegetable is old, dress it up with sauces or seasoning.

- Chill the serving plates to keep the salad crisp.

- Fruit juices, such as pineapple and orange, can be used as salad dressing by adding a little olive oil, nutmeg, and honey.

COOKING FOR A CROWD

❦ BREAKFAST STRATA ❦
(For lg. 2-inch deep casserole pan)
Connie Walther

2 lbs. frozen hash brown
  potatoes or a loaf dried
  bread, cubed
2 c. milk
3 c. shredded Cheddar cheese
1 - 1½ lbs. diced ham or
  ground sausage (cooked and
  drained)

½ c. chopped onion (or to
  taste)
Season to taste with parsley,
  salt, pepper, cayenne
2 tsp. dry mustard
1 dozen eggs
Paprika

Spray baking dish and fill bottom with potatoes or bread. Mix milk, cheese, meat, onions, parsley, salt, pepper, cayenne and dry mustard. Pour over potatoes/bread. Beat eggs well; add to casserole. Sprinkle with paprika. Bake uncovered at 350° for 40-45 minutes. Serves 16-20.

❦ CHICKEN ENCHILADA CASSEROLE ❦
Ruth Manning

36 chicken breast halves
½ c. oregano
6 T. garlic powder
2 T. salt
6 (10 oz.) cans cream of
  mushroom soup
6 (10 oz.) cans cream of
  chicken soup
6 (16 oz.) containers sour
  cream

6 (8 oz.) cans diced mild green
  chilies
2 lg. onions, diced
48 (8-inch) flour tortillas
64 oz. shredded Mexican
  Cheddar cheese mixture,
  divided

Place chicken in a large pot and cover with water. Sprinkle in oregano; add garlic powder and salt. Boil about 20 minutes and shred from bones (save the broth). Mix soups, sour cream and chilies in a large pan. Add only enough reserved broth to slightly thin. Re-season as needed. Simmer on low 15 minutes. Add chicken and onion. Spoon
(continued)

mixture equally in center of each tortilla, top each tortilla with ½ of the shredded cheese, roll tortillas and place in six greased 9 x 13-inch or larger baking pans. Bake in 350° oven for 20 minutes. Remove and sprinkle remaining shredded cheese over top of casseroles. Bake until cheese melts. Serves 48. Optional preparation: Portion out tortillas per number of pans. Take that pan's portion, layer ½ of the tortillas, ½ of chicken mixture, ½ of the cheese. Repeat for second layer. Bake as above.

❦ CHICKEN SALAD FOR 50 ❦
Ruth Manning

Salad:

9 c. cubed cooked chicken
9 c. cooked small pasta shells
8 c. chopped celery
8 c. seedless green grapes, halved

18 hard cooked eggs, chopped
2 (20 oz.) cans pineapple tidbits, drained

In first of two very large bowls combine chicken, pasta shells, celery, grapes, eggs and pineapple tidbits.

Dressing:

4 c. mayonnaise
16 oz. sour cream
16 oz. Cool Whip whipped topping

¼ c. lemon juice
¼ c. sugar
1½ tsp. salt
2 c. cashew halves

In second bowl, whisk the mayonnaise, sour cream, Cool Whip, lemon juice, sugar and salt. Pour over the chicken mixture; toss to coat. Cover and refrigerate at least 1 hour. Stir in cashews just before serving. Yield: 50 (1 c.) servings.

❦ CITRUS PUNCH ❦
Ruth Manning

16 c. pineapple juice
16 c. orange juice
8 c. grapefruit juice

8 c. lemonade
2 qts. ginger ale

(continued)

Combine pineapple, orange, grapefruit juices and lemonade. Just before serving add ginger ale. Serves 65 punch cup servings.

❧ EASY EGG BAKE ❧
Deb Lund

3 loaves of sliced bread
5 lbs. grated Cheddar cheese (divided by 4)
3 lbs. cooked ham, cubed (divided by 4)
1½ gallon milk (6 cups per pan)

4 dozen eggs (1 dozen per pan)
Salt to taste (about ¼ tsp. per pan)
Pepper to taste
Dried mustard, to taste, if desired (about ¼ tsp. per pan)

Spray 4 large baking pans (12 x 18 x 2-inch) with Pam. Layer bread over bottoms of pans, squishing in some pieces, getting as many slices as possible covering the bottom (you will have about ½ loaf left). Sprinkle one-fourth the 5 lbs. of cheese over the bread in each of the 4 pans. Sprinkle one-fourth of the cubed ham on top of the cheese in each of the pans. In large bowl, beat 1 dozen eggs well. Add 6 cups milk and beat well. Stir in seasonings. Pour slowly over bread/cheese/ham in a pan. Cover with plastic wrap tightly and place in refrigerator. Repeat for other 3 pans. Preheat oven to 350° for regular oven and bake for 45 minutes or until done. If using convection oven, preheat to 325° and bake just over 30 minutes, or until done. Cut into 18-24 pieces per pan, serving as many as 96 smaller or 72 larger servings.

❧ FANCY SAUERKRAUT ❧
Julie Concannon

12 oz. pkg. bacon
1½ onions, minced
4 (1 lb.) cans stewed tomatoes, well drained

2 (1 lb.) cans sauerkraut, well drained
1½ c. sugar
Pepper to taste

Cook bacon and cut in bite sized pieces, reserve drippings. Sauté onion in some of the reserved bacon grease and drain. Mix the tomatoes, sauerkraut, sugar, bacon, onions and pepper and place in 2-quart casserole. Bake at 350° for one hour. 18-24 servings.

❦ FRENCH TOAST CASSEROLE WITH FRUIT ❦

Jackie Combes

French Toast

1 loaf (10 oz.) French bread
   cut into 1-inch cubes (10 c.)
8 eggs
3 c. milk
4 tsp. sugar
1 tsp. vanilla extract

¾ tsp. salt, if desired
2 T. butter or margarine,
   cubed
3 T. sugar
2 tsp. ground cinnamon

Place bread cubes in a greased 9 x 13 x 2-inch baking dish. In a mixing bowl, beat eggs, milk, sugar, vanilla and salt if desired. Pour over bread. Cover and refrigerate for 8 hours or overnight. Remove from the refrigerator 30 minutes before baking. Dot with butter. Combine sugar and cinnamon. Sprinkle over top. Cover and bake at 350° for 45-50 minutes or until a knife inserted near the center comes out clean. Let stand for 5 minutes. Serve with syrup if desired. For large baking pan - double recipe. 8 large baking pans feed 200 people. Purchase 20 (10 oz.) or 13 (16 oz.) loaves bread, 14 dozen eggs, 4 gallons milk, 2 lbs. butter.

Sausage, Juice, and Fruit for 200

56 (12 piece) pkgs. sausage
   links
10 gallons orange juice
5 honeydew melons

12 cantaloupe
4 (4lb.) containers strawberries
3 bags seedless grapes

Brown sausage, keep warm. and serve Cut up fruit, mix together, chill, and serve.

121822-12

❦ HOT HAM SANDWICHES ❦
Mary Lou Gustafson

1 stick butter (must be butter)
1 T. dry onion flakes
1 T. prepared mustard
1 T. Worcestershire sauce
1 T. poppy seeds (I only use
  about 1 tsp.)

12 - 16 deli buns
Shaved ham or turkey ham
Sliced Swiss cheese

Heat butter, onion flakes, mustard, Worcestershire and poppy seeds to boiling. Place meat and cheese in the buns. Place buns in 9 x 13-inch pan. Spoon butter mixture over each sandwich. Cover and put in refrigerator overnight. When ready to serve, bake uncovered at 350° for 20 minutes. Serve warm.

❦ MEAT LOAF MINIATURES ❦
Jackie Combes

1 c. ketchup
3 - 4 T. packed brown sugar
1 tsp. ground mustard
2 eggs, beaten
4 tsp. Worcestershire sauce
3 c. Crispix cereal, crushed

3 tsp. onion powder
½ - 1 tsp. seasoned salt
½ tsp. garlic powder
½ tsp. pepper
3 lbs. lean ground beef

In a large bowl, combine ketchup, brown sugar and mustard. Remove ½ cup for topping; set aside. Add eggs, Worcestershire sauce, cereal and seasonings to remaining ketchup mixture; mix well. Let stand for 5 minutes. Crumble beef over cereal mixture and mix well. Press meat mixture into 18 muffin cups (about ⅓ cup each). Bake at 375° for 18-20 minutes. Drizzle with reserved ketchup mixture; bake 10 minutes longer or until meat is no longer pink and a meat thermometer reads 160°. Serve desired number of meat loaves. Cool remaining loaves; freeze. Transfer to freezer bags, freeze up to 3 months. To use frozen meat loaves: Completely thaw in the refrigerator. Place loaves in a greased baking dish. Bake at 350° for 30 minutes or until heated through, or cover and microwave on high for 1 minute or until heated through. Yield: 1½ dozen.

❦ MORNING PECAN CASSEROLE ❦
Ruth Manning

6 (8 oz.) frozen brown and
  serve sausage patties
Nonstick spray coating
6 (16 oz.) loaves raisin bread,
  cubed (about 12 c.)
36 eggs

9 c. milk
9 c. half and half or light
  cream
2 T. vanilla
1½ tsp. ground nutmeg
1½ tsp. ground cinnamon

In a medium skillet, brown the patties on both sides over medium high heat. Drain off the fat. Cut patties into bite-size pieces. Meanwhile, spray 6 (9 x 13-inch) baking dishes with nonstick coating. Divide bread cubes among the dishes. Add divided browned sausage pieces. In a large mixing bowl beat together the eggs, milk, half and half, vanilla, nutmeg and cinnamon. Divide and pour evenly over the bread and sausage pieces, pressing bread and sausage into the egg mixture.

Topping:

6 c. packed brown sugar
6 c. coarsely chopped pecans
3 c. butter or margarine,
  softened

¾ c. maple syrup or maple-
  flavored syrup

In a bowl, combine brown sugar, pecans, butter and maple syrup. Drop by teaspoonfuls evenly over the tops of the egg mixture. Bake in a 350° oven for 35 to 40 minutes or until a knife inserted near center comes out clean. Depending on size of servings, will serve 48 to 60.

❦ OVEN-BAKED FRENCH TOAST ❦
Ruth Manning

18 T. melted butter
18 slices Texas toast bread
18 eggs
3 c. half and half

6 T. granulated sugar
6 T. orange juice
1½ tsp. vanilla
1½ tsp. nutmeg

Divide melted butter among 3 (9 x 13-inch) baking pans. In each pan, place 6 pieces of Texas toast as close together as possible on butter. Beat together eggs, half and half, sugar, orange juice, vanilla and nutmeg. Pour over bread in pans, turning slices over once to coat evenly. Cover and refrigerate over night.

(continued)

121822-12

Topping:

9 T. butter, softened
2 ¼ c. brown sugar

3 c. finely chopped pecans
(optional)

In the morning, melt the butter and combine with brown sugar and pecans, if desired. Divide and top the three casseroles. Bake at 375° for about 25 minutes, or until firm and golden brown.

❦ PARTY SCRAMBLE ❦
Julie Concannon

½ c. butter or margarine, cut up
1 pouch Lipton onion soup and recipe mix
1 c. bite-sized wheat cereal squares
1 c. bite-sized corn cereal squares

1 bag (6 oz.) Pepperidge Farm cheddar cheese goldfish crackers
1 bag (6 oz.) Pepperidge Farm pretzel goldfish crackers
2 c. salted peanuts

Place butter in 2-cup glass measure. Cover with waxed paper; microwave on HIGH 45 seconds or until melted. Stir in soup mix. In 4-quart microwave-safe bowl, combine wheat and corn cereal squares, cheddar cheese and pretzel goldfish crackers and peanuts. Pour butter mixture over cracker mixture; toss to coat well. Microwave; uncovered, on HIGH 5 minutes or until hot, stirring twice during heating. Cool. Store mixture in airtight container. Makes 10 cups.

❦ SCRAMBLED EGGS FOR 100 ❦
Shari Garder

200 eggs
16 tsp. salt
2 lb. butter

20 c. milk
2 pkgs. bacon bits (opt.)
2 c. Cheddar cheese (opt.)

Heat 2 large roasters to 350°. Beat eggs. Heat milk and salt in roasters. Add eggs, butter, and optional cheese and bacon to milk in roasters. Do not stir. Bake for 30 minutes, stir. Bake another 30 minutes, stir. Serve.

❦ SEAFOOD CHOWDER ❦
Ruth Manning

1 lb. bacon, diced
3 med. onions, chopped
12 c. frozen hash brown
  potatoes (cubes, not shreds)
8 c. water
5 lb. frozen seafood mixture
  (can be purchased at Sam's
  Club)*

1 c. butter, melted
2½ T. salt
3 T. minced fresh parsley (I
  use 2 T. dried parsley flakes)
1 tsp. curry powder
1 gallon milk
2 (12 oz.) cans evaporated
  milk

In a large soup kettle or Dutch oven, cook bacon over medium heat until crisp. Remove with a slotted spoon to paper towels; reserve drippings. Sauté onions in drippings until tender. Add potatoes and water; bring to a boil. Cook for 10 minutes. Add seafood. Cook for 10 minutes. Add bacon, butter, salt, parsley and curry powder. Stir in milk and evaporated milk; heat through. About 60 servings. *I thaw seafood mixture in refrigerator overnight. Then I go over it and cut some of the larger ones into smaller pieces.

❦ SLOPPY JOES ❦
Barb Haskins
Ruth Manning

20 lbs. hamburger
#10 can catsup
2 lb. brown sugar

½ - 1 c. onion flakes
8 - 12 oz. mustard
Salt and pepper to taste

Brown hamburger and drain. Put all ingredients together in electric roaster. Stir well. Start at 350°; lower when boiling to simmer. Let simmer about 2 hours. Serves about 100 sandwiches, depending on size of buns. Ruth's version uses 5 c. catsup, 3 c. brown sugar, and adds 15 cans tomato soup.

❦ SLOPPY JOES ❦
Rex Quadhamer

5 lbs. hamburger
1 lg. onion, chopped
¼ c. brown sugar

¼ c. mustard
1 lg. bottle ketchup
4 eggs

(continued)

Cook hamburger and onion until done. Drain fat. Add brown sugar, mustard and ketchup. Beat eggs and add to hamburger mixture. Cook through. Serves 20+.

❦ STUFFED MUSHROOMS ❦
Rose Roberts

50 cleaned and stemmed mushrooms
1 lb. Jimmy Dean's hot sausage

11 oz. cream cheese
1 tsp. garlic powder

Broil mushrooms for 3 minutes. Brown sausage and drain. Add cream cheese and garlic powder to the meat. Stuff the mushrooms. Just before serving, heat in oven for 15 minutes at 350°. This recipe can be prepared ahead of time.

❦ SWEDISH FRUIT SOUP ❦
Rose Roberts
Myrtle Asper
From Our Savior's Cookbook 1968

2 c. minute tapioca
2 qt. water
1 qt. grape juice
2 c. sugar (or more to taste)
½ c. lemon juice

1 lb. prunes
1 lb. raisins
1 can purple plums
2 whole cinnamon sticks

Boil tapioca in water until clear. In separate large pan combine grape juice, sugar, lemon juice and cinnamon sticks. Heat fruits with juices. Add the tapioca and fruits to large pan. Heat through. Remove cinnamon sticks when ready to serve. Apples or other dried fruit may be used in addition to previous if desired. May be frozen. Makes 6 quarts. Makes 50 servings.

❧ TASTEE SANDWICHES ❧
Julie Concannon

5 lbs. lean ground beef
3 med. onions, chopped fine
1 T. salt
1 T. creamed horseradish
1 T. dry mustard
¼ tsp. black pepper
½ c. ketchup

1 c. water
1 heaping T. Accent
   (monosodium glutamate)
Hamburger buns
Sliced cheese, prepared
   mustard, pickles (if desired)

Put meat and onions in a large saucepan. Put salt, creamed horseradish, dry mustard, black pepper and ketchup in a 16 ounce measuring cup. Mix and pour directly over meat. Stir with a wooden spoon. Add 1 cup water to the same measuring cup and stir around to get all the ingredients off the sides. Pour over the meat. Stir Accent into meat mixture. Stir side of pan a lot and stir the raw meat often until meat begins to boil. (This is to assure that the beef breaks down in to small pieces-you don't want large pieces of meat). Cover saucepan and boil 25 minutes. Serve on hamburger buns with a slice of cheese, prepared mustard and/or pickles if desired. After boiling the meat mixture for 25 minutes, this recipe can be put in a crockpot for 4-5 hours. Serves 20-24 or more if you use mini-hamburger buns!

❧ TATER TOT CASSEROLE ❧
Ruth Manning

10 lbs. ground beef
5 (10¾ oz.) cans cream of
   celery soup
5 (10¾ oz.) cans cream of
   mushroom soup
10 T. Worcestershire sauce

5 lg. Vidalia onions, chopped
2½ c. diced celery
10 - 15 c. shredded Cheddar
   cheese
5 (32 oz.) bags frozen tater
   tots

Brown the ground beef, and drain. Mix celery soup, mushroom soup, Worcestershire sauce, onions and celery together; set aside. Place browned beef in equivalent of 5 (9 x 13-inch) baking pans. Sprinkle with cheese. Cover with soup mixture and arrange tater tots on top to cover. Bake at 350° for one hour. Makes about 48 servings.

121822-12

❦ WESTERN STYLE BEANS ❦
Lisa Rieff

8 slices bacon
4 lg. onions, sliced
¾ c. brown sugar
1 tsp. dry mustard
½ tsp. garlic powder
1 tsp. salt

½ c. cider vinegar
2 cans butter beans
1 can green lima beans
1 can kidney beans
1 (27 oz.) can pork and beans

Fry bacon in large skillet. Remove some fat. Add onions, sugar, mustard, garlic powder, salt and vinegar. Cook over medium heat for 20 minutes. Meanwhile, drain all the beans. In casserole pan, combine the skillet ingredients with the beans. Bake at 350° covered for 30 minutes. Remove cover and bake an additional 15-30 minutes, if desired.

Recipe Favorites

121822-12

Grandma's/ Mom's Recipes

Helpful Hints

- Keep eggs at room temperature to create greater volume when whipping egg whites for meringue.

- Pie dough can be frozen. Roll dough out between sheets of plastic wrap, stack in a pizza box, and keep the box in the freezer. Defrost in the fridge and use as needed. Use within 2 months.

- Place your pie plate on a cake stand when ready to flute the edges of the pie. The cake stand will make it easier to turn the pie plate, and you won't have to stoop over.

- When making decorative pie edges, use a spoon for a scalloped edge. Use a fork to make crosshatched and herringbone patterns.

- When cutting butter into flour for pastry dough, the process is easier if you cut the butter into small pieces before adding it to the flour.

- Pumpkin and other custard-style pies are done when they jiggle slightly in the middle. Fruit pies are done when the pastry is golden, juices bubble, and fruit is tender.

- Keep the cake plate clean while frosting by sliding 6-inch strips of waxed paper under each side of the cake. Once the cake is frosted and the frosting is set, pull the strips away, leaving a clean plate.

- Create a quick decorating tube to ice your cake with chocolate. Put chocolate in a heat-safe, zipper-lock plastic bag. Immerse it in simmering water until the chocolate is melted. Snip off the tip of one corner, and squeeze the chocolate out of the bag.

- Achieve professionally decorated cakes with a silky, molten look by blow-drying the frosting with a hair dryer until the frosting melts slightly.

- To ensure that you have equal amounts of batter in each pan when making a layered cake, use a kitchen scale to measure the weight.

- Prevent cracking in your cheesecake by placing a shallow pan of hot water on the bottom oven rack and keeping the oven door shut during baking.

- A cheesecake needs several hours to chill and set.

- For a perfectly cut cheesecake, dip the knife into hot water and clean it after each cut. You can also hold a length of dental floss taut and pull it down through the cheesecake to make a clean cut across the diameter of the cake.

GRANDMA'S / MOM'S RECIPES

❦ AEBLESKIVER ❦
Kathy Christiansen
Ann Christiansen

3 eggs, separated
2 T. sugar (optional)
2 c. buttermilk
2 c. flour
1 tsp. baking powder
½ tsp. salt
Shortening for frying
Applesauce (optional)

Beat egg yolks. Add sugar and buttermilk. Sift together the dry ingredients and add to egg yolk mixture. Add stiffly beaten egg whites. Heat small amount of shortening in each hole of aebleskiver pan over medium heat and when hot, add dough. If desired, put a teaspoon of applesauce on top of dough when half baked. Turn with a fork and finish baking. Serve with jam or syrup.

❦ APPLESAUCE PUFFS ❦
Julie Concannon
From my Mom Judy Montgomery

2 c. packaged biscuit mix
¼ c. sugar
1 tsp. cinnamon
½ c. applesauce
¼ c. milk
1 slightly beaten egg
2 T. cooking oil
¼ c. sugar
¼ tsp. cinnamon
2 T. butter or margarine, melted

Combine the biscuit mix, the first ¼ cup sugar and the teaspoon cinnamon. Add applesauce, milk, egg and cooking oil. Beat vigorously for 30 seconds. Fill greased 2-inch muffin pans ⅔ full. Bake in 400° oven for 12 minutes or until golden. Cool slightly; remove from pans. Mix the second ¼ cup sugar and the ¼ teaspoon cinnamon. Dip tops of muffins in the melted butter then in sugar-cinnamon mixture. 12-18 regular muffins or 36 mini muffins. These are best eaten when they are warm!

❦ ARABIAN SPICE CAKE ❦
Ruth Manning
Marion Hoff (my Mom)

½ c. shortening	1 egg
½ tsp. salt	1 c. brown sugar
¾ tsp. ginger	½ tsp. soda
1 tsp. cinnamon	2 tsp. baking powder
½ tsp. cloves	2½ c. sifted flour
½ tsp. allspice	1 c. thick sour milk (I would
1 tsp. vanilla	use sour cream)

Cream shortening, salt, spices and vanilla. Add egg and gradually add sugar and cream well. Sift soda and baking powder with flour 3 times. Add flour to creamed mixture alternately with milk. Bake 350° in 10 x 10 x 2-inch greased pan for 50 minutes.

❦ AUNT CORA'S POTATOES ❦
Randi VenHuizen

3½ lbs. red potatoes	1 stick butter
Salt to taste	1 lb. Velveeta cheese
1 pt. half and half	1 c. grated Cheddar cheese

Boil potatoes with skins until just done, about 30 minutes or until skins start cracking. Cool with cold water. Peel potatoes. Grate the potatoes. Put a layer of potato in a 9 x 13-inch pan and lightly salt until all potatoes are gone. Melt half and half, butter and Velveeta cheese in a double boiler. Pour over the potatoes. Cover and put in the refrigerator overnight. Sprinkle with grated cheese. Bake uncovered at 350° for 45 minutes.

❦ BAKED APPLE PANCAKE ❦
Kathy Christiansen
Ann Christiansen

3 apples	1 tsp. vanilla
4 T. butter, divided	½ tsp. salt
1 c. flour	¼ tsp. nutmeg
1 c. milk	Powdered sugar
6 eggs	Syrup

(continued)

121822-12

Turn oven to 450° and place cast iron skillet in it while you prepare other ingredients. Cut apples into thin slices. In a heavy skillet, melt 2 T. butter and sauté apples. Place flour, milk, eggs, vanilla, salt and nutmeg in blender in the order given. Blend until well mixed. Remove skillet from oven and melt remaining 2 T. of butter. Quickly arrange sautéed apples in skillet and pour batter over apples. Place in 450° oven and bake for 15 minutes. Reduce oven temperature to 375° and bake 10 minutes longer. Sprinkle with powdered sugar, slice into wedges and serve with syrup.

❦ BARBECUE BURGERS ❦
Julie Concannon
From my Mom Judy Montgomery

1½ lbs. ground beef	1 c. ketchup
¾ c. rolled oats	½ c. water
1 c. milk	3 T. vinegar
1½ tsp. salt	2 T. Worcestershire
1 sm. onion, chopped	2 T. sugar
¾ tsp. pepper	

Mix the ground beef, oats, milk, salt, onion and pepper and shape into patties and place in a baking pan with sides. Mix the ketchup, water, vinegar, Worcestershire and sugar and pour over patties. Bake at 300° for 1½ hours. 6-8 burgers.

❦ BBQ GREEN BEANS ❦
Julie Concannon
From my Mom Judy Montgomery

3 cans green beans, drained	1 c. brown sugar
1 onion, chopped	6 slices bacon, cut in pieces
1 c. ketchup	

Mix the drained green beans, onion, ketchup, brown sugar and bacon pieces in a 2-quart casserole dish. Bake at 275° for 4 hours. Serves 12.

❦ BEEF BRISKET ❦

Julie Concannon
From my Mom Judy Montgomery

Beef Brisket, we purchase 1 lb. per person so we have lots of leftovers!

Liquid smoke (one bottle per brisket)

Celery salt to taste

Garlic salt to taste

Onion salt to taste

Your favorite barbecue sauce

Slice brisket about ¼-inch thick (slices easier if partially frozen or you can ask your butcher to do this for you). Soak brisket overnight in liquid smoke and seasonings which are all sealed in heavy foil together. Do not spread brisket out too thinly or it will dry out during baking. Bake 6 hours at 275°, sealed in foil. Remove from oven, drain off liquid. Spread meat out a bit and liberally cover with barbecue sauce. Bake one more hour uncovered. I am so glad my mom found this recipe. It is melt in your mouth delicious and leftovers are a must for additional meals as is or in sandwiches. You could freeze some leftovers too and enjoy later. My mouth waters just thinking about it. Thanks, Mom!

❦ BUTTER BALLS FOR HOMEMADE CHICKEN NOODLE SOUP ❦

Kathy Christiansen
Ann Christiansen

5 c. dry plain bread crumbs

1 c. melted butter

4 eggs

¼ tsp. salt

1 c. half and half (or cream), warmed slightly

½ tsp. allspice

Put crumbs in large bowl and pour butter over crumbs, add unbeaten eggs, salt and allspice. Pour heated cream over mixture. Mix thoroughly (using hands) until mixture can be formed into walnut sized balls without breaking or crumbling. If they break, may need to add additional cream or egg. At this point these can be frozen for later use or put into fridge to set for 2 to 3 hours. After you have made your noodle soup, drop into a gently simmering soup for about 10 minutes. This is a special treat for many Germans from Russia for Christmas Eve supper.

❦ CHICKEN AND RICE CASSEROLE ❦

Paula Foster
In memory of Jackie Badtke

1 c. rice
8 pieces chicken, i.e. breasts, thighs or drumsticks
Salt and pepper to taste
1 can cream of chicken soup
1 can cream of mushroom or cream of celery soup
1 can clear chicken broth
Paprika

Put rice in a 9 x 13-inch dish. Place chicken on top of rice. Salt and pepper to taste. Pour cream of chicken soup on top, and then the cream of mushroom or cream of celery soup and then the clear broth. Sprinkle paprika over the top. Put foil over the dish and bake at 300° for 3 hours. Take foil off and bake 10 more minutes.

❦ CHICKEN CASSEROLE ❦

Sue Dieter

¾ c. macaroni, uncooked and rinsed
3 c. chicken, cooked and cubed
1 can cream of mushroom soup
1 can cream of chicken soup
¼ lb. American cheese, cubed
¾ c. milk
½ c. diced celery
1 can sliced water chestnuts, drained
2 hard boiled eggs, chopped
Slivered almonds, optional
Chinese noodles, for topping

Rinse and drain the uncooked macaroni (I even double checked with my Mother about the uncooked macaroni!). Mix all ingredients together except Chinese noodles. Mix well and pour into a 9 x 9-inch baking pan. Refrigerate several hours or overnight. Cover with Chinese noodles and bake at 350° for 1½ hours. Recipe can be doubled.

❧ CHIFFON SALAD ❧
Sue Dieter

1 (3 oz.) pkg. lemon jello
1 c. boiling water
1 (8 oz.) pkg. cream cheese
1 c. pineapple juice
1 (8 oz.) can crushed
   pineapple, drained

½ c. celery, finely chopped
½ c. nuts, chopped
1 (8 oz.) Cool Whip

Add jello to boiling water. Stir to dissolve. Add cream cheese. Mix well; then stir in pineapple juice. Cool in refrigerator until syrupy and beginning to set. Fold in pineapple, celery, nuts and Cool Whip. Pour into 7 x 11-inch dish and refrigerate. Cut into squares and serve on lettuce leaf.

❧ COCONUT FRUIT SALAD ❧
Julie Concannon
From my Mom Judy Montgomery

1 can mandarin oranges,
   drained
Coconut, as desired
1 (16 oz.) sour cream

1 can chunk pineapple,
   drained
Mini marshmallows, as desired

Mix all ingredients and refrigerate until serving.

❧ CORN FRITTERS ❧
Dayla Miller

1⅓ c. flour
1½ tsp. baking powder
¾ tsp. salt
1 T. sugar
⅔ c. milk

1 egg, well beaten
1 can whole kernel corn,
   drained
Oil for frying
Maple syrup

Sift together flour, baking powder, salt and sugar. Blend milk and egg, add to dry ingredients. Stir in the drained corn and drop from tablespoon into hot grease, fry until golden brown 4-8 minutes depending upon size. Drain on paper towel and serve with maple syrup. Makes 10-15 fritters depending on size.

121822-12

❦ CREAM CHEESE PARTY MINTS ❦
(Flavor of Choice or Chocolate)
Connie Walther
Leota Williams & Fern McVey

2 oz. cream cheese, room temperature
¼ - ½ tsp. flavoring of choice

Food coloring of choice
1⅔ - 2 c. powdered sugar

Mash cream cheese until smooth. Add flavoring and coloring, mix evenly. Add sugar, a little at a time, to dough consistency. Knead with hands until smooth. Pinch off small amounts at a time to form marble size balls. Roll in sugar, can make thumb print or press into mold of choice. Unmold immediately and lay on wax paper. Makes 40- 50 pieces. Store in air tight container.

Chocolate Mints:

3 tsp. cocoa

⅛ - ¼ tsp. vanilla, to taste

Use cocoa and vanilla instead of flavoring in original mixture.

❦ DANISH DUMPLINGS FOR CHICKEN SOUP ❦
Kathy Christiansen
Ann Christiansen

½ c. butter
1 c. hot water
½ tsp. salt

1 c. flour
4 eggs

In large mixing bowl melt butter in hot water (microwave works good here). Add salt and beat in flour. Let cool. Stir in eggs, one at a time without beating, until mixture is glossy and lemon yellow. Heat a large pot of lightly salted water to simmering. Drop dough mixture by spoonfuls into simmering water. Cook until done (they will rise to top). Remove with slotted spoon and cool on baking sheets. At this time the dumplings can be frozen for later use. When ready to use, drop into simmering homemade chicken soup.

❦ DANISH PASTRIES ❦

Kathy Christiansen
Ann Christiansen

Pastries:

2 pkgs. yeast	2 c. flour
¼ c. lukewarm water	2 beaten eggs
¼ c. sugar	2 c. flour (additional)
1 tsp. salt	⅓ c. butter
1 c. butter, divided	1 c. powdered sugar
1 c. hot milk	1 c. nutmeats ground fine

Soften yeast in lukewarm water for 5 minutes. Then stir until blended. Place sugar, salt and ½ cup butter in mixing bowl and add 1 cup hot milk and stir, mashing butter against the sides of the bowl until broken into small lumps. Cool to lukewarm; stir in 2 cups flour and beat until smooth. Add 2 beaten eggs to yeast. Stir until blended and then add to flour mixture. Stir in the additional 2 cups of flour and blend well. Rub with butter and let rise 1½ hours. Roll dough into rectangle ¼-inch thick and about 8-inches wide, spread with ¼ cup butter, fold 1 end to center and the other end over the 2 layers to make 3 layers. Press edges together. Roll out and repeat this process using ¼ cup more butter. Roll out to 22 x 12-inch rectangle on floured board. Mix together ⅓ cup butter, powdered sugar and finely ground nutmeats for filling. Spread the filling over half the dough along 22-inch side. Fold uncovered dough over dough with the filling and press edge. Cut into ¾-inch strip (crosswise). Twist each strip 4 or 5 times. Hold 1 end on baking sheet and curl remaining strip around center roll as a pinwheel, tucking other end under. Let rise until double in size. Bake in 375° oven for 15 minutes.

Frosting:

Powdered sugar	½ tsp. lemon zest
Warm water	

Combine ingredients to desired consistency and frost pastries while warm.

121822-12

❦ FLANK STEAK ROLL ❦

Julie Concannon
From my One Grandma, Vernon Elce

1½ lb. flank steak	1 tsp. sage
3 med. onions	½ tsp. thyme
½ c. minced suet (or solid vegetable shortening)	Flour
2 c. stale bread crumbs	1 tsp. salt
1 egg	½ tsp. pepper
½ tsp. marjoram	2 T. drippings (from previous meal)

Pound flank steak with meat tenderizer to a scant ½-inch thickness. Peel onions and pour boiling water over and let stand 15 minutes, drain and chop finely. Add the suet, bread crumbs, egg, marjoram, sage and thyme to the onions, mix well and add enough hot water to make moist enough to spread. Lay the steak flat, spread the bread mixture evenly over. Roll up and skewer or tie securely. Roll in flour seasoned with salt and pepper and sear quickly in hot frying pan in which drippings have been melted. Place in a casserole, add ½ cup hot water, cover and cook for one hour at 400°. Remove to a hot platter, take off skewers or string and thicken the gravy in the pan. Serves 6. I had to look up suet! Solid vegetable shortening is about as close as you will come as far as I can tell. My Grandma was born in 1900 which explains the use of the suet! I miss her every single day!

❦ FLEMISH POT ROAST ❦

Kathy Christiansen
Ann Christiansen

4 T. butter, divided	1 tsp. salt
1 T. canola oil	1 tsp. freshly ground black pepper
1 (3 - 4 lb.) beef roast (rump, arm or chuck)	1 (12 oz.) can beer
2 lg. onions, sliced	2 T. all-purpose flour
2 cloves garlic, minced	

In large pot or Dutch oven, melt 2 tablespoons butter with canola oil. Add roast; brown well on all sides. Remove roast from pan; set aside. Add onions and minced garlic to drippings; sauté until golden brown. Return roast to pot. Add salt, pepper and beer. Cover; let simmer for 2 to 2½ hours, adding water if it becomes too dry. Toward end of

(continued)

75 ❦

cooking time, remove remaining 2 tablespoons butter from refrigerator and let soften. When roast is tender, remove to a cutting board. Combine softened butter and flour, then slowly stir mixture into gravy to thicken, using as much as is necessary. Let simmer while you carve the roast, then serve.

❧ FRUIT SALAD ❧
Julie Concannon
From my Mom Judy Montgomery

1 can (21 oz.) peach pie filling
1 can (15 oz.) mandarin oranges, drained
1 can (20 oz.) pineapple tidbits or chunks, drained

1½ c. mini marshmallows
3 bananas, sliced

Mix the peach pie filling, mandarin oranges, pineapple and mini marshmallows and chill until serving time. Just before serving, add sliced bananas.

❧ GRANDMA FERN'S MEAT LOAF ❧
Shirley Schuchard
Carolyn Arch

2 eggs
½ tsp. salt
¼ tsp. pepper
1 T. dried onion
1 (4 oz.) can tomato sauce (for salisbury steak--½ c. milk instead)

20 crackers, crushed
2 lbs. ground beef

Mix eggs, salt, pepper, onion and tomato sauce together. Add crackers and let set a few minutes. Mix together with ground beef, place in loaf pan and bake about 1½ hours at 350°. For salisbury steak: Make into patties and brown (using milk rather than tomato sauce). Put in 9 x 13-inch pan and cover with foil. Bake for about ½ hour. Serve with gravy packet mix prepared according to directions on packet and add can of sliced mushrooms.

🍎 GRANDMA HAZEL'S APPLE COFFEE CAKE 🍎

Lisa Rieff

1 box lemon or yellow cake mix (I use lemon)	⅓ c. brown sugar
	1 T. flour
3 eggs, well beaten	1 c. chopped nuts
1 can Wilderness apple pie filling	1 tsp. cinnamon
	½ stick butter

Mix cake mix with the beaten eggs. Batter will be stiff. Add pie filling and mix well without completely mashing the apples. Pour into a greased and floured 9 x 13-inch pan or two 8 x 8-inch pans. Mix the brown sugar, flour, nuts and cinnamon together. Sprinkle on top of the cake batter. Melt the butter and drizzle on top of cake. Bake at 325° for 35-45 minutes. This is AWESOME served warm.

🍎 GRANDMA'S BROWN SUGAR COOKIES 🍎

Connie Walther
Leota Williams & Fern McVey

Cookies:

1 c. shortening	1 tsp. nutmeg
2 c. brown sugar	1 tsp. baking soda
2 eggs, beaten	1 tsp. salt
½ c. cold coffee	3½ c. sifted flour
1 tsp. cinnamon	½ c. nutmeats (optional)

Measure shortening, stir until creamy. Add sugar and cream well. Stir in beaten eggs and coffee. Add spices, soda, and salt to sifted flour. Sift again. Add to creamed mixture. Add nutmeats, if desired. Drop by teaspoons onto a greased cookie sheet and bake at 350° for 12 - 15 min.

Powdered Sugar Frosting:

½ c. powdered sugar   Milk

Add milk, one teaspoon at a time, to powdered sugar until a syrup-like consistency is reached. When cookies are cool you can drizzle a criss-cross pattern on them with the frosting.

❦ GRANDMA'S OLD FASHIONED SUGAR COOKIES ❦
Nancy Shinrock

Cookies:

2 c. sugar
1 c. thick sour cream
3 eggs, well beaten
2 tsp. vanilla

1 c. margarine or Crisco
1 tsp. baking soda
2 tsp. baking powder
6½ c. flour

Combine all ingredients in order given. Roll out dough about ½-inch thick. Cut with cookie cutters. Bake at 350° for about 12 minutes. Do not over bake or even brown cookies.

Frosting:

1 c. Crisco
2 lbs. powdered sugar
¼ c. milk
¼ c. water

1 tsp. vanilla
1 egg white
1 tsp. lemon juice

Mix all together and spread on cooled cookies.

❦ GRANDMA'S RED HOT SALAD ❦
Brian Vandeventer
Evelyn Smets

1 (3 oz.) pkg. candy red hots
1 (6 oz.) pkg. strawberry or
  raspberry gelatin

1 (16 oz.) can applesauce

Dissolve red hots in the gelatin hot water mixture, then complete gelatin instructions. Add applesauce and chill. For further awesomeness, have whipped cream available when serving!

❦ GRANDMA'S SUMMER SAUSAGE ❦
Connie Walther
Norma Walther

5 lbs. lean ground beef	2½ tsp. garlic powder
5 rounded tsp. Morton Tender	2½ tsp. mustard seeds
Quick salt	2½ tsp. coarse ground pepper
½ c. water	1 tsp. hickory smoked salt

Day 1 - combine all ingredients, mix well and refrigerate. Day 2 and Day 3 - mix well again and refrigerate. Day 4 - mix and separate into 4 rolls, about 2-inches in diameter. Place on broiler pan in 170° oven. Bake 6 hours, turning every 2 hours. Keep refrigerated, then when cool, can wrap in foil to store in refrigerator. Slice and serve with Cheddar and crackers.

❦ GREEN BEAN CASSEROLE ❦
Shari Garder

1 (10¾ oz.) can cream of	29 oz. canned green beans,
mushroom soup	drained; or 18 oz. frozen
¾ c. milk	green beans, thawed
⅛ tsp. pepper	1⅓ c. french fried onions

Mix soup, milk, and pepper in a 1½ qt. baking dish. Stir in beans and ⅔ c. onions. Bake at 350° for 30 minutes or until hot. Stir. Top with remaining ⅔ c. onions. Bake additional 5 minutes until onions are golden brown.

❦ HAM AND TOMATO QUICHE ❦
Julie Concannon
From my Mom Judy Montgomery

1 Pillsbury refrigerated pie crust (from 15 oz. box), softened as directed	1 c. finely chopped cooked ham
3 eggs	1 med. tomato, cut in half, seeded and cut into thin strips
¾ c. milk	3 T. chopped green onions
2 T. flour	1 c. shredded Cheddar cheese
¼ c. grated Parmesan cheese	

(continued)

Heat oven to 400°. Place pie crust in 9-inch glass pie plate as directed on box for one-crust filled pie. Do not prick crust. Bake 8-10 minutes or just until edge begins to brown (if crust puffs up in center, gently push down with back of wooden spoon). Meanwhile, in medium bowl, beat eggs, milk, flour and Parmesan cheese with wire whisk until well blended. Layer ham, tomato, onions and Cheddar cheese in partially baked crust. Pour egg mixture over layers. Cover crust edge with strips of foil to prevent excessive browning; bake 25-35 minutes or until golden brown and knife inserted in center comes out clean. Let stand 10 minutes before serving. Serves 6-8.

❦ HOT PUNCH ❦
Sue Dieter

½ c. sugar
1½ c. water
¼ tsp. cloves
¼ tsp. allspice
¼ tsp. cinnamon

⅛ tsp. nutmeg
⅛ tsp. salt
4 c. cranberry juice
2 c. apple juice

Combine sugar, water, spices and salt. Bring to a boil. Add cranberry and apple juices and simmer until hot.

❦ ICE CREAM DESSERT ❦
Debra Gillespie
Grandma Dorthy Pedersen

1 c. graham crackers
1 c. soda crackers
½ c. butter, melted
1 (6 oz.) pkg. instant chocolate
   pudding

2 c. milk
4 c. vanilla ice cream, softened
1 carton Cool Whip

Crush graham and soda crackers using a rolling pin. Reserve ¼ cup of crumbs for topping. Combine cracker crumbs with butter and press into 9 x 13-inch pan. In large bowl, beat pudding and milk with electric mixer until thick, then fold in softened ice cream. Pour ice cream mixture on crust. Refrigerate to set up, then top with Cool Whip and sprinkle with reserved cracker crumbs. Keep refrigerated until serving time. May vary pudding flavor. Serves: 12.

121822-12

❦ KNOEPHLA SOUP ❦

Kathy Christiansen
Ann Christiansen

2 T. butter
2 - 3 carrots, diced
2 ribs celery, diced
1 sm. onion, diced
2 qt. water
2 T. chicken base
3 - 4 potatoes, peeled and
  diced
3 - 4 bay leaves
½ tsp. black pepper (or to
  taste)
2 c. flour
2 eggs
1 tsp. salt
½ c. milk
1 can cream of chicken soup
1 c. cream

Melt butter over medium-high heat in a large stockpot. Add carrots, celery, and onion. Sauté until the vegetables are crisp tender and onion is beginning to turn translucent. Add water, chicken base, potatoes, bay leaves, and pepper. Bring to a boil, reduce heat, and simmer for 10-15 minutes until the potatoes are tender. Meanwhile, combine flour, eggs, salt and milk and knead until smooth and elastic (if you have a dough hook on your mixer, this is a good time to use it!). Lightly flour your counter and gently roll out dough into a "rope" (approximately 1-inch in diameter). Use a pizza cutter or knife to slice the dough in 1-inch increments. As you slice, add the cut dumplings to the soup. Let simmer for 5 more minutes. Combine cream of chicken soup and cream with a whisk. Add to soup. Let simmer for 2 more minutes. This is a recipe from Mom's Germans from Russia heritage.

❦ LEMON CAKE ❦

Sue Dieter

Cake:

1 lemon cake mix
1 (4 oz.) pkg. lemon instant
  pudding
⅔ c. oil
⅔ c. water
4 eggs

Mix cake mix, pudding, oil, water, and eggs for two minutes. Pour into greased and floured 9 x 13-inch pan. Bake as directed on cake mix package. Remove from oven and poke holes in cake with a fork.

(continued)

Glaze:

Juice of one lg. lemon   1 T. water
2 c. powdered sugar

Mix lemon juice, powdered sugar and water together. Pour over hot cake.

❦ LIME JELLO SALAD ❦
Julie Concannon
From my Grandma Bernice Montgomery

1 sm. pkg. lime jello
1 c. boiling water
1 (3 oz.) pkg. cream cheese
1 pkg. Dream Whip, prepared
1 sm. can crushed pineapple,
   drained

½ c. chopped nuts
½ c. chopped celery
1 c. mini marshmallows

Combine lime jello with boiling water. Cool until partially set. Beat cream cheese and combine with prepared Dream Whip. Stir into jello. Fold in pineapple, nuts, celery and mini marshmallows. Allow to set in refrigerator. This can be prepared in a 2-quart glass casserole dish or 9 x 13-inch glass pan.

❦ MAKE AHEAD MASHED POTATOES ❦
Debra Gillespie
Aunt Jane Simonson

9 lg. potatoes, peeled and
   cubed
½ c. butter, softened
12 oz. cream cheese, softened

½ c. sour cream
Pinch nutmeg
¼ tsp. pepper
½ tsp. salt

Place potatoes in large pot and cover with water. Bring to boil, reduce heat and simmer over medium heat until potatoes are tender. Drain and place in mixing bowl. Beat with an electric mixer until potatoes are light and fluffy. Beat in butter and cream cheese. Beat in the sour cream and seasonings. Scrape into heavily buttered casserole dish. Cover with plastic wrap and refrigerate. To reheat: let set out until potatoes reach room temperature, then bake in 300° oven for 30 minutes.

(continued)

Makes 8 servings. This recipe can be made up to 4 days in advance and refrigerated until needed.

❦ MEXICAN PINWHEELS ❦
(Appetizer)
Connie Walther
Norma Walther

8 oz. sour cream	4 oz. chopped black olives
8 oz. cream cheese, softened	¼ c. finely chopped red
4 oz. green chilies	peppers
1 c. shredded Cheddar cheese	5 (10-inch) flour tortillas
½ c. green onions, chopped	Favorite salsa

Mix all ingredients except tortillas and salsa then spread on torillas. Roll up snuggly, wrap in plastic wrap. Chill at least 2 hours. Take off plastic wrap and slice ½-inch thick. Serve with salsa.

❦ MINCE MEAT ❦
Ruth Manning
Marion Hoff (my Mom)

2 qt. chopped beef	1 c. orange peel
3 qt. chopped apple	1 pt. strong coffee
2 qt. raisins	3 qt. sweet cider
3 qt. sugar	1 T. nutmeg
1 qt. chopped suet	2 T. cinnamon
1 pt. vinegar	1 T. cloves
1 c. molasses	

Put all ingredients together in pan and cook in oven until fruit is tender, stirring occasionally. Note: I'd use my 5 qt. Dutch oven and bake at 300°. I don't know for sure how long, but I remember it seemed like it took quite awhile (2 hours?) and the kitchen smelled wonderful.

🍎 MOM'S APPLE PUDDING WITH BUTTER SAUCE 🍎
Karen Armitage

Apple Pudding:

2 c. sugar
½ c. oleo or butter
2 eggs
4 c. apples, peeled and diced
2 c. flour

2 tsp. cinnamon
2 tsp. baking soda
Dash salt
1 c. nuts, chopped

Cream together sugar, butter and eggs. Add apples. Mix together flour, cinnamon, soda, salt and nuts, and add to creamed mixture. Spread into greased 9 x 13-inch pan and bake 30 minutes at 350°. Cool and serve with warm butter sauce.

Butter Sauce:

½ c. butter
1 c. cream
1 c. sugar

2 tsp. vanilla
1 c. brown sugar

Combine all ingredients in saucepan and heat to boiling. Serve warm over apple pudding.

🍎 MOM'S CHICKEN AND RICE 🍎
Kathy Christiansen
Ann Christiansen

1 stick oleo (margarine)
1 chicken, cut up or equivalent
  chicken parts
½ green pepper, chopped

½ onion, diced
4 chicken bouillon cubes
1 c. regular rice
1½ c. water

Melt oleo in oven safe pan and brown chicken. Remove chicken and then brown green pepper and onion. Crush up bouillon cubes and add to vegetables. Add rice and water to pan, place chicken on top, cover and cook in "slow oven" (300 to 325° ?) for 1½ to 2 hours.

121822-12

❦ NORWEGIAN FLATBREAD ❦
Deb Lund
Helen Lund/Anna Kvinge

1 ¾ c. flour
¾ c. whole wheat flour
¼ tsp. salt
¼ c. canola oil or vegetable oil

¼ tsp. baking soda
1 c. buttermilk (powdered
works fine)

Mix flours and salt together with oil like pie crust. Stir baking soda
into buttermilk, then add to dry ingredients to make a soft dough.
Refrigerate around an hour or so, tightly covered. Roll out on pastry
cloth or floured board, about ¼ of the amount at a time, as thin as
possible. Place on large baking sheet. Prick with a fork. Bake at 350°
for 10 minutes or so--until light brown. Cool on rack and break into
pieces. Store in covered containers. May also freeze. I've also made
this on a lefse grill, which works just fine.

❦ OLD-FASHIONED ROLLED
MOLASSES COOKIES ❦
Harry Naasz

1 ½ c. (or less) white sugar (or
brown)
¾ c. lard, Crisco or whatever
you have
2 eggs
¼ tsp. nutmeg
2 tsp. ginger

1 tsp. cinnamon
¾ c. molasses
¾ c. sour milk (or buttermilk)
1 tsp. soda
Flour, enough to roll out, cut,
bake

Mix all ingredients together. That's all. Don't roll too thin. Don't bake
too long. Good luck. My mother's recipe as she wrote it for me.

❦ ONION CASSEROLE ❦
Connie Walther
Norma Walther

5 med. sweet onions, sliced
½ c. margarine
8 oz. fresh Parmesan cheese

1 tube pkg. Ritz crackers,
crushed

(continued)

Sauté sliced onions in margarine until limp but not brown. Put half of onions in a 1½ qt. casserole. Sprinkle with half of cheese and half of cracker crumbs. Repeat. Bake at 325° for 20 minutes. Add small amount of milk if dry.

❧ PEACH CAKE ❧
Nancy Shinrock

Cake:

1½ c. sugar	2 c. flour
¾ c. oil	1 tsp. cinnamon
2 lg. eggs	Pinch salt
1⅓ c. mashed peaches (canned, fresh, or frozen)	

Mix sugar, oil, and eggs, beat. Stir in peaches. Sift dry ingredients several times and mix with wet ingredients. Bake in oblong pan at 350° for 40 minutes or until done.

Frosting:

1 c. sugar	1 T. flour
1 stick butter	½ c. coconut
1 c. canned milk	½ c. nuts
3 egg yolks	1 tsp. vanilla

Cook sugar, butter, milk, egg yolks, and flour until thick. Then add coconut, nuts, and vanilla. Spread frosting over warm cake.

❧ PEANUT BUTTER FUDGE ❧
Connie Walther
Leota Williams

2 c. sugar	1 c. miniature marshmallows
3 T. butter	1⅓ c. chunky style peanut butter
1 tsp. vanilla	
1 c. evaporated milk	

Combine sugar, butter, vanilla and milk. Bring to a boil and continue to boil for 5 minutes, stirring constantly. Remove from heat and stir in marshmallows and peanut butter until all are blended. Turn into a buttered 9-inch square pan. Cool. Store in air tight container.

121822-12

❦ PECAN SNOW BALLS ❦
Julie Concannon
From my Grandma Bernice Montgomery

1 c. oleo (margarine)	2 c. flour
½ c. sugar	1 tsp. salt
2 tsp. vanilla	Powdered sugar
1 c. chopped pecans	

Cream oleo and sugar. Mix in vanilla and pecans. Stir in flour and salt. Shape into 1-inch balls. Place on ungreased cookie sheet. Bake in 325° oven for 20 minutes. Roll in powdered sugar.

❦ QUICK CAKE ❦
Ruth Manning
My Grandma Olson

2 eggs	Pinch salt
1 c. sugar	½ c. milk
1 c. flour	1 T. butter
1 T. baking powder	

Beat eggs until thick. Add sugar, gradually. Mix flour, baking powder and salt together. Add to first mixture. Beat well. Bring milk and butter to a boil. Add at once to flour and sugar mixture and beat well. Note: no further instructions. I'd put this in a greased 8-inch cake pan and bake at 350° for 25 minutes.

❦ RHUBARB UPSIDE DOWN CAKE ❦
Connie Walther
Leota Williams

3 T. melted butter	2 c. finely diced rhubarb
½ c. sugar	1 white cake mix plus
Red food coloring	ingredients to make cake

Combine butter, sugar, and a few drops of food coloring. Add rhubarb and toss lightly. Spread into a 8¼ x 1¾-inch baking dish. Prepare loaf size cake mix according to directions. Pour over fruit. Bake at 375° for 30-35 minutes. Loosen edges and invert on plate. Let stand 3-5 minutes and lift off pan. Serve with vanilla ice-cream or cool whip.

❧ SAUERKRAUT IN JARS ❧

Kathy Christiansen
Ann Christiansen

2 - 3 lg. heads cabbage   **Vinegar**
Pickling salt

Clean cabbage and shred thin. While cutting cabbage, sterilize 10 to 12 canning quart jars, lids and rings. Fill hot jars with fresh cut cabbage, pressing in tight to fill jars. With handle of butter knife, poke knife down into jars, making several holes. Add 1 tablespoon of salt and 1 tablespoon of vinegar to jars and then fill with boiling water. Poke knife down into jar again and then fill jar again with boiling water. Wipe jar clean and cover tight with hot, new lids. Leave set on a towel on top of cupboard for 2 days for curing. Jars will seal tight on their own.

❧ SLOPPY JOES ❧

Julie Concannon
From my Mom Judy Montgomery

1 lb. ground beef   **1 c. water**
⅔ c. chopped onion   **½ tsp. Worcestershire sauce**
1 tsp. salt   **⅔ c. ketchup**
⅛ tsp. pepper   **Hamburger buns**
1 T. flour

Brown ground beef with onion in skillet. Drain and return to skillet. Add salt, pepper, flour and water to skillet with beef and onion. Cook and stir until thickened. Add Worcestershire sauce and ketchup, simmer until ready to serve. Serve on hamburger buns, open or closed face. 4-8 servings.

121822-12

❦ SNICKERDOODLES ❦

Julie Concannon
From my Mom Judy Montgomery

½ c. soft shortening (I use
  Crisco)
½ c. butter
1½ c. sugar
2 eggs
2¾ c. flour

2 tsp. cream of tartar
1 tsp. baking soda
¼ tsp. salt
2 T. sugar
2 tsp. cinnamon

Mix thoroughly the shortening, butter, sugar and eggs. Mix together
and stir in the flour, cream of tartar, baking soda and salt. Roll into
balls the size of small walnuts. Roll in cinnamon and sugar mixture.
Place 2-inches apart on ungreased baking sheet. Bake at 400° until
lightly browned but still soft, about 8-10 minutes. 5 dozen cookies.

❦ STRAWBERRY RHUBARB BAKE ❦

Sue Dieter

4 c. diced rhubarb, 1-inch
  pieces
½ pt. strawberries, halved
¾ c. sugar
1 (3 oz.) pkg. strawberry jello

1 one layer yellow Jiffy cake
  mix
1 c. water
¼ c. butter

Place rhubarb and strawberries in 9 x 13-inch baking pan. Pour sugar,
jello, yellow cake mix and water over rhubarb and strawberries in that
order. Dot with butter. Bake at 350° for 40 to 45 minutes.

❦ TOOTIE FRUTIE SALAD ❦

Debra Gillespie
Grandma Gerry Zeman

#2 can chunk pineapple
2 T. vinegar
¼ c. sugar
2 tsp. corn starch

4 tart apples
4 bananas
1 c. miniature marshmallows
1 c. walnuts

Drain juice from pineapple into sauce pan. Add vinegar, sugar and
corn starch. Mix well and cook over medium heat, stirring constantly,
until liquid bubbles and is thickened. While this mixture is cooling,

(continued)

cut up apples and bananas and combine in bowl with marshmallows and walnuts. Stir to combine ingredients and pour sauce over fruit. Refrigerate until time to serve.

❦ TWO DAY BUNS ❦
Ruth Manning
My Grandma Olson

11 a.m. day one:
1 cake yeast into 1 c.
lukewarm water
12 noon day one add:
2 c. flour

½ c. shortening
1 scant cup sugar
Salt
Flour for soft dough

Knead batter. Every 2 hours, punch it down. Make into buns and refrigerate. Bake in the morning of day two. Note: no baking time/temperature is given. I'd guess bake at 350° for about 35 minutes. I remember these as having such a great taste.

❦ VEGETABLE CHEESE CHOWDER ❦
(Can add leftover chicken or turkey)
Connie Walther
Norma Walther

3 c. chicken broth
½ c. butter/oleo (margarine)
2 chopped potatoes
½ c. sliced carrot
½ c. chopped celery
½ c. chopped onion

½ c. chopped green pepper
2 c. evaporated skim milk
½ c. flour
1 lb. diced Velveeta cheese
1 T. parsley
Black pepper to taste

Heat broth and butter on medium heat to simmer. Add vegetables. Cook at simmer until vegetables are tender. Combine milk and flour until smooth. Stir slowly into hot vegetable broth. Add cheese, parsley, and pepper. Stir until cheese is melted and soup thickens. Serves 6-8.

121822-12

❦ WESSON OIL DRESSING ❦
Julie Concannon
From my Grandma Bernice Montgomery

½ c. sugar
¼ c. vinegar
⅛ tsp. salt

⅛ tsp. pepper
1 tsp. prepared mustard
1 c. Wesson oil

Mix sugar, vinegar, salt, pepper and mustard in a small saucepan. Cook until slightly thickened, cool a little and beat in Wesson oil. Makes 1½ cups. I have never had this turn out as good as my grandma but it sure makes me think of her!

❦ WORLDS BEST CHOCOLATE CAKE ❦
Nancy Shinrock

Cake:

½ c. unsalted butter
4 oz. unsweetened chocolate, broken up
2½ c. flour
1 c. unsweetened cocoa powder
2 tsp. baking soda

½ tsp. baking powder
1½ tsp. salt
1½ c. sour cream
3 eggs
1 c. water
2 tsp. vanilla extract

Heat oven to 350°. Grease and flour three 9-inch round cake pans. In a microwave safe bowl, melt butter and chocolate together in microwave on high until melted and smooth (about 1 to 1½ minutes), stirring halfway through. Set aside. Mix flour, cocoa, soda, baking powder, and salt in a large bowl until blended. Add sour cream, eggs, water, chocolate mixture, and vanilla. Beat 30 seconds on low speed, until dry ingredients are moistened, increase to medium speed and beat 2 minutes. Pour into prepared pans. Bake for 40 minutes or until cake layers spring back when pressed. Cool layers in pans on rack for 10 minutes. Remove cakes from pans to rack to cool completely.

(continued)

Frosting:

4 oz. unsweetened chocolate,
  broken up
½ c. shortening
½ c. unsalted butter, softened
¼ c. sour cream
⅓ c. milk
2 tsp. vanilla extract

¼ tsp. salt
1 lb. powdered sugar, divided
½ c. unsweetened cocoa
  powder
Garnish with chocolate curls,
  berries

In a microwave safe small bowl, melt chocolate in microwave on high 1 minute. Stir until smooth, set aside. Beat shortening, butter, sour cream, milk, vanilla, salt, 1 c. sugar, and cocoa powder in a medium size bowl until creamy. Gradually beat in remaining sugar and melted chocolate until think and smooth. Frost the cake.

❦ YOLK COOKIES ❦
Julie Concannon
From my Grandma Bernice Montgomery

1 c. butter
1½ c. sugar
4 egg yolks, beaten
1 tsp. vanilla

1 tsp. baking soda
Pinch salt
2½ c. flour

Cream the butter and sugar. Add egg yolks and vanilla. Combine the baking soda, salt and flour and add to butter and egg mixture. Form into small balls and press with fork. Bake at 375° until light brown, 8-10 minutes.

121822-12

Healthy Eating

Helpful Hints

- When preparing a casserole, make an additional batch to freeze for when you're short on time. Use within 2 months.

- To keep hot oil from splattering, sprinkle a little salt or flour in the pan before frying.

- To prevent pasta from boiling over, place a wooden spoon or fork across the top of the pot while the pasta is boiling.

- Boil all vegetables that grow above ground without a cover.

- Never soak vegetables after slicing; they will lose much of their nutritional value.

- Green pepper may change the flavor of frozen casseroles. Clove, garlic, and pepper flavors get stronger when frozen, while sage, onion, and salt become more mild.

- For an easy no-mess side dish, grill vegetables along with your meat.

- Store dried pasta, rice (except brown rice), and whole grains in tightly covered containers in a cool, dry place. Refrigerate brown rice and freeze grains if you will not use them within 5 months.

- A few drops of lemon juice added to simmering rice will keep the grains separated.

- When cooking greens, add a teaspoon of sugar to the water to help vegetables retain their fresh colors.

- To dress up buttered, cooked vegetables, sprinkle them with toasted sesame seeds, toasted chopped nuts, canned french-fried onions, grated cheese, or slightly crushed seasoned croutons.

- Soufflé dishes are designed with straight sides to help your soufflé rise. Ramekins work well for single-serve casseroles.

- A little vinegar or lemon juice added to potatoes before draining will make them extra white when mashed.

- To avoid toughened beans or corn, add salt midway through cooking.

- If your pasta sauce seems a little dry, add a few tablespoons of the pasta's cooking water.

- To prevent cheese from sticking to a grater, spray the grater with cooking spray before beginning.

HEALTHY EATING

❦ ANGEL FOOD PINEAPPLE ORANGE MUFFINS ❦
Ruth Manning

1 box fat free angel food cake mix
1 (14 oz.) can crushed pineapple with juice
1 (10-oz.) can mandarin oranges, drained
Zest of one orange

Preheat oven to 350°. Line muffin pans with 24 paper liners or spray with nonstick cooking spray. Combine cake mix, crushed pineapple and mandarin oranges and mix well. Add orange zest. Fill muffin cups ¾ full. Bake approximately 15 minutes. Calories: 48.

❦ ANGEL LUSH ❦
Julie Concannon

1 can (20 oz.) crushed pineapple in juice, undrained
1 pkg. (4-serv.) jello vanilla flavor fat free sugar free instant pudding
1 c. thawed Cool Whip lite or Cool Whip sugar free whipped topping
1 (10 oz.) pre-made round angel food cake
10 fresh strawberries

Mix pineapple and dry pudding mix in medium bowl. Gently stir in whipped topping. Cut cake horizontally into three layers with a serrated knife. Place bottom cake layer, cut-side up, on serving plate; top with one-third of the pudding mixture. Repeat layers two times. Refrigerate at least 1 hour. Top with berries just before serving. Store leftovers in refrigerator. 10 servings. Per serving: 140 calories, 1 gram fat, 31 grams carbohydrates, 2 grams protein.

🍎 APPLE COLESLAW 🍎
Julie Concannon

¾ c. Kraft fat free mayonnaise
1 T. honey
1 bag (14 oz.) coleslaw blend
(shredded cabbage and
carrots)

2 med. apples (preferably 1
red and 1 green), chopped

Mix mayonnaise and honey in a large bowl. Add coleslaw blend and apples; mix lightly. Refrigerate at least one hour. Makes: 12 servings, about ½ cup each.

🍎 AVOCADO AND BLACK EYED PEA SALSA 🍎
Christie Klos

2 ripe but firm avocados,
diced
½ c. chopped green onion
½ c. chopped cilantro
1 c. chopped Roma tomatoes
1 can shoepeg corn, drained
1 (15 oz.) can black-eyed peas,
drained

¼ c. red wine vinegar
¼ c. olive oil
1 tsp. ground cumin
½ tsp. minced garlic
Salt and pepper to taste

Lightly mix together avocados, green onions, cilantro, tomatoes, corn and black-eyed peas in a bowl. Whisk together vinegar, olive oil, cumin and garlic in a bowl. Pour over salad. Toss and add salt and pepper to taste. Chill for 1 hour to blend flavors.

121822-12

❦ BROCCOLI WILD RICE SOUP/MY LIGHTER VERSION ❦
Julie Concannon

1 pkg. (6 oz.) Uncle Ben's Country Inn Chicken & Wild Rice Mix
5 c. water
3 c. frozen chopped broccoli, thawed
1 med. carrot, shredded

2 tsp. dried minced onion
1 can (10 ¾ oz.) 98% fat free condensed cream of chicken soup, undiluted
1 pkg. (8 oz.) light cream cheese, cubed
Salt and pepper to taste

In a large saucepan, combine rice, contents of seasoning packet and water; bring to a boil. Reduce heat; cover and simmer for 10 minutes, stirring once. Stir in the broccoli, carrot and onion. Cover and simmer for 5 minutes. Stir in soup, cream cheese, salt and pepper. Cook and stir until cheese is melted. Yield: 8 servings (about 2 quarts).

❦ CARROT AND ZUCCHINI MUFFINS ❦
Ruth Manning

1 c. all-purpose flour
½ c. whole-wheat flour
2 T. brown sugar
2 tsp. baking powder
1 tsp. cinnamon
½ tsp. salt
1 tsp. vanilla extract

1 egg
2 egg whites
½ c. finely shredded carrot
½ c. finely shredded zucchini
⅔ c. plain nonfat yogurt
2 tsp. grated lemon zest
¼ c. toasted walnut pieces

Preheat the oven to 400°. Coat a 12-cup muffin pan with cooking spray. In a large bowl, combine the flours, sugar, baking powder, cinnamon and salt. In a medium bowl combine the vanilla, egg and egg whites. Beat well. Add carrots, zucchini, yogurt, lemon zest, and walnut pieces. Add the egg mixture to the flour mixture and beat until just combined. Fill each cup two-thirds full with batter. Bake for 15 to 17 minutes until a tester comes out clean and muffins are lightly browned. Remove muffins from the pan and cool. Serving size: 1 muffin = 1 starch exchange and .5 fat exchange. Calories: 101; calories from fat 21.

❦ CHEESY POTATO SOUP ❦
Debra Gillespie

2 c. potatoes, cubed
2 tsp. beef bouillon
1½ c. water
8 oz. Cheddar cheese

2½ c. milk
2 T. dried bacon bits
1 tsp. parsley flakes
1 T. dried onion flakes

Combine potatoes, beef bouillon and water. Cook about 15 minutes on medium heat until potatoes are tender. Add all remaining ingredients and cook over low heat until cheese is melted. Makes 6 servings. Calories: 290 per 1 cup.

❦ CHICKEN ASPARAGUS ROLL-UPS ❦
Connie Walther
W. Yates
Taste of Home

4 boneless chicken breasts, pounded thin
Salt and pepper (to season chicken breasts, to taste)
1 lb. fresh asparagus, trimmed and washed
2 T. flour

1 garlic clove, minced
Salt to taste (optional)
½ tsp. leaf thyme, divided
¼ tsp. paprika
2 c. white onion, sliced
3 tomatoes, sliced (optional)
½ c. chicken broth

Season pounded chicken with salt and pepper to taste. Split into 2 pieces each. Place 2-3 asparagus spears on each chicken half. Roll up tightly; secure with toothpicks. Set aside. Combine flour, garlic, salt, ¼ tsp. thyme, and paprika. Roll chicken in mixture. Place onion and tomatoes on bottom of 9 x 13-inch pan (reserve part of onion and tomatoes for top). Place chicken over vegetables, top with reserved vegetables. Combine broth and remaining thyme; pour over chicken. Cover pan loosely with foil. Bake at 350° for 30 minutes, basting every 10 minutes. Uncover and bake an additional 10-15 minutes. 8 servings.

121822-12

❦ CHICKEN WITH BALSAMIC VINEGAR, ONIONS & THYME ❦

Julie Concannon

3 T. all-purpose flour
¾ tsp. salt, divided
½ tsp. freshly ground black pepper, divided
1 lb. (four 4-oz. pieces) uncooked boneless, skinless chicken breast
2 tsp. olive oil
1 sm. Vidalia onion, cut in half lengthwise, thinly sliced (about 2 c.)

1 c. reduced-sodium chicken broth
2 T. balsamic vinegar
1 T. fresh, chopped thyme, or less to taste (or ½ tsp. dried)
2 tsp. butter

On a plate, combine flour, ½ teaspoon salt, and ¼ teaspoon pepper. Dredge chicken in flour mixture and turn to coat; shake off any excess. Heat oil in a large nonstick skillet over medium-high heat. Add chicken and cook, flipping once, until golden and cooked through, about 7 minutes; remove to a serving plate and cover to keep warm. Add onion to skillet; sauté over medium-high heat until lightly browned, about 4 minutes. Add broth, vinegar, thyme, and remaining ¼ teaspoon each salt and pepper. Bring to a boil; cook, stirring often, until onions are tender, about 5 minutes. Remove skillet from heat and stir in butter until melted; spoon sauce over chicken. Yields 1 chicken breast and about ¼ cup onion sauce per serving. Serves 4. This is a W.W. recipe and is 5 ppv per serving.

❦ COLORFUL BLACK BEAN SALAD ❦

Christie Klos

Salad:

1 (15 oz.) can black beans, drained
1 (15 oz.) can corn, drained
1 pt. cherry tomatoes, quartered

1 med. sweet pepper, julienne (red, green or yellow)
Bunch of green onions, chopped
Minced cilantro

In a bowl combine beans, corn, tomatoes, peppers, onions and cilantro.

(continued)

Dressing:

3 T. lemon juice
2 T. olive oil
1 garlic clove, minced

¾ tsp. cumin
Salt and pepper to taste

Combine dressing ingredients and pour over salad. Salt and pepper to taste.

❦ GLUTEN-FREE BROWNIES ❦
Julie Concannon

1¼ c. semi-sweet chocolate chips
1 can (15 oz.) garbanzo beans, rinsed and drained
3 egg whites
1 egg
2 T. instant coffee granules, optional

2 T. canola oil
1½ tsp. pure vanilla extract, gluten free
½ c. packed brown sugar
½ tsp. baking powder
Dash salt
½ c. chopped walnuts, optional

In a microwave, melt chocolate chips; stir until smooth. Cool slightly. Meanwhile, place the beans, egg whites, egg, coffee granules if desired, oil and vanilla in a food processor. Cover and process until very smooth. In a small bowl, combine the brown sugar, baking powder and salt; add to bean mixture. Cover and process until combined. Gradually add the chocolate; process until blended. Pour batter into a 9-inch square baking pan coated with cooking spray. Sprinkle with walnuts if desired. Bake at 350° for 30-35 minutes or until a toothpick inserted near the center comes out with moist crumbs (do not overbake). Cool completely on a wire rack. One dozen brownies.

❦ GREEK PIZZA ❦
Julie Concannon

4 (6-inch) pita breads
1 c. reduced-fat ricotta
½ tsp. garlic powder
10 oz. frozen chopped spinach (thawed and squeezed dry)

3 sliced tomatoes
¾ c. crumbled feta
¾ tsp. dried basil

(continued)

Place pita breads on a baking sheet. Combine the ricotta and garlic powder; spread over pitas. Top with the spinach, tomato slices, crumbled feta and basil. Bake at 400° for 12-15 minutes. Serves 4.

❦ MADE OVER CHICKEN TETRAZZINI ❦
Julie Concannon

½ lb. spaghetti, uncooked
1 lb. boneless skinless chicken breasts, cubed
1 med. red pepper, chopped
2 c. sliced fresh mushrooms
4 oz. low fat cream cheese, cubed

¼ c. flour
1 can (14 oz.) fat-free reduced-sodium chicken broth
3 T. grated Parmesan cheese, divided
½ c. 2% milk shredded mozzarella cheese

Preheat oven to 350°. Cook pasta as directed on package (if you break the pasta in half before cooking it makes serving the dish easier). Meanwhile, spray large nonstick skillet with cooking spray. Add chicken, peppers and mushrooms; cook and stir 5 minutes or until chicken is no longer pink. Remove from skillet; set aside. Place cream cheese, flour and broth in skillet. Cook and stir with wire whisk until boiling. Reduce heat to medium-low; simmer 5 minutes, stirring frequently. Drain pasta; return to saucepan. Add cream cheese mixture, chicken mixture and 2 tablespoons of the Parmesan cheese; mix well. Spoon into 2-quart round casserole dish; cover with foil. Bake 25 minutes. Top with mozzarella and remaining 1 tablespoon Parmesan cheese; continue baking, uncovered, 2 minutes or until mozzarella cheese is melted. 6 servings, 1 cup each.

❦ MAKEOVER ZUCCHINI SUPPER ❦
Jessica and Jason Garder

1½ lbs. lean ground beef
½ lb. reduced-fat bulk pork
   sausage
1 lg. onion, chopped
2 med. carrots, chopped
2 celery ribs, chopped
2 c. cubed day-old whole
   wheat bread
½ c. fat free milk
1 T. flour
4 c. chopped zucchini

¾ lb. reduced-fat processed
   cheese (Velveeta), cubed
1 can (10¾ oz.) reduced-fat
   reduced-sodium cream of
   mushroom soup
2 eggs or ¾ c. egg substitute
1 tsp. garlic powder
½ tsp. onion powder
½ tsp. rubbed sage
½ tsp. dried thyme
½ tsp. pepper

In a Dutch oven, cook the beef, sausage, onion, carrot, and celery over medium heat until meat is no longer pink and vegetables are crisp-tender. Meanwhile, in a small bowl, combine bread cubes and milk; set aside. Remove meat mixture from the heat; drain. Stir in flour until blended. Stir in bread mixture and remaining ingredients. Transfer to a 9 x 13-inch baking dish coated with cooking spray. Cover and bake at 350° for 40-45 minutes or until a meat thermometer reads 160°. Uncover and stir. Bake 8-12 minutes longer or until golden brown. 8 Servings.

❦ MEXICAN CHICKEN CHILI ❦
Julie Concannon

1 lb. boneless skinless chicken
   breasts, cubed
1 T. canola oil
2 cans (14½ oz. each) diced
   tomatoes, undrained
2 c. frozen corn
1 can (15 oz.) black beans,
   rinsed and drained

1 can (14½ oz.) reduced-
   sodium chicken broth
1 can (4 oz.) chopped green
   chilies
2 T. chili powder
1 T. ground cumin
½ tsp. salt
¼ tsp. cayenne pepper

In a small skillet, brown chicken in oil (I prefer to just brown the chicken in my non-stick skillet without any oil). Transfer to a 5-quart slow cooker. Stir in the remaining ingredients. Cover and cook on low for 5-6 hours or until chicken is fully cooked and no longer pink. Serves: 6.

121822-12

❦ MEXICAN-STYLE BROWN RICE CASSEROLE ❦

Julie Concannon

Cooking spray
4 c. cooked brown rice
1¼ c. fat-free salsa
1 tsp. ground cumin
15 oz. canned refried beans
10 oz. frozen corn kernels, thawed
4 oz. canned mild green chili peppers, diced

1 T. chili powder
10 oz. chopped frozen spinach, thawed and set to drain in a strainer
¾ c. low-fat shredded Cheddar cheese, divided

Preheat oven to 375°. Coat a 2-quart baking dish with cooking spray. In a large bowl, combine rice, salsa, and cumin. Spoon 2 cups of rice mixture into prepared baking dish and spread out to evenly cover bottom of dish. In another large bowl, combine refried beans, corn, chili peppers, and chili powder. Using a rubber spatula, scrape bean mixture on top of rice layer and smooth out top. Squeeze out any excess water from spinach and then spread on top of bean layer; sprinkle with 6 tablespoons of cheese. Top with remaining rice mixture and smooth out top. Place casserole on a large rimmed baking sheet to catch any spillage. Bake until heated through and bubbling, about 30 minutes. Top with remaining cheese and let sit a few minutes to melt some. Serves 6-8. This is a W.W. recipe and has 8 ppv per serving when serving 6.

❦ ONION-APPLE PORK CHOPS ❦

Julie Concannon

2 boneless pork loin chops (4 oz. each)
¼ tsp. garlic salt
¼ tsp. lemon-pepper seasoning
2 tsp. olive oil
1 med. apple, peeled and thinly sliced

1 sm. onion, thinly sliced
⅓ c. reduced-sodium chicken broth
2 T. maple syrup

Sprinkle chops with garlic salt and lemon-pepper. In a large ovenproof skillet, brown chops in oil. Remove and keep warm. In the same skillet,

(continued)

sauté apple and onion in drippings until tender. Stir in broth and syrup. Bring to a boil. Reduce heat; simmer, uncovered, for 5-7 minutes or until liquid is almost evaporated. Return chops to pan. Cover and bake at 350° for 15-20 minutes or until a thermometer reads 145°. 2 servings.

❧ ORANGE-CILANTRO BLACK BEAN SALAD ❧
Julie Concannon

½ tsp. olive oil
2 cloves garlic, finely chopped
¼ tsp. ground cumin
2 tsp. red wine vinegar
⅛ tsp. salt or to taste
⅛ tsp. pepper or to taste

½ med. red onion, thinly sliced
1 can black beans, rinsed and drained
2 cans no sugar added mandarin oranges, drained
2 T. cilantro, fresh, chopped

In a large bowl, mix the olive oil, garlic, cumin, red wine vinegar, salt and pepper with a whisk. Add the onion, black beans, mandarin oranges and cilantro. Mix well and refrigerate for several hours or overnight. Serves: 4 (about ¾ cup each).

❧ POTATO BAKE ❧
Paula Foster

8 sm. red potatoes
1 sm. onion, chopped
4 cloves garlic, chopped
¼ c. fresh basil leaves, chopped

Salt
Pepper
Olive oil

Cut potatoes into quarters, making sure all pieces are about the same size, place in a 8 x 8-inch pan. Add onion, garlic and basil. Add salt and pepper to taste. Drizzle olive oil over the potato mixture. Cover with foil and bake in a 350° oven for 45 minutes. This can be doubled and put in a 9 x 13-inch pan.

121822-12

❧ PUMPKIN PIE TARTLETS ❧
Julie Concannon

16 (2½-inch) foil baking cups (paper liners removed)
Nonstick cooking spray
¾ c. granulated sugar
1 T. cornstarch
1 tsp. ground cinnamon
½ tsp. ground ginger
½ tsp. salt
2 lg. egg whites
1 can (15 oz.) Libby's 100% pure pumpkin
1 can (12 fl. oz.) Nestle Carnation evaporated fat free milk
1 c. fat free whipped topping
12 sm. gingersnap cookies, broken into pieces, if desired

Preheat oven to 350°. Place baking cups on baking sheet with sides. Spray each cup with cooking spray. Combine sugar, cornstarch, cinnamon, ginger and salt in small bowl. Beat egg whites in large bowl (DO NOT form peaks, just whip until a bit foamy with a hand whisk). Stir in pumpkin and sugar mixture. Gradually stir in evaporated milk. Spoon ¼ to ⅓ cup of mixture into each prepared cup. Bake for 25 to 28 minutes or until knife inserted near centers comes out clean. Cool on baking sheet for 20 minutes. Refrigerate for at least 1 hour. Top each with whipped topping and gingersnap crumbs (if desired). Store leftovers in refrigerator. 16 servings.

❧ SEASONED TILAPIA FILLETS ❧
Julie Concannon

2 tilapia fillets (6 oz. each)
Parkay spray butter
1 tsp. McCormick's Montreal steak seasoning
½ tsp. dried parsley flakes
¼ tsp. dried thyme
¼ tsp. paprika
⅛ tsp. onion powder
⅛ tsp. salt
Dash garlic powder

Place fillets in a 9 x 9-inch baking dish sprayed with non-stick spray. Spray Parkay on each fillet to moisten. In a small bowl, combine the steak seasoning, parsley flakes, thyme, paprika, onion powder, salt and garlic powder; sprinkle over fillets. Cover and bake at 425° for 15 minutes. Uncover and bake 5-8 minutes longer or until fish flakes easily with a fork. 2 servings.

❦ SIZZLIN' CHICKEN SKEWERS ❦
Connie Walther
Food and Family

1 lb. boneless skinless chicken
  breast halves
⅓ c. hot water
¼ c. teriyaki/BBQ sauce
¼ c. light creamy peanut
  butter

¼ c. low sodium soy sauce
¼ c. chopped cilantro
2 tsp. honey Dijon mustard

Cut chicken into 12 thin strips. Mix water, teriyaki sauce, peanut butter, soy sauce, cilantro and mustard. Pour HALF of mixture into gallon resealable plastic bag. Add chicken, seal bag. Shake to coat. Refrigerate 2 hours to marinate. Refrigerate remaining sauce for dipping. Thread chicken onto 12 skewers in a ribbon fashion. Discard remaining marinade. Grill on medium high heat 7-10 minutes, or until chicken is cooked through. Serve with brown rice or spinach noodles for a complete meal, along with your favorite steamed vegetable or salad.

❦ TILAPIA FLORENTINE ❦
Julie Concannon

1 pkg. (6 oz.) fresh baby
  spinach
6 tsp. canola oil, divided
4 tilapia fillets (4 oz. each)
2 T. lime juice

2 tsp. garlic-herb seasoning
  blend
1 egg, lightly beaten
½ c. part-skim ricotta cheese
¼ c. grated Parmesan cheese

In a nonstick skillet, cook spinach in 4 teaspoons oil until wilted; drain. Meanwhile, place tilapia in a greased 13 x 9-inch baking dish. Drizzle with lime juice and remaining oil. Sprinkle with seasoning blend. In a small bowl, combine the egg, ricotta cheese and spinach; spoon over fillets. Sprinkle with Parmesan cheese. Bake at 375° for 15-20 minutes or until fish flakes easily with a fork. 4 servings.

❦ TILAPIA WITH CORN SALSA ❦
Julie Concannon

4 tilapia fillets (6 oz. each)
1 T. olive oil
¼ tsp. salt
¼ tsp. pepper
1 can (15 oz.) black beans, rinsed and drained
1 can (11 oz.) whole kernel corn, drained
¾ c. light Italian salad dressing
2 T. chopped green onion
2 T. chopped sweet red pepper

Brush both sides of fillets with oil; sprinkle with salt and pepper. Place on a broiler pan. Broil 4 to 6-inches from the heat for 5-7 minutes or until fish is completely opaque and firm. Meanwhile, in a bowl, combine black beans, corn, salad dressing, green onion and sweet red pepper. Serve with the fish. 4 servings.

❦ WHITE BEAN DIP AND PARMESAN PITA CRISPS ❦
Rose Roberts

White Bean Dip:

1 can (15 - 19 oz.) white kidney (cannellini) beans, rinsed and drained
⅓ c. plain nonfat yogurt
1 T. fresh lemon juice
1 T. extra virgin olive oil
1 tsp. anchovy paste
¼ tsp. salt
¼ tsp. pepper

In food processor with knife blade attached, purée beans with yogurt, lemon juice, oil, anchovy paste, salt, and pepper until smooth. Spoon dip into small container with tight-fitting lid. Can be refrigerated up to 2 days. Serve with Parmesan Pita Crisps. 1½ cups dip.

Parmesan Pita Chips:

3 T. olive oil
¾ tsp. ground cumin
¼ tsp. ground red pepper (cayenne)
5 (5- to 6-inch) whole wheat or white pitas with pockets
½ c. coarsely grated Parmesan cheese
Salt (optional)

(continued)

Preheat oven to 350°. In cup, with fork, mix oil, cumin, and pepper. With knife or kitchen shears, carefully split each pita in half. Brush 1 side of pita halves with oil mixture. Cut each half into 8 wedges (triangles). Arrange wedges, oiled-side up, in 2 ungreased 15½ x 10½-inch jelly-roll pans. Sprinkle with Parmesan, and salt if you like. Place pans on 2 oven racks and bake crisps 12 to 15 minutes or until golden, rotating pans from upper to lower racks halfway through baking for even browning. Cool crisps in pans on wire racks. Store crisps in tightly covered container or large self-sealing plastic bag up to 1 week. 80 crisps.

121822-12

Holiday Favorites

Helpful Hints

- Unbaked cookie dough can be covered and refrigerated for up to 24 hours or frozen in an airtight container for up to 9 months.

- Bake one cookie sheet at a time on the middle oven rack.

- Decorate cookies with chocolate by placing cookies on a rack over waxed paper. Dip the tines of a fork into melted chocolate and wave the fork gently back and forth to make line decorations.

- Some cookies need indentations on top to fill with jam or chocolate. Use the rounded end of a honey dipper.

- Dip cookie cutters in flour or powdered sugar and shake off excess before cutting. For chocolate dough, dip cutters in baking cocoa.

- Tin coffee cans make excellent freezer containers for cookies.

- If you only have one cookie sheet on hand, line it with parchment paper. While one batch is baking, load a second sheet of parchment paper to have another batch ready to bake. Cleanup will be easier.

- When a recipe calls for packed brown sugar, fill the correct size measuring cup with sugar and use one cup size smaller to pack the brown sugar into its cup.

- Cut-up dried fruit often sticks to the blade of your knife. To prevent this problem, coat the blade of your knife with a thin film of vegetable spray before cutting.

- Instead of folding nuts into brownie batter, sprinkle on top of batter before baking. This keeps nuts crunchy instead of soggy.

- Only use glass or shiny metal pans. Dark or nonstick pans will cause brownies to become soggy and low in volume.

- When making bars, line pan with aluminum foil and prepare as directed. The bars can be lifted out, and cleanup is easy.

- Cutting bars is easier if you score the bars right as the pan leaves the oven. When the bars cool, cut along the scored lines.

- Use a double boiler for melting chocolate to prevent it from scorching. A slow cooker on the lowest setting also works well for melting chocolate, especially when coating a large amount of candy.

- Parchment paper provides an excellent nonstick surface for candy. Waxed paper should not be used for high-temperature candy.

HOLIDAY FAVORITES

❦ BIRDS' NESTS WITH JELLY BEANS ❦
Julie Concannon

6 lg. shredded-wheat biscuits, crumbled
¼ c. butter or margarine, softened
¼ c. firmly packed light brown sugar
2 T. honey
½ tsp. ground cinnamon
Miniature jelly beans

Heat oven to 375°. Grease 8 muffin-pan cups. In large bowl mix crumbled biscuits, butter, brown sugar, honey, and cinnamon. Divide mixture evenly among muffin cups. With moistened fingertips, gently push mixture into bottoms and up sides of cups to form baskets. Bake 10 minutes or until golden brown. Transfer pan to wire rack and cool completely. Carefully remove baskets from pan. Fill with jelly beans. 8 baskets.

❦ BUNNY ROLLS ❦
Julie Concannon

Frozen dinner roll dough
Raisins

Thaw rolls overnight in refrigerator (or according to package directions). To make each roll: Place 1 thawed roll on greased cookie sheet (dough should be cold). Gently press to form a 2½-inch circle, about ½-inch thick. Form nose from small part of a second roll. Divide remaining second roll into 2 parts to make ears. Make whiskers with knife tip and press raisins in dough to form eyes. Let dough rise according to package directions. Bake in 350° oven for 15 minutes or until golden brown. Makes 6 bunny rolls.

❦ CANDY CANE CHEESECAKE ❦
Julie Concannon

Cheesecake:

1⅓ c. chocolate cookie crumbs
2 T. granulated sugar
¼ c. butter or margarine, melted
1½ c. sour cream
½ c. granulated sugar
3 eggs
1 T. all-purpose flour

2 tsp. vanilla extract
¼ tsp. peppermint extract
3 pkgs. (8 oz. each) cream cheese, softened
2 T. butter, softened
⅔ c. crushed peppermint candy
Sweetened whipped cream

Preheat oven to 325°. Combine cookie crumbs, 2 tablespoons sugar and ¼ cup melted butter and press into the bottom of a 9-inch springform pan. Set aside. In blender or food processor, blend sour cream, ½ cup sugar, eggs, flour and extracts until smooth. Add cream cheese and 2 tablespoons butter, blending until completely smooth. Stir in crushed candy. Pour into crust. Bake on lowest rack of oven for 50 to 60 minutes, or until firm. Allow to cool (cheesecake may crack while cooling), then refrigerate overnight. To serve, use knife to loosen sides of cheesecake from pan; remove springform.

Sweetened Whipped Cream:

½ c. heavy cream
¼ c. granulated sugar

¾ tsp. vanilla extract

Place heavy cream, sugar and vanilla in a large mixing bowl. Beat at high speed until soft peaks form. Spread top of cheesecake with sweetened whipped cream. 10-12 servings.

❦ CHRISTMAS ROSE SWEET ROLLS ❦
Julie Concannon

1 (14 oz.) jar spiced apple rings, well drained
1 (11 oz.) can Pillsbury refrigerated soft breadsticks

1 c. powdered sugar
1 T. milk
½ tsp. vanilla

(continued)

Heat oven to 350°. Place apple rings in food processor bowl with metal blade or blender container, process until smooth. Remove dough from can. Unroll but do not separate dough. Spread puréed apples evenly over dough. Cut rolls at perforations and re-roll. Place rolls in muffin tins which are slightly sprayed with nonstick spray. Bake at 350° for 15-20 minutes or until golden brown. In small bowl combine powdered sugar, milk and vanilla; making sure to only add enough milk for desired drizzling consistency. Drizzle over warm rolls. 12 rolls.

❦ CORN CASSEROLE ❦
Dayla Miller

1 can whole corn, undrained	1 pkg. Jiffy Corn Mix
1 can cream style corn	1 stick margarine or butter,
1 c. sour cream	softened
1 sm. onion, chopped	Salt and pepper to taste
3 eggs	1 c. shredded Cheddar cheese

Mix all ingredients together. Pour into greased 13 x 9-inch pan. Bake at 350° for 1 hour.

❦ CRANBERRY CAKE DESSERT ❦
Kelly Duffy
Audrey Roe

Cake:

2 T. butter	3 tsp. baking powder
1 c. sugar	½ tsp. salt
1 tsp. vanilla	1 c. whole cranberries
2 c. flour	1 c. milk

Cream together the butter, sugar and vanilla. Mix together flour, baking powder and salt. Add cranberries alternately with the milk to the sugar mixture. Bake at 350° in a 9 x 9-inch pan for 30 minutes or until center is firm. Serve with the warm brown sauce.

Brown Sauce:

½ c. butter	1 c. brown sugar
½ c. cream	

(continued)

Boil butter, cream and brown sugar together for 3 minutes, stirring constantly. The baked cake freezes well and the sauce may be prepared ahead and reheated when serving. A favorite Christmas dessert.

❦ CRANBERRY FRUIT SALAD ❦
Dayla Miller

1 (6 oz.) pkg. strawberry jello
¾ c. sugar
2 c. hot water
2 c. pineapple juice
1 c. sour cream
2½ c. crushed pineapple, drained (save juice)

2 apples, chopped
2 c. ground fresh cranberries
2 med. oranges, chopped
1 c. chopped walnuts

Combine jello and sugar with hot water, stir until dissolved. Add pineapple juice, blend in sour cream and chill until partially set. Add remaining ingredients. Pour into mold or dish and chill until firm.

❦ CRANBERRY JELLO SALAD ❦
Dayla Miller

1 (3 oz.) pkg. raspberry jello
1 c. hot water and ½ c. cold water
1 apple, diced

½ c. pineapple chunks
1 can whole cranberry sauce
¼ c. chopped nuts

Combine jello and hot water and stir until dissolved, add cold water. Chill until partially thickened. Add in remaining ingredients and chill until firm. I use, in place of cold water, some of the pineapple juice.

CRANBERRY-ALMOND COFFEE CAKE

Ruth Manning
King Arthur Flour Baker's Companion

Coffee Cake:

½ c. butter
1 c. sugar
2 lg. eggs
1 c. buttermilk or plain yogurt
1 tsp. almond extract
1 tsp. baking powder
1 tsp. baking soda

2 c. all-purpose flour (King Arthur's unbleached)
½ tsp. salt
1 (10¾ oz.) whole berry cranberry sauce
½ c. blanched slivered or sliced almonds, toasted*

*Spread almonds in an ungreased 9-inch round cake pan, and bake in a preheated 350° oven for 8 to 10 minutes or until golden brown. Grease and flour a 10-cup (9 to 9½-inch) tube pan or bundt pan. In a large bowl, beat the butter and sugar until smooth. Beat in the eggs, then the buttermilk or yogurt and almond extract. Scrape the sides and bottom of the bowl and beat briefly again, to make sure everything is well combined. Add the baking powder, baking soda, flour and salt, stirring just to blend. Spoon half of batter into pan. Spread half of cranberry sauce evenly on top of the batter; spread remaining batter over that and top with remaining cranberry sauce. Sprinkle toasted almonds evenly over sauce. Bake the cake for 55 minutes, tenting it with foil for the final 15 minutes. When it's done, a cake tester inserted into the thickest part will come out clean, and the top will spring back when you press it gently. Remove the cake from the oven and cool it in pan for 5 minutes. After 5 minutes, turn it out of the pan onto a rack set over a piece of parchment.

Glaze:

¾ c. powdered sugar
2 T. milk

½ tsp. almond extract

Stir together glaze ingredients. Drizzle the thin glaze over the warm cake. Let the cake cool completely before serving. Serves 14 to 16.

❦ DARK PFEFFERNUSS ❦
(German Christmas Cookie)
Paula Foster
In memory of Jackie Badtke and
Grandma Reifschneider

½ tsp. cinnamon
½ tsp. ground cloves
½ tsp. allspice
½ tsp. salt
½ tsp. cream of tartar
3½ c. flour
½ tsp. soda
½ c. shortening

¼ c. brown sugar packed
1 egg
½ c. molasses (dark Brer
  Rabbit)
3 drops of anise oil
½ tsp. vinegar
1 T. hot water

Mix cinnamon, ground cloves, allspice, salt and cream of tartar and
then add this to the flour and the baking soda. Mix in remaining
ingredients in order. Knead the dough and then by large serving
spoonfuls, roll dough into ropes. Cut the dough into 1-inch pieces and
place on cookie sheet, 1-inch apart. Bake at 350° for 10 to 15 minutes.
Cool on wire racks.

❦ FANCY DEVILED EGGS ❦
Connie Walther
Sue Crabtree
Taste of Home

6 hard boiled eggs, finely
  chopped
3 bacon strips, cooked and
  crumbled
¼ c. light mayonnaise

1 tsp. minced onion
½ tsp. salt
Pepper to taste
¼ tsp. prepared mustard
1 c. shredded Cheddar cheese

Combine the first seven ingredients until creamy. Shape into 1-inch
balls. Roll in Cheddar cheese. Cover and refrigerate until serving.
Yields about 2 dozen.

121822-12

❦ FESTIVE HOLIDAY BARK ❦
Julie Concannon

16 oz. vanilla-flavored candy coating, chopped
2 c. sm. pretzel twists

½ c. red and green candy-coated chocolate pieces

Line cookie sheet with waxed paper. Melt candy coating in medium saucepan over low heat, stirring constantly. Add remaining ingredients; toss to coat. Spread mixture thinly on waxed paper-lined cookie sheet. Let stand until set. Break into pieces. 42 pieces. You could use different colored candy-coated chocolate pieces to change this up for different holidays (Easter, 4th of July, Halloween colors for example!).

❦ FRUIT CAKE ❦
Ruth Manning

1 lb. pitted dates, sliced
1 c. seedless raisins
⅔ c. butter
1¼ c. brown sugar
1¼ c. hot water
2 eggs
1 lb. candied mixed fruits
1 c. chopped walnuts

3 c. sifted flour
1 tsp. cinnamon
½ tsp. nutmeg
1 tsp. soda
1 tsp. baking powder
½ tsp. salt
Candied cherries
Citrus peel

Combine dates, raisins, butter, brown sugar and water in saucepan and simmer for 5 minutes. Cool in a mixing bowl. Beat in eggs and add candied fruits and nuts. Sift together dry ingredients. Fold gradually into the first mixture, beating well after each addition. Pour into greased loaf pans. Bake at 275° for 90 minutes. Remove from pan. Garnish with candied cherries and citrus peel. Makes 2 loaf pans.

❦ GLUWEIN ❦
Ruth Manning

1 qt. red wine
1 c. water
1 - 2 c. sugar

1 - 2 sticks of cinnamon
½ tsp. whole cloves
Thinly sliced lemon

Combine all ingredients and simmer for 15 minutes. Serves 10 to 12. A popular winter drink from our life in Germany.

GRAND MARNIER SWEET POTATOES

Lisa Rieff

3 lbs. canned yams or sweet potatoes
3 T. melted butter
¾ c. white sugar
Splash orange juice
½ tsp. nutmeg, divided
14 oz. can sweetened condensed milk
3 T. Grand Marnier
¼ tsp. salt
1 egg
5⅓ T. butter
1 c. brown sugar
⅓ c. flour
1 c. chopped pecans

Mash potatoes with 3 tablespoons melted butter in large bowl with mixer. Add white sugar, orange juice, ¼ teaspoon nutmeg, condensed milk, Grand Marnier, salt and egg. Beat at medium speed until smooth. Pour into a lightly greased 9 x 13-inch pan. Melt the 5⅓ tablespoons butter in a small bowl. Add brown sugar, flour, ¼ teaspoon nutmeg and the pecans. Combine and sprinkle over the potatoes. Bake at 425° uncovered for 20 minutes. Remove and cover with foil. Continue baking for 10 minutes.

HALLOWEEN BARS

Lynnette Nore
Mr. Food's Favorite Cookies

½ c. (1 stick) butter
1½ c. graham cracker crumbs
1 can (14 oz.) sweetened condensed milk
12 oz. pkg. semisweet chocolate chips
1 c. peanut butter chips
½ c. candy corn

Preheat oven to 325°. Place butter in a 9 x 13-inch baking dish and melt in the oven. Remove the dish from the oven and distribute the melted butter evenly over the bottom. Sprinkle the graham cracker crumbs evenly over the melted butter; pour the sweetened condensed milk evenly over the crumbs. Top with the chocolate chips and peanut butter chips; press down firmly. Bake for 25 to 30 minutes until golden. Sprinkle with the candy corn and gently press the candies into the uncut bars. Cool, then cut into bars. Makes 2-3 dozen bars.

121822-12

❦ HALLOWEEN PIZZA ❦
Julie Concannon

1 (20 oz.) pkg. Pillsbury refrigerated sugar cookie dough
½ c. creamy peanut butter

1 c. candy corn
½ c. raisins
2 - 4 T. Pillsbury vanilla frosting supreme, melted

Heat oven to 350°. Line 12-inch pizza pan with foil; grease foil. Cut cookie dough into ¼-inch slices; press slices into bottom of foil-lined pan to form crust. Bake at 350° for 15-20 minutes or until deep golden brown. Cool completely. Carefully remove foil from cookie pizza. *Spread cookie with peanut butter; sprinkle evenly with candy corn and raisins. Drizzle melted frosting over pizza. Cut into wedges or squares. *It is easier to cut pizza after peanut butter is on and before candy and raisins, just leave intact as much as possible. 16-24 servings.

❦ HOLLY CRACKLES ❦
Lynnette Nore
Mr. Food's Favorite Cookies

½ c. (1 stick) butter
30 lg. marshmallows
1 - 1½ tsp. green food coloring
1½ tsp. vanilla extract

4 c. cornflakes cereal
Red hot cinnamon candies for decorating

In a medium-sized saucepan, melt the butter and marshmallows over moderate low heat, stirring constantly. When melted, remove from heat and stir in 1 teaspoon of food coloring and the vanilla. Add more food coloring if desired. Stir in cornflakes. Drop the mixture, 1 teaspoon at a time, onto waxed paper. Decorate with the red hot candies. Let stand 30 minutes until cool. Note: 1½ teaspoons food coloring makes these very dark. Also, you can use pastel food coloring and jelly beans to call them Birds Nests in the spring.

❦ IRISH BEEF STEW ❦
Debra Gillespie
Katie Gillespie (Debra's daughter)

1 ¼ lbs. well marbled chuck beef stew meat, cut into 1-inch pieces	1 T. sugar
	1 T. dried thyme
	2 bay leaves
¼ c. olive oil	1 T. Worcestershire sauce
Salt and pepper	2 T. butter
6 lg. garlic cloves, minced	3 lbs. red potatoes, cut into ½-inch thick pieces (7 c.)
6 c. beef stock or canned beef broth	
	2 c. carrots, cut into ½-inch thick pieces
1 c. Guinness beer	
1 c. fine red wine	1 lg. onion, chopped
2 T. tomato paste	2 T. fresh parsley, chopped

Brown beef in olive oil in heavy pan, salt and pepper slightly. Add garlic and sauté 1 minute. Add beef stock, beer, wine, tomato paste, sugar, thyme, bay leaves and Worcestershire sauce. Stir to combine. Bring to boil. Reduce heat to medium-low, cover and simmer 1 hour, stirring occasionally. While meat and stock are simmering, melt butter in another large pot or skillet. Sauté potatoes, carrots, and onions for 20 minutes. Add vegetables to the beef stew. Simmer uncovered until all ingredients are tender. Discard bay leaves and spoon off fat. Garnish each serving with chopped parsley and serve with a hearty bread. May prepare stew 2 days ahead. This is a dark stew, full bodied. It is a tasty meal to serve on St. Patrick's Day. Serves 6-8.

❦ IRISH CHOCOLATE MINT DESSERT ❦
Julie Concannon

Brownies:

1 c. (2 sticks) butter or margarine	4 eggs
	¾ c. Hershey's cocoa
2 c. granulated sugar	1 c. all-purpose flour
2 tsp. vanilla extract	½ tsp. baking powder

Heat oven to 350°. Line a 13 x 9 x 2-inch baking pan with foil and grease the foil (for ease in removing from pan). Place butter in large

(continued)

microwave-safe bowl. Microwave at MEDIUM (50%) 2 minutes or until melted. Stir in granulated sugar and vanilla. Add eggs; beat well. Add cocoa, flour and baking powder; beat until well blended. Pour batter into prepared pan. Bake 30-35 minutes or until wooden pick inserted in center comes out clean. Cool completely on wire rack.

Mint Cream Center:

2⅔ c. powdered sugar
½ c. (one stick) butter
1 T. plus 1 tsp. water

1 tsp. mint extract
4 drops green food color

Combine powdered sugar, butter, water, mint extract and food color. Beat until smooth. Spread evenly on brownies. Cover; refrigerate until cold.

Chocolate Glaze:

6 T. butter
1 c. Hershey's Special Dark
   chocolate chips or Hershey's
   semi-sweet chips

Place butter and chocolate chips in small microwave-safe bowl. Microwave at MEDIUM (50%) 1 minute or until mixture is smooth when stirred. Cool slightly; pour over chilled dessert. Cover; refrigerate at least 1 hour before serving. Lift out of pan and remove foil carefully before cutting. Cover; refrigerate leftover dessert. 24 larger servings or 48 smaller servings (this is quite rich).

❧ IRISH SODA BREAD ❧
Ruth Manning

3½ c. all-purpose flour
½ c. sugar
2 T. caraway seeds
2 tsp. baking powder
1 tsp. salt

½ tsp. baking soda
2 eggs
16 oz. sour cream
¾ c. raisins

In a large bowl, combine the flour, sugar, caraway seeds, baking powder, salt and baking soda. In a small bowl, whisk eggs and sour cream together. Stir into dry ingredients just until moistened. Fold in raisins. Spoon into a greased 9-inch springform pan. Bake at 350° for 40-45 minutes or until a toothpick inserted near the center comes out clean.

(continued)

Cool on a wire rack for 15 minutes before removing sides of pan. Cut into wedges; serve warm. Yield: 1 loaf (12 wedges).

❦ JELLO SPRITZ COOKIES ❦
Ruth Manning

4 c. sifted all-purpose flour	1 tsp. vanilla
1 tsp. baking powder	1 c. sugar
1½ c. butter, softened	1 (3 oz.) pkg. jello, any flavor
1 egg	Additional jello

Sift flour and baking powder. Cream butter, egg and vanilla together. Gradually add sugar and 1 box of jello, mixing well after each addition until smooth. Add flour and baking powder and mix well. Force dough through cookie press onto ungreased baking sheets. Sprinkle with additional jello. Decorate as desired with gumdrops, candied fruit bits, etc. Bake at 400° for 10 to 14 minutes. Store in loosely covered container. Note: at Christmas divide dough in half and mix ½ pkg. of cherry jello in one half and ½ pkg. lime jello into second half of the dough.

❦ LEFSE (NO POTATOES) ❦
Ruth Manning

1 pt. half and half	2 tsp. salt
¼ c. lard (I use butter)	3 c. flour, divided

Heat half and half and lard (butter) to boiling. Add salt and 1 c. flour; stir vigorously as mixture will be thick and mushy. Chill. When cold, knead in remaining flour. Shape dough into rolls. Chill for 15 minutes. Slice. Roll out paper thin. Bake on preheated grill until lightly browned. Makes about 12 "rounds."

121822-12

❦ LIBBY'S PUMPKIN PIE ❦

Julie Concannon
Libby's

¾ c. sugar
½ tsp. salt
1 tsp. ground cinnamon
½ tsp. ground ginger
¼ tsp. ground cloves
2 lg. eggs

1 can (15 oz.) Libby's 100%
Pure Pumpkin
1 can (12 oz.) evaporated milk
1 unbaked 9-inch deep dish pie
shell

Mix sugar, salt, cinnamon, ginger and cloves in small bowl. Beat eggs in large bowl. Stir in pumpkin and sugar-spice mixture. Gradually stir in evaporated milk. Pour into pie shell. Bake in preheated 425° oven for 15 minutes. Reduce temperature to 350°, bake 40-50 minutes or until knife inserted near center comes out clean. Cool on wire rack for 2 hours. Serve immediately or refrigerate. While this is right off the Libby's can, this is our very favorite pumpkin pie at Thanksgiving!

❦ NORWEGIAN NUT COOKIES ❦

Lynnette Nore

1 c. butter
6 T. sugar
1 egg yolk
1 tsp. vanilla

2 c. sifted flour
1 c. sliced pecans
Cinnamon sugar, optional

Beat butter and sugar until creamy with electric mixer. Add egg yolk and vanilla, beat. Add sifted flour. Add pecans. With hands make into small, oval-shaped rolls approximately the size of a finger. Bake at 350° for 12-15 minutes or until set. Cool slightly. Roll in cinnamon sugar.

❦ PEPPERMINT DESSERT ❦

Shari Garder

25 Oreo cookies, crushed
¼ c. margarine, melted
½ gal. peppermint ice cream,
softened

1 c. powdered sugar
¼ c. margarine
1 pkg. chocolate chips
1 sm. can evaporated milk

Mix crushed cookies and margarine. Press into a 9 x 13-inch pan. Freeze. Spread softened ice cream over the crust. Freeze hard. Melt

(continued)

powdered sugar, margarine, chocolate chips, and evaporated milk in a saucepan. Cool. Pour over ice cream and freeze.

❦ PUMPKIN LAYER CAKE ❦
Lisa Rieff

1 pkg. yellow cake mix	8 oz. cream cheese, softened
15 oz. can pumpkin, divided	1 c. powdered sugar
½ c. milk	8 oz. Cool Whip, thawed
⅓ c. vegetable oil	Caramel ice cream topping
4 eggs	½ c. pecans, chopped
1½ tsp. allspice, divided	Whipped cream

Grease and flour two 9-inch round cake pans. Beat cake mix, 1 cup of pumpkin, milk, oil, eggs, and 1 teaspoon allspice in large bowl on medium until smooth. Pour evenly into pans and bake 20-22 minutes at 350°. Cool completely. Meanwhile, beat cream cheese in medium bowl until smooth. Add powdered sugar, remaining pumpkin and remaining allspice. Mix well then fold in Cool Whip. Remove cake from pans and cut each one in half to make 4 layers total. Stack layers on plate spreading ⅓ of frosting on each layer. DO NOT frost the top layer. Garnish each piece by drizzling with caramel, sprinkling with pecans and adding whipped cream.

❦ SCANDINAVIAN SANDBAKKELS ❦
Ruth Manning

1 c. butter, room temperature	1 egg
¾ c. sugar	1 tsp. almond extract
¼ c. powdered sugar	2½ c. all-purpose flour

In a large bowl, beat butter, sugar and powdered sugar with electric mixer on medium speed until fluffy. Add egg and almond extract; beat well. Add flour; beat on low until combined. Chill for 2 to 3 hours or until dough is easy to handle. Pinch off a heaping teaspoon of chilled dough for mold and place dough in the center of a sandbakkel mold. Press the dough evenly on the inside of the mold, spreading it as thin as possible on the bottoms and up sides of the mold. Repeat for the remaining dough. Place the filled molds on a cookie sheet. Bake in a 350° oven for 12 to 15 minutes until edges of cookies turn light brown. Cool. Loosen cookies from molds by tapping bottoms of molds with

(continued)

121822-12

a spoon. Remove cookies from molds. Cookies can be filled like tart shells. Makes about 36 (2-½") cookies.

❦ SPARKLE POPCORN ❦
Julie Concannon

Twin pack of Vic's white
   popcorn
1 pkg. almond bark
1 jar dry roasted peanuts

1 jar sprinkles (blue for 4th of
   July)
2 theater boxes of Hot
   Tamales candies

Place popcorn in two separate large mixing bowls and add ½ jar of roasted peanuts to each bowl and 1 box of Hot Tamales to each bowl. Divide almond bark in half and melt one half according to package directions. Pour melted bark over popcorn mixture in one bowl and stir to coat. Sprinkle with ½ jar of sprinkles and stir some more. Repeat with other bowl. Cool. About 27 cups total. The blue and red in this version make it fun for the 4th of July. You can change up the color of sprinkles and the candy for different holidays. You could try pink sprinkles and jelly beans for Easter, orange sprinkles and Mike & Ike's for Halloween, etc.

❦ SPOOKY CINNAMON ROLLS ❦
Julie Concannon

1 can Pillsbury refrigerated
   cinnamon rolls with icing
2 drops red food color

2 drops yellow food color
1 sm. tube black decorating
   gel

Heat oven to 400°. Bake cinnamon rolls as directed on can. Meanwhile, add both food colors to container of icing; blend well to make orange icing. Frost warm rolls with icing. Pipe decorating gel in spiral around top of each frosted roll. To form spider web design, start at center of each roll and draw toothpick through gel to edge of roll, spacing lines about 1-inch apart at edge of roll. 8 rolls.

121822-12

❧ SPRITZ COOKIES (CHRISTMAS TREES) ❧
Lynnette Nore

1 c. shortening	2¼ c. sifted flour
¾ c. sugar	¼ tsp. baking powder
1 egg	¼ tsp. salt
1 tsp. almond extract	Green food coloring

Cream shortening and sugar well. Beat in egg and almond extract. Gradually blend in flour, baking powder and salt which have been sifted together and tint the dough with a few drops of green food coloring. Mix well. Fill press and form cookies on ungreased cookie sheets. Bake at 350° for 8 minutes. Remove at once to cooling racks.

❧ ST. PATRICK'S DAY CHEESE-CRUSTED BISCUITS ❧
Ruth Manning

2 c. flour	1 c. shredded Kerrygold
2 tsp. baking powder	Cheddar cheese, divided
½ tsp. baking soda	⅔ c. buttermilk
½ tsp. salt	½ c. chopped walnuts
2 c. cold unsalted Kerrygold	2 tsp. dried sage
Pure Irish Butter, cut into	¼ tsp. freshly ground pepper
½-inch cubes	

Heat oven to 425°; lightly grease a baking sheet. In a medium bowl, stir together flour, baking powder, baking soda and salt. Add butter. Cut butter into flour mixture with pastry blender or fork until mixture resembles coarse meal. Stir in ½ c. of the cheese, buttermilk, walnuts, sage and pepper. Stir until mixture forms a ball, adding a little more flour if dough is too sticky. Turn out dough on a very lightly floured board and press to shape into a square 1-inch thick. Sprinkle with ¼ c. of the remaining cheese, pressing lightly into surface. Turn dough and repeat with the remaining cheese. Cut into 12 pieces and place on baking sheet. Bake on center rack of oven 10 to 12 minutes or until golden. Makes 12 biscuits.

121822-12

❦ ST. PATRICK'S DAY SCALLOPED POTATOES ❦
Ruth Manning

2 T. Kerrygold (Irish) butter
1 sm. onion, minced
2 med. garlic cloves, minced
   (about 2 tsp.)
3 c. heavy cream (I use half
   and half)
1 c. whole milk
4 sprigs fresh thyme

2 bay leaves
2 tsp. salt
½ tsp. ground black pepper
4 lbs. russet potatoes, peeled
   and cut into ⅛-inch slices
I c. shredded Kerrygold white
   sharp Cheddar cheese (about
   4 oz.)

Heat oven to 350°. Meanwhile, melt butter in large Dutch oven over medium-high heat until foaming subsides, about 1 minute. Add onion and sauté until it turns soft and begins to brown, about 4 minutes. Add garlic and sauté until fragrant, about 30 seconds. Add cream, milk, thyme, bay leaves, salt, pepper, and potatoes and bring to simmer. Cover, adjusting heat as necessary to maintain light simmer, and cook until potatoes are almost tender (paring knife can be slipped into and out of center of potato slice with some resistance), about 15 minutes. Remove and discard thyme sprigs and bay leaves. Transfer potato mixture to 3-quart gratin dish and sprinkle with cheese. Bake until cream has thickened and is bubbling around sides and top is golden brown, about 20 minutes. Cool for 5 minutes before serving. Serves 8 to 10. You can use "non-Irish" Cheddar cheese and butter, but the flavor isn't as good.

❦ SWEET & SPICY MIXED NUTS ❦
Connie Walther

1 lg. egg white
⅓ c. sugar
1 tsp. kosher salt
½ tsp. ground cinnamon
¼ tsp. cayenne pepper

¼ tsp. cumin
½ tsp. smoked paprika
3 c. unsalted mixed nuts or
   almonds

Heat oven to 325°. Line a rimmed baking sheet with foil. In large bowl, whisk together egg white and dry ingredients. Add the nuts and toss to coat. Spread nuts evenly on prepared pan. Bake 30-35 minutes, stirring twice, until nuts are dry. Transfer to a clean sheet of foil and

(continued)

let cool. Can store the nuts at room temperature for up to 2 weeks. Great for individual bagged gifts. Makes 3 cups.

❦ SWEET POTATO CASSEROLE ❦
Dayla Miller

Sweet Potatoes:

3 c. cooked sweet potatoes
2 eggs, beaten
1 c. sugar
1 T. vanilla

5 T. softened margarine or
 butter
¼ c. flour

Blend ingredients until smooth. Pour into 9-inch round baking dish.

Topping:

1 c. brown sugar
⅓ c. flour

5 T. margarine or butter
1 c. chopped pecans

Blend ingredients and crumble onto potato mixture. Bake at 350° for 30 minutes or until bubbly and brown.

❦ THANKSGIVING CRANBERRY COBBLER ❦
Julie Concannon

1 deluxe yellow cake mix
½ tsp. ground cinnamon
¼ tsp. ground nutmeg
1 c. (2 sticks) butter, softened
½ c. chopped nuts

1 can (21 oz.) peach pie filling
1 can (16 oz.) whole cranberry
 sauce
Vanilla ice cream

Preheat oven to 350°. Combine dry cake mix, cinnamon and nutmeg in bowl. Cut in butter with pastry blender or two knives until crumbly. Stir in nuts; set aside. Combine peach pie filling and cranberry sauce in ungreased 13 x 9 x 2-inch pan; mix well. Sprinkle crumb mixture over fruit. Bake at 350° for 45 to 50 minutes or until golden brown. Serve warm with ice cream. 16 servings.

121822-12

❦ WHITE PFEFFERNUSS ❦
(German Christmas Cookie)
Paula Foster
In memory of Jackie Badtke and
Grandma Reifschneider

½ c. shortening	1 tsp. baking powder
1 c. sugar	½ tsp. cardamom
2 eggs	1 tsp. salt
1 tsp. vanilla	2½ c. flour

Mix ingredients in order (Jackie put baking powder, salt and cardamom into the flour first). Chill dough. Taking large serving spoon size of dough, roll into a long rope. Cut the dough into small pieces about 1-inch each. Leave about 1-inch of space between cookies on cookie sheet. Bake in a 350° oven for 10 to 15 minutes. Cool cookies on wire racks. Store covered.

Recipe Favorites

121822-12

Main Dishes & Meats

Helpful Hints

- Certain meats, like ribs and pot roast, can be parboiled before grilling to reduce the fat content.

- Pound meat lightly with a mallet or rolling pin, pierce with a fork, sprinkle lightly with meat tenderizer, and add marinade. Refrigerate for 20 minutes and cook or grill for a quick and succulent meat.

- Marinating is a cinch if you use a plastic bag. The meat stays in the marinade and it's easy to turn. Cleanup is easy; just toss the bag.

- It's easier to thinly slice meat if it's partially frozen.

- Adding tomatoes to roasts naturally tenderizes the meat as tomatoes contain an acid that works well to break down meats.

- Whenever possible, cut meat across the grain; this will make it easier to eat and also give it a more attractive appearance.

- When frying meat, sprinkle paprika on the meat to turn it golden brown.

- Thaw all meats in the refrigerator for maximum safety.

- Refrigerate poultry promptly after purchasing. Keep it in the coldest part of your refrigerator for up to 2 days. Freeze poultry for longer storage. Never leave poultry at room temperature for over 2 hours.

- When frying chicken, canola oil provides a milder taste, and it contains healthier amounts of saturated and polyunsaturated fats. Do not cover the chicken once it has finished cooking because covering will cause the coating to lose its crispness.

- One pound of boneless chicken equals approximately 3 cups of cubed chicken.

- Generally, red meats should reach 160° and poultry should reach 180° before serving. If preparing fish, the surface of the fish should flake off with a fork.

- Rub lemon juice on fish before cooking to enhance the flavor and help maintain a good color.

- Scaling a fish is easier if vinegar is rubbed on the scales first.

- When grilling fish, the rule of thumb is to cook 5 minutes on each side per inch of thickness. For example, cook a 2-inch thick fillet for 10 minutes per side. Before grilling, rub with oil to seal in moisture.

MAIN DISHES AND MEATS

BEEF

❦ APRICOT MEAT LOAF ❦
Harry Naasz
Mrs. R.C. Swain

Meat Loaf:

2 lbs. ground beef	2 eggs
1 c. dried apricots, chopped	1½ tsp. salt
½ c. dry bread crumbs	⅛ tsp. pepper

Combine ground beef, apricots, bread crumbs, eggs, salt and pepper and shape into roll. Place on greased shallow baking pan and bake for 1 hour at 350°.

Glaze:

½ c. brown sugar	1 tsp. water

Heat brown sugar and water until sugar is melted and spread over hot meat loaf.

❦ ASIAN BEEF NOODLES ❦
Mike Klos

1 lb. beef round tip	¼ c. steak sauce
1 jalapeño pepper, diced	1 med. carrot, shredded
1 T. olive oil	2 T. green onions, chopped
1 pkg. beef flavor instant ramen noodles	¼ c. chopped peanuts

Cut steak into strips. In bowl combine beef, jalapeño pepper and olive oil. Toss to coat. Break noodles into 4 pieces. Reserve seasoning packet. Cook noodles following packet directions. Drain. Heat skillet and add beef mixture. Cook until no longer pink. Remove beef to plate. In same skillet, combine noodles, steak sauce, carrot, green onions and reserved seasoning packet. Cook until hot, then return beef. Mix and sprinkle with peanuts.

❦ B & G BURGERS (SLOPPY JOES) ❦
Dayla Miller

Seasoning:

4 oz. ketchup	5 tsp. salt
3 heaping T. mustard	3 tsp. Worcestershire sauce
3 heaping T. cream style horseradish	½ tsp. pepper

Combine all of the seasoning ingredients in a jar or cup. The seasoning ingredients should fill the cup, if not, add more ketchup and mix together.

Burgers:

5 lbs. hamburger	1 yellow onion, chopped
1 heaping tsp. Accent	

Put the hamburger and onion into large pan or kettle, add seasoning mixture. Fill the seasoning jar with water and pour onto mixture of hamburger and seasoning. Add Accent and stir thoroughly with wooden spoon over medium heat, continue to stir until meat is broken finely apart. Increase the heat until it comes to a boil. Let boil 25 minutes. Stir every few minutes. Serve on buns. Great with mustard and pickles. If too much grease, I have drained a bit. I have added extra ketchup, mustard and horseradish as well.

6-29-12
Millers
c Edna
good

❦ BARBEQUE MEATBALLS ❦
Shari Garder

Meatballs:

2 lbs. ground beef	1 c. oatmeal or 1 c. instant rice
Chopped onion	Salt and pepper to taste
½ c. milk	

Mix all together. Shape into meatballs and place in 9 x 13-inch pan.

Sauce:

2 c. catsup	2 T. Worcestershire sauce
⅓ c. brown sugar	Salt and pepper to taste
2 T. mustard	

(continued)

121822-12

Mix all sauce ingredients together. Pour over meatballs. Bake at 350° for 1 hour.

❦ BEAN CASSEROLE ❦
Judy Egr

½ lb. bacon, chopped
½ lb. hamburger
1 onion, chopped
1 can B & M beans, drained
1 can Bush beans, drained

1 can kidney beans, drained
½ c. catsup
¼ tsp. mustard
1 tsp. vinegar
½ c. brown sugar

Brown bacon, hamburger and onion together. Add remaining ingredients. Bake at 350° for 30 minutes.

❦ BEEF BURGUNDY ❦
Judy Egr

1½ lbs. sirloin, cut in 1-inch
   cubes
2 T. butter
2 cans golden mushroom soup
⅛ tsp. pepper

½ c. red wine (Burgundy)
12 sm. white onions (may use
   frozen)
2 T. parsley
1 lb. wide noodles, cooked

Brown meat in butter. Add remaining ingredients except noodles. Cover and simmer for 1 hour or until meat is tender. Stir occasionally. Serve over cooked noodles. Makes 6 servings.

❦ BEEF BURGUNDY ❦
Mary Lou Gustafson
From my sister Annette Kurimay

5 lb. beef stew meat
Salt and pepper
4 cans onion soup
3 cloves garlic, finely diced

2 c. Burgundy wine
3 sm. cans mushrooms,
   drained

Season beef with salt and pepper then brown meat. Spray a large kettle with Pam. Transfer meat into the kettle and add the 4 cans of soup, diced garlic, wine and mushrooms. Cover and cook for 4 hours in a 325° oven. Serve over rice.

❦ BEEF ENCHILADAS ❦
Brenda Mac

1 ⅓ lbs. hamburger
½ med. onion, chopped
1 can Old El Paso mild
  enchilada sauce
1 can cream of tomato soup

1 can cream of mushroom
  soup
2 c. shredded Cheddar cheese,
  divided
1 pkg. (10 count) flour tortillas

Brown hamburger with onion and drain off grease. Mix together enchilada sauce, cream of tomato soup and cream of mushroom soup. Add ½ cup enchilada sauce mix to hamburger mixture and ½ cup cheese. Fill each flour tortilla with beef mixture (2 heaping tablespoons) and roll tight. Place the 10 tortillas in a cake pan and top with remaining enchilada sauce and remaining cheese. Bake at 350° for 20 minutes or until bubbly.

❦ BEEF STROGANOFF ❦
Rex Quadhamer

1 lb. hamburger
1 sm. onion, chopped
8 oz. frozen noodles

2 cans cream of mushroom
  soup, undiluted
8 oz. container sour cream

Cook hamburger and onion until done. Drain fat. Cook noodles according to directions on package. Drain. Add to hamburger. Add cream of mushroom soup and sour cream and mix thoroughly. Heat through.

❦ BEEF STROGANOFF ❦
Shari Garder

1 lb. stew meat
1 stick margarine
2 cans cream of mushroom
  soup

16 oz. sour cream
Rice or egg noodles

Sauté stew meat in margarine in slow cooker for 2 hours. Add soup and continue to cook on low. Shortly before ready to serve add sour cream. Heat until warm. Serve over rice or egg noodles.

121822-12

❦ BEEF, RICE AND BEAN ENCHILADAS ❦
Lisa Rieff

1 lb. ground beef	1 can refried beans
1 pkg. taco seasoning	3 c. shredded Cheddar cheese,
2 c. water	divided
1 pkg. (Lipton/Knorr) Spanish	1 lg. can enchilada sauce
or Mexican flavored rice	Flour tortillas

Brown and drain beef in a large skillet. Add taco seasoning, water and rice package. Bring to a boil, cover and simmer 7 minutes. Add can of beans and 1 cup cheese. Mix well. Lightly grease two 9 x 13-inch pans. Add enough enchilada sauce to both pans to cover the bottom. Fill tortillas and roll, placing seam side down in pan. Cover with remaining sauce and cheese. Bake at 350° for 25-30 minutes. You can freeze one pan for later use.

❦ CABBAGE ROLLS CASSEROLE ❦
Cheyrle Badtke

2 lbs. hamburger	2 pkg. crescent rolls
2 pkgs. dry onion soup mix	2 c. Cheddar or Swiss cheese
½ c. water	
1 (8 oz.) pkg. shredded	
cabbage	

Brown hamburger meat. Drain. Add onion soup mix, water and cabbage and cook for 15 minutes. Take one pkg. of crescent rolls and line the bottom of a greased 9 x 13-inch pan. Spread beef and cabbage mixture over the crescent rolls. Spread on the cheese and top with the second can of crescent rolls. Bake at 350° for 30 minutes.

❦ CAVATINI PIZZA CASSEROLE ❦
Shari Garder

1½ lb. hamburger	1 sm. can mushrooms
12 - 16 oz. twist macaroni	6 oz. sliced pepperoni
1 (32 oz.) jar spaghetti sauce	1 c. mozzarella cheese

(continued)

Brown hamburger and drain. Cook macaroni and drain. Simmer hamburger, sauce, and mushrooms. Add to macaroni and put in 9 x 13-inch pan. Cover with pepperoni. Bake at 350° for 35 minutes. Add cheese to top and bake 10 more minutes. May add peppers, onions, or celery if desired. Serves 6-8.

❧ CHEESEBURGER PIE ❧
Nancy Shinrock

1 lb. ground beef
1 c. chopped onion
½ tsp. salt
1 c. shredded Cheddar cheese

2 eggs
½ c. Bisquick
1 c. milk

Heat oven to 400°. Grease 9-inch pie plate. Cook beef and onion until beef is brown, drain. Spread in pie plate. Sprinkle with salt and cheese. Stir eggs, Bisquick, and milk until blended. Pour into pie plate. Bake 25 minutes. 6 servings.

❧ CHUCKWAGON BEEF AND BEANS ❧
Mike Klos

1 lb. lean ground beef
1 green pepper, chopped
1 (15 oz.) can barbecue beans, undrained
1 (15 oz.) can Great Northern white beans, drained

⅓ c. barbecue sauce
2 T. prepared mustard
½ c. water
1 can buttermilk biscuits

In skillet cook beef until browned. Drain off fat and return to skillet. Stir in green pepper, barbecue beans, white beans, barbecue sauce, mustard and water. Heat to boil. Cut biscuits in half and place on top of mixture. Reduce heat to medium-low. Simmer for 15 minutes or until biscuits are cooked. They will not brown. They will be like dumplings.

121822-12

❦ CRUNCHY CHEESERONI CASSEROLE ❦
Cathy Aden

2 c. uncooked elbow macaroni
1 ring kielbasa, diced/chopped
¾ c. chopped green pepper
1 can (10¾ oz.) cream of
  mushroom soup

1 can (10¾ oz.) condensed
  tomato soup
2 cups cubed Colby cheese
1 can (3 oz.) french fried
  onions

Cook and drain macaroni according to package directions. Stir in kielbasa, green pepper, soups and Colby cheese. Top with french fried onions. Bake at 350° for 45-60 minutes.

❦ EASY BEEF ENCHILADA'S ❦
Nancy Shinrock

1 lb. ground beef
1 can (19 oz.) enchilada sauce,
  divided

1½ c. shredded cheese, divided
1 pkg. (8.2 oz.) flour tortillas

Heat oven to 375°. Lightly grease 13 x 9-inch glass baking dish. In 10-inch skillet cook beef over medium-high heat, stirring occasionally until thoroughly cooked. Drain meat. Stir in ¾ c. of enchilada sauce and 1 c. of the cheese. Spoon enchilada filling into tortillas, roll and place seams side down in baking dish. Pour remaining enchilada sauce over top, sprinkle with remaining cheese. Bake 15 to 20 minutes or until hot. Makes 10 enchilada's.

❦ FARMERS DELIGHT ❦
Cheyrle Badtke

1½ lb. ground beef
½ c. chopped onion
1 (8 oz.) pkg. noodles
1 can chicken with rice soup
1 can cream of mushroom
  soup

½ soup can of water
1 can cream style corn
¼ lb. diced American cheese
1 sm. jar pimento

Brown meat and onions. Cook and drain noodles. Combine with meat mixture. Stir in soups, water, corn, cheese and pimento. Bake at 350° for one hour. Cover for first ½ hour. Serves 8.

❦ FOOLPROOF STANDING RIB ROAST ❦
Kathy Christiansen

1 rib roast (with ribs)	Pepper
Salt	Garlic powder

Allow roast to stand at room temperature for 1 hour. Preheat oven to 375°. Mix 2 parts salt, 1 part pepper and 1 part garlic powder together. Rub roast generously with seasoning mixture. Place roast on a rack in the pan with the rib side down and the fatty side up. Roast for 1 hour. Turn off oven. Leave roast in oven but do not open oven door for 3 hours. About 30 (perfect medium rare) to 40 minutes (a little more medium) before serving time, turn oven to 375° and reheat the roast. Important: Do not remove roast or re-open the oven door from time roast is put in until ready to serve.

❦ FOOTBALL STEW ❦
Rose Roberts
Shirley Roberts

1½ lbs. meat, cubed	½ tsp. garlic
3 med. potatoes, cubed	½ tsp. salt
2 carrots, sliced	Pepper, to taste
2 stalks celery, chopped	¼ head shredded cabbage
½ lg. onion, chopped	1 can tomato soup
1 container mushrooms, sliced	1 can beef broth
2 T. tapioca	1 can water

Layer the meat, potatoes, carrots, celery, onion, sliced mushrooms, tapioca, garlic, salt, pepper and cabbage in that order in a casserole dish. Combine the tomato soup, broth and water and pour over the layered ingredients. Bake at 250° for 5 hours. Can be done in a crock pot.

❦ FRENCH DIP SANDWICH ❦
Jill Hild

1 beef roast	1 pkg. onion soup mix
1 can beer	½ tsp. garlic powder
1 can beef broth	Hoagie buns
2 T. sugar	

(continued)

Combine all ingredients except buns in crock pot, cook on low 24 hours. Serve on hoagie buns.

❦ GERMAN PIZZA ❦

Connie Walther
Audrey Nolt
Taste Of Home

1 lb. ground beef
½ med. onion, diced
½ green pepper, diced
Salt and pepper
2 T. margarine
6 med. potatoes, peeled and
　shredded

3 eggs, beaten
⅓ c. milk
2 c. shredded Cheddar or
　mozzarella cheese

Brown beef with onion and green pepper, add salt and pepper to taste. Remove meat mixture and drain. Melt margarine, add potatoes and additional salt to taste. Press down slightly and add beef mixture. Combine eggs and milk and pour over all. Cook on medium heat, until potatoes are tender, about 30 minutes. Top with cheese; cover to melt cheese. Serves 4-6.

❦ HAMBURGER STROGANOFF ❦

Heidi Meyer

½ - 1 lb. ground beef
½ - 1 T. minced onion
⅛ tsp. garlic powder
2 T. flour
1 tsp. salt
½ tsp. paprika

1 can cream of mushroom
　soup
½ c. water
1 c. sour cream
Cooked rice or wavy noodles

Brown ground beef with minced onion and garlic powder. Drain grease. Coat meat with flour, salt, and paprika. Add in soup, water, and sour cream. Heat thoroughly. Serve over white rice or wavy noodles.

❦ ITALIAN MEATBALL AND BISCUIT BAKE ❦
Julie Concannon
From my sister Jana Mabie

1 bag (16 oz.) frozen cooked Italian style meatballs

1 can Pillsbury Grand homestyle refrigerated buttermilk biscuits

1 jar (14 oz.) tomato pasta sauce

1½ c. shredded mozzarella cheese

Heat oven to 375°. Spray a 9 x 13-inch (3 qt.) glass baking dish with cooking spray. In a large microwave safe bowl, microwave the meatballs on medium for 3-5 minutes or until thawed. Separate dough into 8 biscuits; cut each biscuit into 8 pieces and place in the bowl with the meatballs. Gently stir in pasta sauce to coat. Spoon and spread mixture in baking dish. Bake 30-40 minutes or until edges are deep golden brown and biscuit pieces are no longer doughy on the bottom. Sprinkle with cheese and bake 2-5 minutes longer or until cheese is melted. Cool 10 minutes before serving.

❦ ITALIAN MEATBALLS ❦
Rose Roberts

4 lbs. ground beef

1 lb. ground pork sausage

2 tsp. salt

½ c. Romano cheese

½ c. Parmesan cheese

2 T. parsley

1 tsp. pepper

1 c. of bread crumbs

½ tsp. chopped garlic

5 eggs

Spaghetti sauce

Combine ground beef, ground pork, salt, cheeses, parsley, pepper, bread crumbs, garlic and eggs and form into balls. Brown under broiler that has a drip pan. Add to spaghetti sauce to heat through. This is a recipe from one of my student's Italian grandmother.

❦ JEANNE'S SLOPPY JOES ❦

Mary Lou Gustafson
From my friend Jeanne Svatos

1 lb. hamburger	¼ tsp. pepper
1 med. onion, diced	1 tsp. prepared mustard
½ c. ketchup	½ c. cold water
½ tsp. chili powder	

Brown hamburger and onion, drain and return to stove. Add remaining ingredients and simmer. Serve on hamburger buns.

❦ JOES TO GO ❦

Nancy Shinrock

1 lb. lean ground beef	¼ c. packed brown sugar
½ c. finely chopped onion or 2	1 T. white vinegar
T. dried minced onion flakes	1 T. yellow mustard
½ tsp. garlic salt	1 (8 oz.) can tomato sauce
⅛ tsp. pepper	6 hamburger buns
½ c. chili sauce	

In a large skillet, cook and stir ground beef and onion until beef is brown. Drain meat. Add garlic salt, pepper, chili sauce, brown sugar, vinegar, mustard, and tomato sauce. Bring to a boil, reduce heat. Simmer uncovered 10 minutes, stirring occasionally. Serve in warmed hamburger buns.

❦ LASAGNE ❦

Shawn Lorenzen

1 lb. ground beef	1 lb. cottage cheese
1 jar spaghetti sauce	½ c. grated Parmesan cheese
¾ c. water	3 c. shredded mozzarella
1 tsp. sugar	cheese
Salt to taste	
8 oz. pkg. lasagna noodles,	
uncooked	

Brown beef and drain. Add spaghetti sauce, water, sugar, and salt. Simmer several minutes. In a 9 x 13-inch pan, layer ½ the sauce, ½ the noodles, ½ the cheeses. Repeat layers. Cover with foil. Bake at 350° for 55-60 minutes. Let set 10 minutes before cutting.

❦ MEAT LOAF ❦
Lisa Meyer

2 lb. ground beef	1 egg
1 envelope dry onion soup mix	1 c. milk
3 slices bread, crumbled	Ketchup

Mix all ingredients. Place in baking dish. Top with ketchup. Bake 1 hour at 375°.

❦ MEAT LOAF ❦
Julie Concannon

1½ lbs. ground beef (I use 85/ 15)	1 T. Worcestershire sauce
	1 tsp. salt
3 slices bread, torn into pieces	½ tsp. dry mustard
1 c. milk	¼ tsp. pepper
1 egg	½ tsp. garlic salt
1 sm. onion, finely chopped (about ¼ c.)	¼ c. ketchup
	2 T. packed brown sugar

Mix ground beef, torn bread, milk, egg, onion, Worcestershire, salt, mustard, pepper and garlic salt. Place mixture in ungreased loaf pan, 9 x 5 x 3-inches. Cook, uncovered, in 350° oven for one hour. Drain fat off meat loaf and cover with a mixture of ¼ cup ketchup and 2 tablespoons packed brown sugar. Continue baking for ½ hour or until done (at least 160° on meat thermometer).

❦ MEAT LOAF ❦
Judy Egr

1 lb. ground beef	¼ tsp. pepper
½ lb. ground pork	¼ tsp. celery salt
1 c. dry bread crumbs	¼ tsp. garlic salt
1¼ c. milk	¼ tsp. dry mustard
1 egg, beaten	¼ tsp. sage
1 T. dry minced onion	1 T. Worcestershire sauce
1¼ tsp. salt	

Mix all ingredients thoroughly. Spread in greased loaf pan. Bake at 350° for 1½ hours.

❦ 138

❦ MEAT LOAF ❦
Dennis Hindemith

1 tsp. Tabasco sauce
1 egg
1 c. tomato juice or milk
2 c. soft bread crumbs
½ c. finely chopped onion

2 T. finely chopped parsley
¼ tsp. thyme
1½ tsp. salt
2 lb. ground beef

Add Tabasco sauce to egg and tomato juice or milk in mixing bowl and beat until blended. Stir in bread crumbs. Add onion, parsley, thyme, salt and ground beef and mix with fork until blended. Form into loaf in shallow baking pan or pack into a 9 x 5 x 3-inch loaf pan. Bake in a 350° oven for 1 hour and 15 minutes. 8-10 servings.

❦ MEAT LOAF CORDON BLEU ❦
Marjorie Keiser

1 egg
½ c. tomato sauce
1½ oz. meat loaf seasoning
   mix (optional)
2 lbs. ground beef
2 c. soft bread crumbs

8 thin slices boiled or baked
   ham
8 slices Swiss cheese
3 or 4 oz. can mushrooms,
   drained

Beat together egg, tomato sauce and seasoning mix. Add ground beef and bread crumbs; mix lightly. Roll or pat out on waxed paper to 18 x 9-inch rectangle. Top with layers of ham, cheese and mushrooms. Carefully roll up, enclosing filling. Seal all edges well. Place in shallow baking pan. Bake at 350° for one hour. Serves 8 to 10.

❦ MEATBALL DINNERS ❦
(In Foil Baskets)
Connie Walther
Brian Walther

Foil
1½ lbs. lean ground beef
3 potatoes, cleaned and cut
   into med. pieces
1 med. onion, sliced
Carrots, sliced

Corn, frozen
Black pepper
1 can fat-free cream of chicken
   soup
1 can fat-free cream of
   mushroom soup

Make 4 foil baskets by folding up sides. Roll ground beef into meat balls. Place 4-5 medium size meat balls on each foil piece. Leave space for potatoes and onions. On one side of meat; place slices of carrot, on the other side, put about ½ cup corn. Place potatoes and onions on top. Pepper to taste. Mix soups together and spoon over potatoes and meat. Fold sides at top and seal ends. Grill on medium heat for 45-50 minutes. Check meat after 30 minutes. Can also be baked in oven.

❦ MEATBALLS ❦
Rex Quadhamer

1 lb. hamburger
6 double crackers, crushed
2 - 3 slices onion, diced
⅓ c. milk

1 egg, beaten
¾ c. ketchup
½ c. hot water
2 tsp. brown sugar

Combine hamburger, crackers, onion, milk and egg in a large bowl. Mix thoroughly and make into meatballs. Cook either in a skillet or bake in oven at 350° until done. Combine ketchup, water and brown sugar and add to meatballs. Heat through.

❦ MONGOLIAN BEEF ❦
Heidi Meyer

4 tsp. oil	2 petite sirloin steaks
1 tsp. ginger, ground	½ c. cornstarch
1 tsp. garlic powder	Oil for frying
1 c. soy sauce	1 bunch green onions, cut into
1 c. water	1-inch pieces
¾ c. brown sugar	Cooked white rice

Heat 4 tsp. oil in medium saucepan over medium heat. Do not let the oil get too hot. Add ginger and garlic. Add soy sauce and water quickly before the garlic scorches. Add brown sugar and stir. Heat to medium and boil 2-3 minutes. Remove from heat. Slice steak against the grain in ¼-inch slices. Dip in cornstarch and let sit 10 minutes. Heat oil in frying pan until hot but not smoking. Add beef and sauté 2 minutes while stirring. Do not overcook. Remove onto paper towels and discard oil. Place meat back in pan and simmer 1 minute. Add sauce and stir for 1 minute. Add onions and cook for 1 minute. Remove to bowl but leave extra sauce behind. Serve on cooked white rice.

❦ NOAH'S FAVORITE BROCCOLI & BEEF STIR-FRY ❦
Julie Concannon

½ lb. boneless tender beef steak	1 lb. fresh broccoli
1 T. cornstarch	1¼ c. water
4 T. soy sauce, divided	4 tsp. cornstarch
1 tsp. sugar	3 T. vegetable oil, divided
1 tsp. minced fresh ginger root	1 onion, chunked
1 clove garlic, minced	Hot cooked rice

Cut beef across grain into thin slices. Combine 1 tablespoon each cornstarch and soy sauce with sugar, ginger and garlic in small bowl; stir in beef. Let stand 15 minutes. Meanwhile, remove flowerets from broccoli; cut in half lengthwise. Peel stalks; cut crosswise into ⅛-inch slices. Combine water, 4 teaspoons cornstarch and remaining 3 tablespoons soy sauce; set aside. Heat 1 tablespoon oil in hot wok or large skillet over high heat. Add beef and stir-fry 1 minute; remove. Heat remaining 2 tablespoons oil in same pan. Add broccoli and onion;

(continued)

stir-fry 4 minutes. Stir in beef and soy sauce mixture. Cook and stir until mixture boils and thickens. Serve immediately over rice. 2-3 servings.

❦ NORWEGIAN MEATBALLS ❦
Ruth Manning

5 lb. ground beef	1 tsp. ginger
1 lb. ground pork	1 tsp. allspice
2 eggs	Salt and pepper
1 c. milk	¼ c. grated onion
2 T. cornstarch	Cooking oil
1 tsp. nutmeg	

Combine ground beef and ground pork. Add eggs and milk and mix well. Add cornstarch, nutmeg, ginger, allspice, salt and pepper and onion and mix well. Shape into balls, and fry on all sides in oil. Simmer until done (I brown and cook them in the oven at 375°).

❦ PIKES PEAK ROAST ❦
Joe Combes

1 (10 oz.) can Rotel tomatoes	1 tsp. garlic powder
2 (10.75 oz.) cans cream of mushroom soup	1 c. chopped green onions
	1 tsp. ground black pepper
1 (10.75 oz.) can golden mushroom soup	3 - 5 lb. Rump roast
1 (1.5 oz.) pkg. dry onion soup mix	

In a 16 qt. roaster or cast iron Dutch oven, mix all the gravy ingredients and dilute with water to the consistency that you like your gravy. Add roast. Place in a 350° oven for 1½ hours. Remove and turn roast and place back in the oven for 1 hour. Remove roast and slice in ¼-inch slices across the grain. Place back in the gravy, cover and bake for 45 minutes to 1 hour. A 5 lb. roast will serve 12 to 14 people.

121822-12

❦ POPPIN' FRESH BARBECUES ❦
Jane Hawkins

1 lb. ground beef
½ c. barbecue sauce
1 T. instant minced onion
2 T. brown sugar

1 can of 10 refrigerated
   biscuits (Hungry Jack)
¾ c. grated Cheddar cheese

In a large skillet brown the ground beef. Drain well. Add barbecue sauce, onion and brown sugar. Separate biscuit dough into 10 biscuits. Place one in each greased muffin cup, pressing dough up to the edge of the cup. Put hamburger mixture in each cup. Sprinkle with cheese. Bake at 400° for 10-12 minutes until golden brown.

❦ PRIME RIB ❦
Judy Egr

10 lb. prime rib   Season as desired

Bring prime rib to room temperature (about 4 hours). Set oven to 375°. Roast for 1 hour. Turn oven off and let stand in oven for at least 2 hours. DO NOT OPEN DOOR! Approximately 1 hour before serving, turn oven to 350°. Cook for: Rare--40 minutes, Medium--50 minutes, Well--60 minutes. Take out and let sit for about 15 minutes before slicing.

❦ QUICK SUPPER ❦
Jill Hild

1 lb. hamburger
1 can vegetable beef soup

2 c. instant mashed potatoes

Brown hamburger in a skillet, drain off any grease. Add can of soup to the beef (do not add any water). Grease a small baking dish and place mixture into dish. Place large spoonful of potatoes on top of the mixture. Place in 350° oven. Bake 15-20 minutes, until slightly brown. This can be stretched by using 2 cans of soup.

❦ ROUND STEAK ❦
Heidi Meyer

1 pkg. Lipton onion soup mix
Round steak
1 can cream of golden
  mushroom soup

1 can milk

Sprinkle the dry onion soup mix on the bottom of a 9 x 13-inch pan. Lay the round steak on top. Mix 1 can cream of golden mushroom soup with 1 can of milk in a small bowl. Pour mixture over round steak. Cover pan with foil and bake at 350° for 1½ hours.

❦ SEVEN-UP CASSEROLE ❦
Carol Novak
Renae Rich
Rachel Novak

2 potatoes, thinly sliced
1 onion, thinly sliced
3 - 4 carrots, thinly sliced
1 celery stalk, sliced
Peas, frozen or canned

1½ lbs. ground beef, browned
  lightly
½ tsp. salt
1 (8 oz.) can tomato sauce

Grease a baking dish. Place one layer of each ingredient (potatoes, onion, carrots, celery, peas and ground beef) in the order given above. Sprinkle with salt and cover with tomato sauce. Bake, covered, at 350° for 1½ hours. Remove cover to brown for a few minutes.

❦ SIMPLIFIED LASAGNA ❦
Mary Lou Gustafson

1½ - 2 lb. Italian sausage or
  hamburger
1 onion, chopped
1 T. crushed garlic
1 T. oregano
1 T. sweet basil
1 sm. can tomato paste

1 lg. can tomato sauce
1 can tomato soup
10 lasagna noodles
1 pkg. sliced mozzarella cheese
2 c. shredded mozzarella
  cheese

Brown meat with chopped onion. Drain and add spices and canned tomato ingredients to meat in large pan. Simmer for 1 hour. Boil 10

(continued)

❦ 144

121822-12

lasagna noodles. Drain and rinse. Layer in a 9 x 13-inch baking dish in the following manner: Noodles, ½ sauce, ½ shredded cheese, noodles, ½ sauce, ½ shredded cheese, noodles, sliced mozzarella. Cut into serving size squares. Bake 20 -25 minutes. Let set for a few minutes before serving.

❦ SLOPPY JOES ❦
Connie Walther
Brian Walther

2 lbs. lean ground beef	½ c. catsup
1 med. onion, finely chopped	1 can tomato soup
Garlic powder	1 tsp. chili powder
Ground black pepper	1 tsp. sugar

Brown beef and onion. Season with garlic powder and pepper to taste. Add remaining ingredients and simmer to heat through.

❦ STIR-FRIED BEEF GYROS IN PITA POCKETS ❦
Mike Klos

2 tsp. olive oil	4 pita pockets, halved crosswise
1 med. onion, thinly sliced	2 tomatoes, thinly sliced
1 lb. beef round tip steaks, cut into strips	½ c. prepared cucumber ranch dressing
2 garlic cloves, crushed	
1 tsp. oregano	

Heat olive oil in pan until hot. Add onion. Stir-fry 3 to 4 minutes. In same pan add beef, garlic, and oregano. Stir-fry until beef is no longer pink. Fill pita pockets with equal amounts of beef mixture and tomatoes. Drizzle with dressing.

❦ STUFFED PEPPERS ❦
Jackie Combes

6 med. green peppers
1 lb. ground beef
¼ c. chopped onions
2 c. hot cooked rice
1 (8 oz.) jar Cheez Whiz
 process cheese spread

Dash of pepper
Dash of basil
¼ c. dry bread crumbs
1 T. margarine, melted

Remove tops and seeds from peppers. Parboil 5 minutes; drain. Brown meat; drain. Add onion; cook until tender. Stir in rice, cheese spread and seasonings; fill peppers. Place in baking dish; top with crumbs tossed with margarine. Bake at 350°, 40 minutes. 6 servings.

❦ STUFFED SHELLS ❦
Kathy Christiansen
Tami Watts-McPhail

1 box jumbo shells (you'll need
 25 shells)
1 lb. ground beef or turkey
2 cloves minced garlic
1 tsp. salt
½ tsp. pepper
1 tsp. onion powder
2 tsp. Italian seasoning
⅓ c. reserved pasta cooking
 water

¼ c. grated Parmesan cheese
1 egg, lightly beaten
2 c. grated mozzarella or
 grated Cheddar cheese,
 divided
16 oz. marinara sauce (see
 recipe for Tami's Marinara
 Sauce)

Cook shells according to package directions. Reserve ⅓ cup pasta cooking water, draining the rest, and set aside. Preheat oven to 350°. Cook ground beef or turkey until no longer pink, drain and return to the pot. Stir in seasonings, reserved pasta cooking water, Parmesan cheese, egg and 1 cup of cheese (cook's choice). Cover the bottom of a 9 x 13-inch baking dish with a layer of marinara sauce. Spoon the beef mixture into the cooked shells until full, then lay in the dish. Spoon remaining marinara sauce over the stuffed shells and top with remaining 1 cup cheese. Bake, loosely covered in foil, in a 350° oven for 30 minutes, or until sauce is bubbling and cheese is melted. Remove foil and broil for a few minutes until the cheese is golden brown.

121822-12

❦ TACO HOT DISH ❦
Shari Garder

1 pkg. crescent rolls
1 lb. hamburger
½ med. onion, chopped
1 pkg. taco seasoning
8 oz. can tomato sauce
1 c. sour cream
2 c. grated Cheddar cheese
Crushed Doritos or Fritos
Shredded lettuce, tomato and/
   or avocado

Line bottom of 9 x 13-inch ungreased pan with crescent rolls to form a crust. Bake at 375° until lightly browned. Brown the hamburger and onion. Drain well. Add the taco seasoning and tomato sauce. Place on top of the rolls. Spread with the sour cream. Place cheese on top. Bake an additional 25 minutes. Top with crushed Doritos or Fritos. You may also top with lettuce, tomato and avocado.

❦ TACO PIE ❦
Nancy Shinrock

1½ lb. ground beef
⅓ c. finely chopped onion
1 pkg. taco seasoning
1 (4 oz.) can diced green
   chilies, drained
1 c. biscuit baking mix
   (Bisquick)
2 eggs
½ c. milk
2 tomatoes, sliced
1 c. grated mild Cheddar
   cheese
1 (8 oz.) carton sour cream
1 tomato, chopped
Shredded lettuce to garnish pie

Heat oven to 400°. In a large skillet, cook and stir ground beef and onion until beef is brown. Drain. Combine beef with taco seasoning mix and spread in a 10-inch pie pan. Sprinkle with chilies. Beat biscuit baking mix, eggs, and milk until smooth. Pour milk mixture over beef. Bake uncovered for 35 minutes. Top with sliced tomatoes, sprinkle with cheese. Bake until golden brown an additional 8-10 minutes. Top with sour cream, chopped tomato, and shredded lettuce. Cut into slices and serve.

❦ TAMI'S MARINARA SAUCE ❦

Kathy Christiansen
Tami Watts-McPhail

1½ T. olive oil
1 lg. or 2 med. yellow onions, chopped
4 cloves garlic, minced
1½ T. dried Italian seasoning
1 tsp. salt
½ tsp. pepper
28 oz. can chopped tomatoes
2 (14.5 oz.) cans tomato sauce

12 oz. can tomato paste
Bottle of V-8 hot and spicy juice
1 tsp. sugar
3 T. chopped parsley
2 - 3 bay leaves
2 - 4 c. water
1 - 1½ c. grated Romano cheese

Heat olive oil in a large pot (like a BIG soup kettle). Sauté chopped onions until translucent, then add garlic, Italian seasoning, salt and pepper and sauté all for an additional minute or two. Stirring constantly, add in chopped tomatoes (undrained), tomato sauce, tomato paste and V-8 juice. As mixture comes to a bubble, add in sugar, parsley and bay leaves. Depending on mixture's consistency, add in water and Romano cheese (too thick, less water; too thin, more cheese). Bring all to a boil, cover and turn down to low. Let simmer all day (if you can wait) or put in a crockpot on low.

❦ TAMI'S MEATBALLS ❦

Kathy Christiansen
Tami Watts-McPhail

1½ c. panko bread crumbs
½ - ¾ c. milk or half and half
1 lb. ground beef
1 lb. ground pork
1 T. Italian seasoning
1½ tsp. salt

1 tsp. pepper
3 T. chopped parsley
2 eggs, beaten lightly
1 c. grated Romano cheese
1 c. grated Parmesan cheese

Put bread crumbs in a small bowl. Starting with ½ cup of milk (or half and half), pour it over the bread crumbs and mix. If mixture appears too dry, add more milk (half and half). Let mixture sit for about 10 minutes. In a large bowl, combine the meats, Italian seasoning, salt, pepper, parsley, eggs, cheeses, and the bread crumb mixture. Mix well to combine, but don't over mix. Using a ¼ cup measure, form meatballs. Bake meatballs in a 350° oven for 45 minutes. Add to sauce (see Tami's Marinara Sauce) or let cool and freeze.

121822-12

❦ TATER TOT CASSEROLE ❦
Shari Garder

1 lb. ground beef
2 cans green beans, drain 1
   can

2 cans cream of mushroom or
   cream of celery soup
1 - 2 lb. bag frozen tater tots

Brown ground beef, drain. Mix together meat, beans, and soup and place in 9 x 13-inch pan. Place tater tots over top. Bake at 350° for 45 minutes.

❦ TATER TOT CASSEROLE ❦
Lisa Rieff

1½ lbs. ground beef
Salt and pepper
1 onion, chopped (optional)
1 can corn

1 bag (32 oz.) frozen tater tots
2 cans cream of chicken soup
1 can chicken rice soup
½ c. water

Cook and drain ground beef and onion (if using it). Sprinkle bottom of 9 x 13-inch pan with salt. Spread hamburger into pan. Sprinkle with salt and pepper. Drain corn and spread on top of meat. Put frozen tater tots on top of corn. In a large bowl mix the 3 cans of soup with the water. Pour over the tater tots. Bake at 350° for 1 hour.

❦ TEXAS HASH ❦
Shawn Lorenzen

1 c. chopped onion
1 green pepper, chopped
2 T. oil
1 lb. ground beef
1 tsp. salt
1 tsp. pepper

½ tsp. chili powder
¾ c. uncooked rice
1 jar Gramma's stewed
   tomatoes (or 2 cans)
2 T. sugar

Sauté onions and green pepper in oil, add ground beef and brown. Add all ingredients to casserole, bake at 350° for 1½ hours.

MEATLESS

❦ ANGEL HAIR WITH SUN-DRIED TOMATOES AND GOAT CHEESE ❦
Rose Roberts

1 (10 oz.) jar sun-dried tomatoes packed in oil, chopped (oil reserved)
1 sm. onion, chopped
4 garlic cloves, minced
¼ c. tomato paste
⅔ c. dry white wine
8 oz. angel hair pasta

Salt and freshly ground black pepper
2 oz. soft fresh goat cheese, coarsely crumbled, or cream cheese
2 T. chopped fresh Italian parsley leaves

Heat 2 tablespoons of the oil from the sun-dried tomatoes in a heavy large skillet over medium heat. Add the onion and sauté until tender, about 3 minutes. Stir in the garlic and sauté until fragrant, about 1 minute. Add the tomato paste and cook for 2 minutes, stirring constantly. Add the wine and sun-dried tomatoes and simmer until the liquid reduces by half, about 2 minutes. Meanwhile, bring a large pot of salted water to a boil. Add the pasta and cook until al dente, stirring occasionally, about 5 minutes. Drain, reserving ½ cup of cooking liquid. Add the pasta to the tomato mixture and toss to coat, adding some reserved cooking liquid to moisten. Season the pasta, to taste, with salt and pepper. Sprinkle with the goat cheese and parsley and stir. Mound the pasta into bowls and serve. May add shrimp at the end if desired. 4-6 servings.

❦ CHEESE SPREAD ❦
Dayla Miller

1 lb. American cheese, cut up
½ lb. Cheddar cheese, cut up or shredded
6 hard boiled eggs, chopped

½ c. relish
Garlic salt to taste
Mayonnaise to make spreadable

Mix all ingredients together. Serve on favorite bread, rye is good with this.

❦ EASY MANICOTTI ❦
Shirley Schuchard

1 container (15 oz.) part-skim
  ricotta cheese
1 pkg. (10 oz.) frozen chopped
  spinach, thawed, squeezed
  dry
2 c. shredded part-skim
  mozzarella cheese, divided
¼ c. grated Parmesan cheese
2 tsp. Italian seasoning
¼ tsp. ground black pepper
1 pkg. (8 oz.) dry manicotti
  shells, uncooked
1 can (26.5 oz.) Hunt's
  traditional pasta sauce,
  divided
Pam original no-stick cooking
  spray

Preheat oven to 375°. Combine ricotta cheese, spinach, 1 cup of the mozzarella cheese, Parmesan cheese, Italian seasoning and black pepper in medium bowl; mix well. Stuff 3 tablespoons cheese mixture in each uncooked manicotti; set aside. Pour half of the sauce in the bottom of sprayed 13 x 9 x 2-inch baking dish. Arrange stuffed manicotti in single layer over sauce; pour the remaining sauce evenly over top. Sprinkle remaining mozzarella cheese evenly over sauce. Cover tightly with foil sprayed with cooking spray. Bake 1 hour 15 minutes or until pasta is tender. Let stand, covered, 10 minutes before serving. 7 servings (2 manicotti each).

❦ PESTO FOR PASTA ❦
Jill Hild

1 c. firmly packed fresh basil
  leaves
½ c. firmly packed parsley
  sprigs w/stems removed or
  torn fresh spinach
½ c. grated Parmesan or
  Romano cheese
¼ c. pine nuts, walnuts or
  almonds
1 lg. clove garlic, quartered
¼ tsp. salt
¼. olive oil
12 oz. fettuccine or spaghetti

For pesto: In a blender or food processor combine basil, parsley, cheese, nuts, garlic and salt. Cover and pulse until a paste forms, stopping several times and scraping sides. With machine running slowly, gradually add oil and mix to consistency of soft butter. Cook and drain pasta. Toss pasta and sauce, serve immediately. Can store in refrigerator 1-2 days or freeze up to 3 months. Can also serve pesto on toasted bread.

❦ SUMMER DAY LUNCHEON ❦
Shirley Schuchard

3 - 4 Grandchildren	1 loaf bread
1 Sunshiny Day	1 jar strawberry jam
1 jar peanut butter	1 container kool-aid over ice

Best served at park with trees and swings.

❦ VEGETABLE FRITTATA ❦
Dennis Hindemith

1 T. vegetable oil	1 T. chopped fresh parsley
1 c. broccoli flowerets	¼ tsp. salt
1 med. carrot, shredded (½ c.)	¼ tsp. red pepper sauce
1 med. onion, chopped (½ c.)	1 c. shredded Cheddar cheese
¼ c. sliced ripe olives	(4 oz.)
4 lg. eggs	1 T. grated Parmesan cheese
¼ c. milk	

Heat oil in 10-inch skillet over medium-high heat. Cook broccoli, carrot, onion and olives in oil about 5 minutes, stirring frequently, until vegetables are crisp-tender. Meanwhile beat eggs, milk, parsley, salt and pepper sauce thoroughly with fork or wire whisk until a uniform yellow color. Pour egg mixture over vegetables. Sprinkle with cheeses and reduce heat to low. Cover and cook about 10 minutes or until set in the center. Cut into wedges. Serve immediately. 4 servings.

PORK

❦ BACON EGG SALAD CROISSANTS ❦
Julie Concannon

6 hard-cooked eggs, chopped	⅛ tsp. pepper
⅓ c. diced celery	⅓ c. crumbled cooked bacon
⅓ c. fat free mayonnaise	4 lettuce leaves
1 tsp. prepared mustard	4 tomato slices
¼ tsp. salt	4 croissants, split

(continued)

121822-12

In a bowl, combine the eggs, celery, mayonnaise, mustard, salt and pepper. Fold in bacon. Place a lettuce leaf, tomato slice and ½ cup egg salad on bottom half of each croissant and then replace top. Also very good served on whole wheat bread. 4 servings.

❦ BAKED SPAGHETTI ❦
Rex Quadhamer

1 lb. Italian sausage links	½ c. Parmesan cheese
8 oz. spaghetti	8 oz. shredded mozzarella
24 oz. jar spaghetti sauce	cheese

Cook Italian sausage in a skillet. While the sausage is cooking, boil spaghetti according to package directions. Drain and empty into a casserole dish. When the sausage is cooked, cut into ¼-inch slices. Add to the cooked spaghetti. Pour in spaghetti sauce and add Parmesan cheese. Stir together to mix ingredients. Top with mozzarella cheese. Bake in a 350° oven for 30 minutes.

❦ BROWN SUGAR PORK CHOPS WITH ONIONS ❦
Amy Kragnes

2 tsp. vegetable oil	¼ c. orange juice
4 boneless pork chops	2 T. brown sugar
¼ tsp. black pepper	¼ tsp. crushed red pepper
1 med. onion, thinly sliced	

In a large skillet, heat oil over medium heat. Sprinkle chops with black pepper. Cook chops in hot oil for 6 to 8 minutes, until brown on outside and slightly pink in center, turning once halfway through cooking time. Remove chops from skillet; cover and keep warm. In same skillet, cook onion over medium heat for 3 minutes or until tender. Push onion aside. Add orange juice and brown sugar. Cook and stir for 1 minute or until sugar is dissolved. Stir onions into sauce. Spoon sauce over chops; sprinkle with crushed red pepper.

❦ CHEESE AND HAM-STUFFED LOAF ❦
Leah Klos

1 lg. loaf French bread
1 (3 oz.) pkg. cream cheese, softened
½ c. sour cream
1 (10 oz.) pkg. frozen spinach, thawed and squeezed dry
Bunch of green onions, chopped
Red or green pepper, chopped
1 c. shredded Cheddar cheese
1 lb. ham, chopped into bite size pieces

Preheat oven to 375°. Slice off top of loaf; set aside. Pull out soft inside of loaf, leaving a thick shell. Mix together cream cheese and sour cream until smooth. Stir in spinach, onions, pepper, Cheddar cheese and ham. Blend well. Spoon mixture into hollow loaf. Replace top. Wrap tightly with foil. Bake 30-35 minutes or until heated through. Cut into diagonal slices and serve.

❦ HAM AND SWISS QUICHE ❦
Renae Rich
Rachel Novak

1 (9-inch) pie crust
2 T. olive oil
1 onion, finely chopped
¼ tsp. salt
Pinch of ground nutmeg
4 eggs
¾ c. half and half
1 c. grated Swiss cheese (about 4 oz.)
¾ c. diced, cooked ham

Preheat oven to 375°. Place the crust in a pie pan. In a large skillet, heat olive oil over low heat for 1 minute. Add onion and cook, stirring occasionally for about 15 minutes or until onion is lightly browned. Season with salt and nutmeg. Set aside to cool slightly. In a mixing bowl, beat together the eggs and half and half. Spoon the onion mixture evenly over crust. Sprinkle the cheese and ham over the onions. Pour in the egg mixture. Bake quiche for about 1 hour or until set. Allow to cool 10 minutes. You may want to use foil to cover the edge of the crust to prevent burning.

121822-12

❦ PORK CHOP CASSEROLE ❦

Kathy Christiansen
Sharon Christiansen

2 (1 oz.) pkgs. dry onion soup mix	1 (4.5 oz.) can mushrooms, drained
3 c. water	Salt and pepper to taste
2 c. instant rice	6 (¾-inch thick) pork chops

Preheat oven to 350°. In a medium size bowl, mix dry onion soup mix and water until dissolved. Pour mixture into a 10 x 15-inch baking dish. Add rice and mushrooms and mix to distribute well. Salt and pepper to taste. Add pork chops in a single layer on mixture. Push pork chops down into mixture and make sure they are covered with it. Cover baking dish tightly with aluminum foil and bake in a preheated oven for 1 hour. Quick and easy dinner. Put it in the oven and go and read a book!

❦ PORK CHOPS MEXICALI ❦

Jesse Brewer

6 pork chops	1 can (8 oz.) tomato sauce
1 tsp. salt	1½ c. water
¾ c. uncooked regular rice	½ c. Cheddar cheese, shredded
1½ - 2½ T. taco seasoning mix	

Brown pork chops. Arrange in 9 x 13-inch pan and season with salt. Sprinkle rice around chops. Combine taco seasoning mix, tomato sauce and water and pour over chops and rice. Cover tightly with foil and bake 1 to 1¼ hours in 350° oven. Remove 10 minutes before done and sprinkle with cheese. Cover and continue baking for 10 minutes more.

❦ PORK, CHICKEN, OR SALMON MARINADE ❦

Deb Lund

3 T. catsup	½ tsp. garlic powder
3 T. orange juice	½ tsp. onion powder
2 T. soy sauce	¼ tsp. ground ginger
1 T. lemon juice	Ground pepper, to taste
1 T. honey	

(continued)

Mix together all ingredients and place in bowl with chicken, pork, or salmon. Marinade in refrigerator at least 4 hours. Be sure marinade covers the meat, or turn occasionally to cover all sides of meat or fish. Cook on grill or in oven as desired.

❧ ROASTED PORK WITH APPLES AND POTATOES ❧
Valerie Florea

1 T. apple jelly	10 pearl onions
1½ tsp. packed brown sugar	1 T. olive oil
¼ tsp. ground ginger	¾ tsp. salt
2 apples, cored and cut into 1-inch slices	¾ tsp. pepper
	¾ T. minced fresh rosemary
1 lb. small red potatoes, halved	3 lb. boneless pork loin

Preheat oven to 450°. Stir together apple jelly, brown sugar and ginger; set aside. Combine apples, potatoes, onions, olive oil, salt, pepper and rosemary. Place pork in center of roasting pan; arrange apple mixture around pork in a single layer. Roast 15 minutes. Reduce oven temperature to 350°. Roast another 20 minutes; stir apple mixture. Spread apple jelly glaze on pork; continue to roast 15 to 20 minutes or until center of pork loin reaches 145°.

❧ SECRET INGREDIENT SAUCY CHOPS ❧
Julie Concannon

4 bone-in pork loin chops (7 oz. each)	2 T. steak sauce (I use A. 1.)
	1 T. molasses
½ tsp. salt	¼ tsp. garlic powder
½ tsp. pepper	¼ tsp. dried thyme
1 T. canola oil	1 oz. semisweet chocolate, chopped
¾ c. strong brewed coffee	

Sprinkle pork chops with salt and pepper. In a large nonstick skillet, cook chops in oil over medium heat for 4-6 minutes on each side or until a thermometer reads 160°. Remove and keep warm. Add the coffee, steak sauce, molasses, garlic powder and thyme to the pan. Bring to a boil; cook until liquid is reduced by half. Whisk in chocolate until melted. Return pork chops to pan; heat through. 4 servings.

❧ 156

❦ SMOKED PORK LOIN ❦
Rex Quadhamer

3 lb. pork loin
Misty's Bar-B-Q seasoning

Wood chips for smoker

I use an electric Brinkman's smoker. It runs at about 210°. Season the pork loin with the Misty's Bar-B-Q seasoning. Start the smoker with your choice of wood chips (I use either apple or hickory). Put in a meat thermometer and cook to 165-170°. It takes approximately 3 hours.

❦ SMOTHERED PORK CHOPS ❦
Debra Gillespie

8 Potatoes
6 Pork Chops
Flour

2 cans cream of mushroom
soup
1½ soup cans of milk

Peel potatoes, cut into thick slices, and place in bottom of a Dutch oven. Coat pork chops in flour and brown in skillet. Arrange pork chops on top of potatoes. Combine soup and milk and pour over chops. Place lid on Dutch oven and bake for 1½ to 2 hours at 350°.

❦ STROMBOLI (MAKES 2) ❦
Judy Egr

2 tubes crescent rolls
Ham and/or turkey
Pepperoni

Provolone cheese
Mozzarella cheese, shredded
1 egg, beaten

Roll out crescent rolls. Layer in center: ham and/or turkey (I use both), pepperoni and cheeses. Roll up. Score long sides (1 to 2-inch strips). Close up ends. Brush with beaten egg with a little water added to it. Bake at 350° for 30 minutes, until golden brown.

🍒 STUFFED ANAHEIM PEPPERS 🍒
Lisa Rieff

6 - 8 lg. Anaheim peppers
Olive oil
1 lb. mild pork sausage
1 c. Romano cheese, divided

½ c. Italian flavored bread crumbs
1 egg
Marinara sauce

Preheat oven to 350°. Wash peppers. Make a slice the length of the pepper and slightly pull apart. Remove the seeds. Brush with olive oil and bake to soften as you prepare the stuffing. Brown sausage and drain. Add ½ cup of cheese, bread crumbs and the egg. Mix together. Remove the peppers from the oven and when cooled for handling, stuff the peppers with the filling. Cover with the Marinara and sprinkle the remaining cheese on top. Continue to bake for about 20-30 minutes.

🍒 SUMMER RIBS 🍒
Kathy Christiansen

2 T. brown sugar
3 T. kosher salt
1 T. chili powder
½ tsp. black pepper
½ tsp. red pepper
½ tsp. Old Bay seasoning
½ tsp. dried thyme

½ tsp. onion powder
½ tsp. garlic powder
1 - 2 slabs of pork ribs (not country style)
6 - 8 oz. Cola (NOT diet)
Your favorite barbecue sauce

In a bowl, combine all dry ingredients and mix well. Place each slab of baby back ribs on a piece of heavy-duty aluminum foil, shiny side down. Sprinkle each side generously with the dry rub. Pat the dry rub into the meat. Refrigerate the ribs for a minimum of 1 hour, but better if overnight. Preheat oven to 250°. Mix Cola (amount depends on thickness of barbecue sauce) with 1 to 1½ cups of barbecue sauce to make a braising liquid. Place the ribs on a baking sheet. Open one end of the foil on each slab and pour half of the braising liquid into each foil packet. Tilt the baking sheet in order to equally distribute the braising liquid. Braise the ribs in the oven for 2½ hours. Toward the end of the braising time, preheat BBQ grill to medium heat. Remove ribs from oven and carefully loosen foil. Grill over medium heat for 3 to 4 minutes per side, brushing with barbecue sauce as desired. This was adapted from Alton Brown's recipe.

121822-12

❦ THE BEST PORK CHOPS YOU WILL EVER TASTE ❦
Jason Garder

3 c. fine dry Italian bread crumbs
1 sm. pkg. dry Italian dressing mix
1 T. garlic powder
2 T. fresh grated Parmesan cheese
Ranch dressing
6 lg. loin pork chops

Mix bread crumbs, dressing mix, garlic powder and Parmesan cheese together in a large bowl. Pour a layer of ranch dressing onto a plate. Take one pork chop at a time and coat with ranch dressing. Then place pork chop into the bowl with bread crumbs and coat well on all sides. Place breaded pork chops in 9 x 13-inch pan coated with cooking spray. Bake at 350° for 50-60 minutes. Jason likes to marinate the pork chops in the ranch dressing.

POULTRY

❦ BRUSCHETTA AND CHEESE STUFFED CHICKEN BREASTS ❦
Julie Concannon

1 can (14½ oz.) diced tomatoes with basil, garlic and oregano, undrained
1¼ c. shredded low-moisture part-skim mozzarella cheese, divided
¼ c. chopped fresh basil or 1 teaspoon dried basil
1 pkg. (6 oz.) stuffing mix for chicken
8 sm. boneless skinless chicken breast halves
⅓ c. roasted red pepper Italian with Parmesan dressing

Heat oven to 350°. Mix tomatoes, ½ cup cheese and basil in medium bowl. Add stuffing mix; stir just until moistened. Place 2 chicken breasts in large freezer-weight resealable plastic bag. Pound with meat mallet or side of heavy can until chicken is ¼ inch thick. Remove from bag; place, top-sides down, on cutting board. Repeat with remaining chicken. Spread chicken with stuffing mixture. Starting at 1 narrow

(continued)

end, tightly roll up each breast. Place, seam-sides down, in 13 x 9-inch baking dish. Drizzle with dressing. Bake 40 minutes or until chicken is done (165°). Sprinkle with remaining cheese; bake 5 minutes or until melted. 8 servings.

❦ BRUSCHETTA CHICKEN BAKE ❦
Julie Concannon

1 can (14½ oz.) diced
  tomatoes, undrained
1 pkg. (6 oz.) Stove Top
  stuffing mix for chicken
½ c. water
2 cloves garlic, minced

1½ lbs. boneless skinless
  chicken breasts, cut into
  bite-sized pieces
1 tsp. dried basil leaves
1 c. 2% milk shredded
  mozzarella cheese

Heat oven to 400°. Mix tomatoes, stuffing mix, water and garlic just until stuffing mix is moistened. Layer chicken, basil and cheese in 3-quart casserole or 13 x 9-inch baking dish. Top with stuffing. Bake 30 minutes or until chicken is done. 6 servings, 1 cup each.

❦ CHICKEN A LA ORANGE ❦
Brenda Mac

1 lg. whole chicken or 2 sm.
  chickens
½ c. butter, melted
1 med. onion, sliced into rings
1 tsp. salt
½ tsp. garlic salt

6 oz. frozen orange juice
  concentrate
½ c. water
1 T. brown sugar
1 tsp. paprika

Lightly salt and pepper chicken and place in roasting pan. Combine melted butter, onion, salt, garlic salt, orange juice, water, brown sugar and paprika in sauce pan. Bring to boil and simmer 5 minutes. Pour ½ cup sauce over chicken and bake 45 minutes at 375°. Drain off grease and orange sauce. Pour another ½ cup sauce over and bake another 30 minutes or until chicken is done, leaving lid off last 30 minutes to brown. I like to serve with Uncle Ben's long grain wild rice cooked as directed. Serve by drizzling remaining orange sauce over rice and chicken.

❦ CHICKEN & RICE ❦
Dayla Miller

1 can cream of chicken soup
1 c. mayonnaise
1 (5 oz.) can evaporated milk
1 T. lemon juice **see below **
2 tsp. Greek seasoning **see below **
4 - 6 cooked chicken breasts cut up or Rotisserie chicken cut up
3 c. cooked rice
1 (4 oz.) can sliced mushrooms, drained
1½ c. crushed Corn Flakes
¼ c. slivered almonds (optional)
¼ c. melted butter or margarine

** I have used 1 cup Caesar salad dressing in place of lemon juice and 2 tsp. Greek seasoning ** In a large bowl, combine soup, mayonnaise, milk, lemon juice and seasoning or Caesar dressing, mix well and set aside. Combine cooked chicken, rice and mushrooms and mix well. Spoon into baking dish. In small bowl mix corn flakes, almonds and butter and spread over top of casserole. Bake at 350° for 30-45 minutes, uncovered.

❦ CHICKEN AND MUSHROOM PASTA ❦
Lisa Rieff

8 oz. penne pasta
12 oz. chicken breast, cut into strips
Salt and pepper
2 T. olive oil, divided
3 garlic cloves, minced
3 c. sliced mushrooms
1 med. onion, thinly sliced
½ c. chicken broth
¼ c. dry white wine
1 c. cherry tomatoes, halved
¼ c. fresh basil, cut into thin strips
3 T. fresh snipped oregano
¼ c. shredded Parmesan cheese

Cook pasta al dente, drain and return to pan to keep warm. Meanwhile, season chicken with salt and pepper. Heat 1 T. of the oil in a large skillet over medium-high heat. Add the chicken and garlic and cook about 3-5 minutes until chicken is done. Remove from pan and keep warm. Add remaining 1 T. of oil to pan. Add mushrooms and onion. Cook until tender. Add broth and wine. Bring to a boil and reduce

(continued)

heat. Boil gently about 2 minutes or until liquid is reduced by half. Add pasta, chicken, tomatoes, basil and oregano to mushroom mixture. Toss gently to combine. Sprinkle with Parmesan cheese and pepper. Makes about 6 servings.

❦ CHICKEN AND RICE ❦
Heidi Meyer

4 chicken breasts, bone in, with skin
¼ c. butter
1 can cream of mushroom soup

2 cans cream of chicken soup
1½ c. uncooked white rice
Salt and pepper

Melt butter in 9 x 13-inch pan. Coat raw chicken in melted butter and set aside. Mix soups and rice with remaining butter in pan. Lay chicken on top. Salt and pepper. Bake uncovered at 325° for 1¾ to 2 hours.

❦ CHICKEN AND WILD RICE CASSEROLE ❦
Lisa Rieff

½ c. melted butter
¼ c. flour
12 oz. evaporated milk
1 c. chicken broth
1½ tsp. salt
3 c. cooked and shredded chicken

1 box (6 oz.) cooked Uncle Ben's wild rice
1 c. sliced mushrooms
Sliced almonds

Melt butter in skillet. Add flour and whisk. Add milk, broth and salt to make a sauce. Remove from heat. Add the chicken, rice and mushrooms. Pour into greased 9 x 13-inch pan. Bake at 350° for 30 minutes. Sprinkle with almonds and serve.

121822-12

❦ CHICKEN ARTICHOKE PASTA ❦

Mary Lou Gustafson
From my friend Adrienne Van Winkle

Cooked chicken (3 - 4 breasts),
  cut into bite size pieces
1 can sliced mushrooms
2 T. crushed garlic
1 red onion, chopped
Olive oil
3 cans artichoke hearts,
  drained and chopped

1 bag fresh spinach
1 - 2 jars Alfredo sauce
⅓ cup Parmesan or Romano
  cheese
Cooked penne pasta

Sauté chicken, mushrooms, garlic and onion in a little olive oil. Simmer 10-15 minutes. Add the artichoke hearts and then the fresh spinach. Put lid on until spinach wilts. Add Alfredo sauce and Parmesan or Romano cheese and serve with penne pasta.

❦ CHICKEN CACCIATORE ❦

Rose Roberts
Kitty Massara

3 lbs. chicken pieces
Flour
Olive oil
2 cloves garlic, minced
2 med. onions, sliced
1 lb. 12 oz. Italian style
  tomatoes
1 lg. green pepper, sliced
  thinly
1 lg. red pepper, sliced thinly

2 T. chopped parsley
½ tsp. crumbled thyme
½ tsp. oregano
½ tsp. pepper
1 bay leaf
⅔ c. dry red wine or ½ c.
  chicken broth
2 T. vinegar
Fresh spinach, as desired
Fresh mushrooms, as desired

Brown chicken pieces that have been tossed in flour in olive oil in an oven safe skillet. Remove chicken and brown garlic and onions until tender in same pan. Return chicken to pan and add Italian tomatoes, green and red pepper, parsley, thyme, oregano, pepper, bay leaf, red wine or chicken broth and vinegar. Bake covered for 1 hour at 325°. Add fresh spinach and mushrooms during last 5 minutes. Remove bay leaf before serving. Other vegetable ideas include zucchini, celery or artichoke hearts.

❦ CHICKEN FINGERS ❦
Joe Combes

1½ c. mayonnaise
¼ c. honey
2 T. roughly chopped dill
2 T. lemon juice
1 T. dry mustard powder
Kosher salt
Fresh ground pepper
2 lb. boneless, skinless chicken breasts, cut into 3 x 1-inch strips

1 T. sugar
1 T. kosher salt
1 T. fresh ground pepper
1½ tsp. garlic powder
1 tsp. paprika
1 tsp. dry mustard powder
1 c. flour
4 eggs, lightly beaten
3 c. panko bread crumbs
Canola oil

For dipping sauce: Whisk mayonnaise with honey, dill, lemon juice, and mustard powder in medium bowl. Season with salt and pepper and stir together until smooth. Set aside. Toss chicken, sugar, salt, pepper, garlic powder, paprika, and mustard powder in medium bowl or zip lock bag. Set aside. Place flour, eggs, and bread crumbs in 3 separate bowls, set aside. Pour oil to a depth of 2-inches into a 6 quart Dutch oven. Heat over medium heat (7) until deep fry thermometer reads 325°. Working in batches, coat chicken in flour, shake off excess, dip in eggs, coat in breadcrumbs. Fry chicken until golden brown and crisp, about 3 minutes. Transfer to paper towels to drain. Serve with dipping sauce.

❦ CHICKEN LASAGNA FLORENTINE ❦
Lisa Rieff

½ box lasagna noodles
1 pkg. frozen spinach
2 c. cottage cheese
1 egg, lightly beaten
½ c. butter
½ c. flour
½ tsp. salt

½ tsp. basil
20 - 24 oz. chicken broth
2½ c. cooked chicken, shredded
12 slices mozzarella cheese
½ c. Parmesan cheese, shredded

Cook and drain noodles. Cook and drain spinach. Mix cottage cheese into beaten egg. Melt butter in large skillet. Whisk in flour, salt and basil. Stir in 20 ounces of chicken broth. Whisk until mixture thickens

(continued)

121822-12

and comes to a boil (it should be like loose gravy, add more broth if it is too thick). Remove from heat and add chicken. Lightly grease a 9 x 13-inch pan. Place ⅓ of chicken mixture in pan. Layer with half the noodles, half the cottage cheese, half the spinach and half the mozzarella cheese. Repeat layers ending with last ⅓ of chicken mixture. Sprinkle with the Parmesan. Bake at 375° for 45 minutes. Let rest before cutting.

❦ CHICKEN MARSALA ❦
Heidi Meyer

¼ c. flour
½ tsp. garlic salt
¼ tsp. pepper
½ tsp. dried oregano
4 boneless, skinless chicken
   breasts

1 T. olive oil
1 T. butter
1 c. fresh mushrooms, sliced
½ c. Marsala wine

In a medium bowl, stir together flour, garlic salt, pepper, and oregano. Dredge chicken in the mixture to lightly coat. Heat olive oil and butter in large skillet over medium heat. Fry the chicken in the skillet for 2 minutes, or until lightly browned on one side. Turn chicken over, and add mushrooms. Cook about 2 minutes, until the other side of chicken is lightly browned. Stir mushrooms so that they cook evenly. Pour Marsala wine over the chicken. Cover skillet, and reduce heat to low. Simmer for 10 minutes, or until chicken is no longer pink and juices run clear.

❦ CHICKEN PICCATA ❦
(With Lemon, Capers, and Artichoke Hearts)
Valerie Florea

1 tsp. salt
1 tsp. pepper
4 boneless, skinless chicken
  breasts, cut into strips
3 cloves garlic, minced
1 T. butter
Olive oil
½ c. dry white wine
½ c. chicken broth
Juice from ½ lemon

Lemon zest
Juice from ½ lime
Lime zest
Fresh mushrooms
Shallots
2 (13 oz.) cans artichoke
  hearts, quartered
1 (13 oz.) can diced tomatoes
¼ c. drained capers
Fresh parsley

Salt and pepper chicken to taste. Sauté garlic in butter and olive oil combination. When golden brown, add chicken and sauté. Add wine and chicken broth and simmer. Add juice and zest of lemon and lime. In another pan sauté mushrooms and shallots in butter and olive oil and then add to chicken. Add artichoke hearts, diced tomatoes, capers and fresh parsley. Simmer until heated through.

❦ CHICKEN SOUVLAKI ❦
Valerie Florea

Souvlaki Marinade:

Garlic clove, minced
3 T. olive oil
2 T. freshly chopped dill leaves
2 tsp. Italian seasoning

1 T. lemon juice
4 boneless skinless chicken
  breasts

In large bowl whisk together garlic, olive oil, dill leaves, Italian seasoning and lemon juice. Add the chicken and toss to coat. Cover and let marinate for at least 30 minutes or overnight in the refrigerator. Heat a large skillet over medium-high heat. Place the marinated chicken in the pan and cook until the chicken is cooked through, about 10 to 12 minutes.

(continued)

Tzatziki Sauce:

1 sm. cucumber, diced	2 tsp. lemon juice
2 T. freshly chopped dill leaves	2 tsp. hot sauce
1 (8 oz.) container plain yogurt	

Mix together all sauce ingredients. Refrigerate and allow flavors to blend for 30 minutes. Sauce will be served at the table with the chicken and each person may add to their plate.

Toppings:

Pita Bread	1 tomato, chopped
Olive oil	1 med. onion, thinly sliced
5 lg. romaine leaves, chopped	

Turn oven on to broil. Just before time to serve souvlaki, lightly coat pita bread with olive oil on both sides. Lightly toast pita bread in oven. Serve the souvlaki with the pita bread, tzatziki sauce, romaine, tomato and onion. Greek potatoes are a wonderful addition to this meal. See recipe in "Vegetables and Sides."

❦ CILANTRO CREAM CHICKEN ❦
Lisa Rieff

4 chicken breasts	3 oz. cream cheese, cubed
Seasoning for chicken	1 T. lime juice
3 T. butter	½ c. chopped cilantro
¾ c. heavy cream	

Pound chicken for even cooking and liberally season with your choice of seasoning (salt and pepper, Cajun spices, seasoned salt, etc). Melt butter in large skillet over medium-high heat. Brown the chicken on both sides. Remove the chicken and turn to low heat. Add the cream and cream cheese to pan, whisking together until blended. Add lime juice and cilantro. Return chicken to pan. Cover and simmer about 15 minutes turning chicken over halfway through. Serve with sauce over the chicken.

❦ CREAMED CHICKEN CASSEROLE ❦
Lynda McGraw

Casserole:

3 lbs. chicken, cooked and
  boned

8 - 12 oz. sour cream
1 can cream of chicken soup

Combine chicken, sour cream and soup and place in a 9 x 13-inch pan or its equivalent.

Topping:

1 - 2 sleeves Ritz crackers,
  crushed finely

1 - 1½ c. melted butter
¼ c. poppy seeds

Combine ingredients for topping and put on top of casserole. Bake at 325° for 30 minutes or until heated through and topping is browned. Serve hot with vegetables of your choice, salad, bread/rolls and drink. Can be made ahead and put in to cook at the time you want (30+ minutes).

❦ FIREMAN'S CHICKEN ❦
Lynda McGraw
JoAnn Niemann

1 can cream of celery soup
1 c. white rice

4 - 6 boned chicken breasts
1 onion dry soup mix

Line cookie sheet with heavy duty foil. Pour soup on foil lined cookie sheet. Sprinkle rice on that. Lay chicken on the rice. Sprinkle dry onion soup mix over all. Wrap foil up around all ingredients tightly and seal by crimping foil together at the top. Bake at 350° for 45 to 60 minutes. This can be made up and kept in the refrigerator until you are ready to bake. Serve with vegetable, rolls, salad and drink.

121822-12

❦ GRILLED CHICKEN KABOBS ❦
Valerie Florea

½ c. olive oil
¼ c. lemon juice
3 garlic cloves, minced
2 tsp. honey
Thyme
Dash of basil
1 tsp. crushed red pepper flakes (more or less for your taste)
1 tsp. pepper
1 tsp. salt
4 boneless, skinless chicken breasts, cut into cubes
Desired vegetables or fruit; examples: tomatoes, peppers, onions, pineapple

In a small bowl, combine olive oil, lemon juice, garlic, honey, thyme, basil, red pepper flakes, pepper and salt. Pour ¾ of marinade over cut chicken to soak up flavors. Cover and refrigerate for at least 4 hours. Drain, discarding marinade that was over chicken. Place chicken on skewers and alternate with vegetables and fruit as desired. Grill over medium-low heat, turning and basting with reserved marinade for 12 minutes or until juices run clear.

❦ GRILLED CHICKEN WITH PROSCIUTTO AND BASIL ❦
Valerie Florea

4 boneless, skinless chicken breasts, about 8 oz. each
1 tsp. salt
1 tsp. minced garlic
½ tsp. freshly ground black pepper
4 thin slices prosciutto
4 thin slices provolone cheese
Large basil leaves, about 8
Butcher's twine
Olive oil
2 c. tomato sauce (spaghetti sauce)

Pound out the chicken breasts to about ¼-inch thick. Season each piece of chicken on both sides with salt, garlic and pepper. Lay a slice of prosciutto on each piece of chicken. Than lay a slice of cheese and 2 basil leaves on top of prosciutto. Carefully roll up the chicken, keeping it snug. Tie 2 pieces of butcher's twine around each piece. Lightly brush each rolled piece of chicken with oil. Grill the chicken over direct medium heat until golden on all sides, about 12 minutes, turning a quarter turn every 3 minutes. Remove from the grill and let rest for

(continued)

3 to 5 minutes. Meanwhile, in a small saucepan over medium-high heat, warm the tomato sauce. Remove the twine from the chicken pieces; cut into slices and serve warm on a pool of sauce. Garnish with pieces of basil.

❧ GRILLED ORANGE CHICKEN WITH MANGO PEACH SALSA ❧
Valerie Florea

4 boneless skinless chicken
  breasts
Pinch of salt and pepper
Clove of garlic, minced
½ c. plus 2 T. orange juice,
  divided
2 T. olive oil
½ tsp. rosemary

1 bay leaf
2 peaches, peeled, pitted and
  chopped
1 mango, peeled, pitted and
  chopped
½ c. chopped red bell pepper
2 green onions, finely chopped
1 T. diced fresh cilantro

Season chicken breasts with salt and pepper. Then combine chicken, garlic, ½ c. orange juice, olive oil, rosemary and bay leaf in plastic bag to marinate for at least 1 hour or up to 8 hours. Meanwhile, in a small bowl, make salsa by combining peaches, mango, red bell pepper, green onion, remaining 2 T. orange juice and cilantro. Cover and chill salsa until serving time. Preheat grill. Remove chicken from marinade and discard marinade. Grill chicken breasts turning once, about 20 minutes or until internal temperature reaches 160°. Serve grilled chicken topped with salsa.

❧ ONE-PAN POTATOES AND CHICKEN TERIYAKI ❧
Dennis Hindemith

4 med. potatoes, cut into thin
  wedges and microwaved 8-10
  min. until tender
1 lb. boneless and skinless
  chicken breasts, cut into ½-
  inch slices

2 tsp. vegetable oil
½ c. sliced green onions
¼ c. prepared teriyaki sauce

(continued)

While potatoes cook: In large skillet toss and brown chicken in oil over high heat 5 minutes. Add potatoes. Sauté and toss until potatoes are lightly browned. Add onions and teriyaki sauce. Toss until heated through. Time: 20 minutes. Servings: 4. Per serving: 280 cal., 9 g. fat, 45 mg. chol., 740 mg. sodium, 28 g. carb., 21 g. pro.

❦ ORANGE CHICKEN ❦
Heidi Meyer

1½ c. uncooked white rice	¼ c. vinegar
3 c. water	⅔ c. orange juice
3 boneless, skinless chicken breasts, cut in bite sized pieces	1 tsp. garlic powder
	⅔ c. brown sugar
1 egg, beaten	1 T. onion flakes
Flour to coat	2 T. cornstarch in 2 T. water, mixed
1½ c. water	Oil to fry chicken, about 1-inch in bottom of frying pan
2 T. soy sauce	

Place uncooked rice in large sauce pan and add 3 cups of water. Bring rice to a boil. Then cook for about 15 minutes on medium low heat. Coat chicken pieces in egg and flour and let sit. In a medium sauce pan add water, soy sauce, vinegar, and orange juice. Heat until boiling. Add garlic powder, brown sugar, onion flakes, and cornstarch mixture. Reduce to medium heat and stir occasionally. Fry chicken pieces in 1-inch of hot oil until very crispy. Place on paper towel to soak up extra oil. Place fried chicken pieces in a bowl and add sauce to cover. Serve over cooked white rice.

❦ OVEN-FRIED CHICKEN ❦
Julie Concannon
Barefoot Contessa/Food Network

2 chickens (3 lbs. each), cut in 8 serving pieces (I use 5 - 6 legs and	2 c. all-purpose flour
	1 T. kosher salt
	1 T. freshly ground black pepper
4 split breasts cut in two for a total of 13 - 14 pieces)	Vegetable oil or vegetable shortening
1 qt. buttermilk	

(continued)

Place the chicken pieces in a large bowl and pour the buttermilk over them. Cover with plastic wrap and refrigerate overnight. Preheat oven to 350°. Combine the flour, salt, and pepper in a large bowl. Take the chicken out of the buttermilk and coat each piece thoroughly with the flour mixture. Pour the oil into a large heavy-bottomed stockpot (I use a large cast-iron skillet) to a depth of 1-inch and heat to 360° on a thermometer. Working in batches, carefully place several pieces of chicken in the oil and fry for about 3 minutes on each side until the coating is a light golden brown (it will continue to brown in the oven). Don't crowd the pieces (I only put 3-4 pieces in the skillet at one time). Remove the chicken from the oil and place each piece on a metal baking rack set on a sheet pan. Allow the oil to return to 360° before frying the next batch. When all the chicken is fried, bake for 30 to 40 minutes, until the chicken is no longer pink inside. Serve hot.

❦ PENNE GORGONZOLA WITH CHICKEN ❦
Ruth Manning

1 pkg. (16 oz.) penne pasta
1 lb. boneless skinless chicken
   breasts, cut into ½-inch
   pieces
1 T. olive oil
1 lg. garlic clove, minced
¼ c. white wine
1 c. heavy whipping cream
¼ c. chicken broth

2 c. crumbled Gorgonzola
   cheese
6 - 8 fresh sage leaves, thinly
   sliced
Salt and pepper to taste
Grated Parmigiano-Reggiano
   cheese and minced fresh
   parsley

Cook pasta according to package directions. Meanwhile, in a large skillet over medium heat, brown chicken in oil on all sides. Add garlic; cook 1 minute longer. Add wine, stirring to loosen browned bits from pan. Add cream and broth; cook until sauce is slightly thickened and chicken is no longer pink. Stir in the Gorgonzola cheese, sage, salt and pepper; cook just until cheese is melted. Drain pasta; toss with sauce. Sprinkle with Parmigiano-Reggiano cheese and parsley. Yield: 8 servings.

121822-12

❦ PLUMP AND JUICY CHICKEN BREASTS ❦
Sandy Hall

½ c. all-purpose flour
1 tsp. poultry seasoning
4 skinless boneless chicken
  breasts
1 T. butter
1 T. olive oil

¼ c. (or more as needed)
  Marsala wine
1 c. chopped onion
4 slices of mozzarella cheese
  (use shredded if that is all
  you have)

Mix flour and poultry seasoning. Roll chicken breasts in flour mixture to cover all sides. Melt butter with the olive oil in skillet over medium high heat. Fry the chicken in the hot butter-oil mixture for 5 minutes on each side. You may want to play with the 5 minute time element depending on the thickness of the chicken breasts. Remove chicken from pan and set aside, keeping chicken warm. Deglaze the pan with Marsala wine. Add chopped onions. Sauté over high heat for 5 minutes. This is the point where you will see if you need to add more wine. Return chicken breasts to the skillet, baste with drippings, put cheese on the breasts, cover with lid and cook for another 2½ minutes; keep lid on tight, do not lift lid during this time. After the 2½ minutes remove pan from heat, keeping lid on, let skillet stand for 10 minutes with lid on. Did I mention that you are not to lift the lid for 12½ minutes?

❦ POPPYSEED CHICKEN ❦
Karen Armitage

6 chicken breast halves,
  cooked, skinned and pulled
  into strips
2 cans condensed cream of
  chicken soup
¼ c. water
1 c. sour cream

8 oz. Monterey Jack cheese,
  grated
3 T. poppy seeds, divided
2 packaged stacks of Ritz
  crackers, crushed
1½ sticks butter, melted

Preheat oven to 350°. Arrange chicken in bottom of 9 x 13-inch baking dish. Season to taste with salt and pepper. Stir together soup and water in saucepan and heat over medium heat to remove all lumps. Remove from heat and add sour cream. Stir in cheese and 1½ T. of the poppy seeds and pour over the chicken. Mix together remaining poppy seeds,

(continued)

cracker crumbs and melted butter. Sprinkle over chicken and bake for 30 minutes. Reduced fat version: substitute low-fat cream of chicken soup, low-fat sour cream, low-fat cheese, and use 1 stack of crackers with only 3 T. butter.

❣ SESAME CHICKEN ❣
Nancy Shinrock

1 egg, beaten
1 T. water
4 skinned and boned chicken breasts
¾ c. bread or cracker crumbs
¼ c. butter

1 T. soy sauce
2 T. butter, melted
½ c. chicken broth
Sesame seeds
Prepared rice

Combine beaten egg and water and dip chicken in the mixture, coat with crumbs. Sauté in ¼ cup butter. Place in baking dish. Make sauce of soy sauce, 2 tablespoons melted butter and chicken broth. Brush chicken with sauce and sprinkle with sesame seeds. Bake at 350° for 35-40 minutes, basting with remaining sauce. Serve over rice.

❣ SMOTHERED CHICKEN ❣
Carol Novak

2 boneless, skinless chicken breasts
Dried oregano
Salt
Garlic powder
Black pepper
Cayenne pepper

1 T. oil
1 med. onion, sliced
2 bell peppers (any color), sliced
1 c. shredded cheese (½ mozzarella and ½ Cheddar is good)

Preheat oven to 350°. Cut chicken breasts in half to make 4 portions. Pound thin. Sprinkle with desired dry spices, using those above or any that you desire. Bake uncovered for approximately 25 minutes. While chicken is cooking, heat the oil in a large skillet. Cook onions and peppers until tender. When chicken is cooked through, spoon vegetables over chicken and sprinkle with cheese. Put back into oven until cheese melts.

❣ 174

❦ SOUR CREAM CHICKEN ENCHILADAS ❦
Julie Concannon

2 cans cream of chicken soup
1 can chopped green chilies
1 bunch chopped green onions
½ pt. sour cream
2 boneless skinless chicken
  breasts, cooked and cubed

1 pkg. (10 count) flour tortillas
¼ lb. grated sharp Cheddar
  cheese

Heat together the soup, chilies, green onions, sour cream and chicken. Fill tortillas with 2 tablespoons of chicken mixture, roll up and place in 9 x 13-inch baking dish. Pour remaining mixture on top. Top with cheese. Bake at 350° for 30 minutes. Let sit for 5 minutes before serving. 10 servings.

❦ SWEET AND SOUR CHICKEN ❦
Nancy Shinrock

1 lb. boneless chicken breasts
¾ c. fat free chicken broth
1 (15½ oz.) can pineapple
  chunks in juice
1 green pepper, cut in thin
  strips
1 red pepper, cut in thin strips

1 carrot, sliced diagonally
¼ c. vinegar
2 tsp. sugar
2 T. cornstarch
2 T. soy sauce
3 c. hot cooked rice

Cut chicken in 1-inch cubes. Heat chicken broth to boiling in large skillet, add chicken. Simmer 5 to 10 minutes, stirring occasionally. Add undrained pineapple chunks, green pepper, red pepper, carrots, vinegar and sugar, bring to a boil. Stir cornstarch into soy sauce until smooth, then stir into skillet mixture. Bring to boiling, stirring constantly. Lower heat. Cover and simmer 10 minutes. Serve over hot cooked rice. 4 servings.

❦ TASTY ITALIAN CHICKEN ❦
Kathy Christiansen
Rita Bigelow

½ c. chopped onion
1⅛ tsp. paprika, divided
3 tsp. olive oil, divided
1¼ c. water
¼ c. tomato paste
1 bay leaf
½ tsp. reduced sodium chicken bouillon granules

½ tsp. Italian seasoning
¼ c. all-purpose flour
1½ tsp. grated Parmesan cheese
½ tsp. salt
¼ tsp. garlic powder
¼ tsp. dried oregano
1½ lbs. chicken tenderloins

In a small saucepan, sauté onion and ⅛ teaspoon paprika in 1 teaspoon oil until tender. Stir in the water, tomato paste, bay leaf, bouillon and Italian seasoning, bring to a boil. Reduce heat; simmer, uncovered, for ten minutes. Meanwhile, in a large resealable plastic bag, combine the flour, Parmesan cheese, salt, garlic powder, oregano and remaining paprika. Add chicken; seal bag and shake to coat. In a large nonstick skillet coated with cooking spray, cook half of the chicken in 1 teaspoon oil for 2-3 minutes on each side or until no longer pink. Remove and keep warm; repeat with remaining chicken and oil. Remove bay leaf from sauce. Serve sauce with chicken. Yield: 6 servings.

❦ TERIYAKI CHICKEN ❦
Nancy Shinrock

1 T. soy sauce
1 c. brown sugar
1 cloves garlic, pressed
4 shakes ground ginger (about ½ tsp.)
½ c. white wine

¼ tsp. onion powder, optional
¼ tsp. seasoned salt, optional
1 T. olive oil
1 chicken bouillon cube
4 chicken breasts
Prepared rice

Combine soy sauce, brown sugar, garlic, ginger, white wine, onion powder, seasoned salt, olive oil and bouillon cube. Pour over chicken breasts and marinate at least one hour. Grill, basting once or twice with marinade. Be careful not to over cook. Serve with rice.

121822-12

❦ THAI GREEN CURRY WITH CHICKEN (OR SHRIMP) ❦
Dave Egr

1 green bell pepper, chopped
1 zucchini, chopped
1 onion, chopped
1 c. frozen peas
8 oz. chicken (or shrimp or both)

1 tsp. olive oil
1 can coconut milk (or ¾ c. skim milk with ¼ c. water)
3 tsp. green curry paste

Sauté chopped up veggies, peas and cut up chicken (or shrimp whole) in olive oil. Add coconut milk and curry paste, simmer on medium for 10 minutes. Serve over rice. 4 servings. 252 calories per serving. You can spice it up with cayenne, diced up jalapeño, garlic powder, or other spices to taste.

❦ TURGETTI ❦
Marjorie Keiser

1¼ c. spaghetti (break into 2-inch pieces)
2 c. cut up cooked turkey or chicken
¼ c. pimento
¼ c. chopped red pepper
¼ c. chopped green pepper
½ c. diced onion

1 can mushroom soup
½ c. broth (I use a little more)
½ tsp. salt
⅛ tsp. pepper
2 c. or more grated Cheddar cheese, divided
Small amount black olives, chopped

Cook spaghetti, drain; add turkey, pimento, peppers and onion. Add soup, broth, salt, pepper and 1¼ cup grated cheese and olives. Toss with fork. Sprinkle remaining cheese on top. Refrigerate overnight. Bake at 350° for 45 minutes. We like extra cheese on it. If using chicken it would be called Chigetti, I suppose.

❦ TURKEY PUFFS ❦
Kay Keiser

2 cans crescent rolls
3 c. cooked turkey (or chicken)
½ c. shredded Cheddar cheese
1 can mushroom stems and
   pieces, drained and chopped

½ c. sour cream
¼ tsp. thyme (optional)
Salt and pepper to taste
3 T. sour cream
Turkey gravy

Pat crescent rolls flat, cut into 12 squares. Mix turkey, cheese, mushrooms, ½ c. sour cream, thyme, salt and pepper and place heaping tablespoonful onto center of each dough square. Fold corners up to center and seal seams tight to make a packet. Place on ungreased pan. Bake at 425° until golden brown, about 20 minutes. Mix 3 tablespoons sour cream with turkey gravy. Serve gravy over top.

SEAFOOD

❦ BAKED SHRIMP AND FETA WITH PASTA ❦
Jody Manning

1 tsp. olive oil
¾ tsp. dried oregano
½ tsp. salt
¼ tsp. crushed red pepper
1 lb. frozen, uncooked shrimp
   that have been peeled and
   deveined
2 - 3 cloves garlic, peeled and
   minced

½ c. dry white wine
1 lg. can diced tomatoes
¾ c. (3 oz.) feta cheese
4 c. hot cooked linguine or
   other type pasta
¼ c. minced fresh flat-leaf
   (Italian) parsley leaves

Preheat oven to 350°. Heat oil in large nonstick skillet over medium high heat. Add oregano, salt, crushed red pepper, shrimp and garlic. Sauté for 3 minutes. Spoon shrimp mixture into 11 x 7-inch baking dish coated with cooking spray. Add wine to skillet and cook over low heat until reduced to ¼ c. (about 3 minutes). Stir into tomatoes and pour over shrimp mixture. Sprinkle with cheese and bake at 350° for 10 minutes. Serve over pasta and sprinkle with parsley. 4 servings.

121822-12

❦ BEER BOILED SHRIMP ❦
Rose Roberts

2 lemons, thinly sliced
1 onion, thinly sliced
¼ c. olive oil
1 T. salt

1 box shrimp/crab boil
2 cans beer
12 c. water to cover
5 lbs. shrimp

Bring lemons, onion, olive oil, salt, shrimp/crab boil, beer and water to a boil and simmer for 5 minutes. Add shrimp and boil for approximately 10 minutes. Drain liquid only.

❦ FISH TACOS ❦
Joe Combes

Beer Batter:

1 c. flour
2 T. cornstarch
1 tsp. baking powder

½ tsp. salt
1 egg
1 c. beer

In a large bowl, combine flour, cornstarch, baking powder and salt. Blend egg and beer, then quickly stir into the flour mixture (don't worry about a few lumps).

White Sauce:

½ c. plain yogurt
½ c. mayonnaise
1 lime, juiced
1 jalapeño pepper, minced
1 tsp. minced capers

½ tsp. oregano
½ tsp. ground cumin
½ tsp. dill weed
1 tsp. ground cayenne pepper

In a medium bowl, mix together yogurt and mayonnaise. Gradually stir in fresh lime juice until consistency is runny. Season with jalapeño, capers, oregano, cumin, dill and cayenne.

Tacos:

1 qt. oil for frying
1 lb. cod fillets, in 2 - 3 oz.
  pieces

1 (12 oz.) pkg. corn tortillas
Shredded cabbage

Heat oil in deep fryer to 375°. Dust fish pieces lightly with flour. Dip into beer batter, and fry until crisp and golden brown. Drain on paper

(continued)

towels. Lightly warm tortillas. Place fish in tortilla, top with shredded cabbage and white sauce.

❦ FRIED WALLEYE ❦
Joe Combes

Walleye fillets
1 c. flour
2 eggs, whipped
2 c. bread crumbs

1 T. Cajun seasoning
A few shakes of pepper
Cooking oil

Dry fish, toss with flour, coating both sides. Dip floured fillets in whipped eggs. Coat fillets in the bread crumbs. Put Cajun seasoning and pepper into a one gallon zip lock bag. Add the fillets to the bag and shake until they are coated. Cover the bottom of a skillet with oil, turn to medium heat. Cook fillets on each side for 3 minutes or until slightly browned.

❦ GRILLED SHRIMP ❦
Shari Garder

½ c. olive oil
6 T. lemon juice
2 T. soy sauce
2 T. parsley

1½ tsp. tarragon
1 tsp. garlic powder
1 lb. shrimp

Mix well all ingredients except shrimp for marinade. Put shrimp in lidded container and pour marinade over top. Shake now and then. Either skewer or place in disposable pan and grill for approximately 5 minutes.

❦ SALMON SALAD ❦
Joe Combes

½ tsp. salt
1 tsp. ground coriander
1 tsp. ground cumin
½ tsp. Spanish style paprika
1 tsp. brown sugar
1 tsp. garlic powder
2 (6 oz.) salmon fillets

6 - 8 c. salad greens
2 carrots, grated
4 T. chopped dates
2 T. toasted pine nuts
Country French Vinaigrette
   dressing

Make spice rub by combining salt, coriander, cumin, paprika, brown sugar and garlic powder. Mix well. Make Country French Vinaigrette dressing (you can get the mix at Penzey's spice store). Rub the salmon evenly with the spice rub. Grill, broil, or pan sear the salmon to your desired level of doneness, skin side up for 3 minutes, then skin side down for 5 minutes over medium heat. While the salmon cooks, divide the salad greens between two plates. Sprinkle with the carrots, dates and pine nuts. Place the salmon fillets on top of the salads and drizzle with dressing. Serve extra dressing on the side.

❦ SEAFOOD ALFREDO ❦
Jackie Combes

1 pkg. (12 oz.) bow tie pasta
2 garlic cloves, minced
2 T. olive or vegetable oil
8 oz. imitation crab meat
8 oz. cooked shrimp
1 T. lemon juice

½ tsp. pepper
1 jar (16 oz.) Alfredo sauce
½ c. frozen peas, thawed
¼ c. shredded Parmesan
   cheese

Cook pasta according to package directions. Meanwhile, in a large skillet, sauté garlic in oil until tender. Stir in the crab, shrimp, lemon juice and pepper. Cook and stir for 1 minute. Add Alfredo sauce and peas. Cook and stir until heated through. Drain pasta, top with the seafood mixture and sprinkle with Parmesan cheese. Yield: 4-6 servings.

❦ SHRIMP BROCCOLI ALFREDO ❦
Deb Lund

8 oz. pasta (fettuccine works well)

¾ - 1 lb. shrimp, peeled and with tails removed (raw or cooked)

3 - 4 c. fresh or frozen broccoli florets

½ c. butter (no substitute)

½ c. cream or half and half (I use half and half)

¾ c. Parmesan cheese

½ tsp. garlic salt

1 T. chopped parsley

Dash pepper (to taste)

Cook the pasta in a large pot until al dente, drain, and keep hot in the cooking pot. Cook shrimp, if raw, and broccoli until broccoli is tender crisp. Do not over cook. Melt butter in glass container. Add cream or half and half, Parmesan cheese, and seasonings. Heat until hot, stirring occasionally (I use the microwave, a minute at a time). Add shrimp and broccoli to pasta in the pot; then add the Alfredo sauce. Stir gently to distribute sauce, and serve. May substitute chicken for shrimp.

❦ TILAPIA ❦
Shari Garder

1 stick margarine

Tabasco sauce

Worcestershire sauce

8 pieces tilapia

Dill weed

Lemon pepper

Melt margarine, 1 shot of Tabasco sauce, and 5 shots of Worcestershire sauce in electric skillet. Add tilapia, dill weed and lemon pepper to skillet. Cook until fish is browned and flaky.

❦ TUNA NOODLE CASSEROLE ❦
Julie Concannon

6 T. butter

6 T. flour

¾ tsp. salt

⅜ tsp. pepper

3 c. milk

½ pkg. (3 c. uncooked) med. egg noodles

2 cans tuna, drained

8 oz. frozen peas, thawed

Crushed potato chips

Make a white sauce by melting butter in a saucepan and whisking in flour, salt and pepper. Add milk and stir until thickened. Cook egg noodles according to package directions, drain. Combine the white

(continued)

sauce, noodles, tuna and peas in a 2-quart casserole dish. Top with crushed potato chips if desired. Bake at 350° for ½ hour.

Recipe Favorites

Salads & Soups

SALADS & SOUPS

SALAD

❦ APPLE SALAD ❦
Cheyrle Badtke

6 - 8 apples   12 oz. Cool Whip
6 regular Snickers bars

Cut apples and Snickers bars into bite size pieces. Mix in Cool Whip and serve.

❦ APPLE SNICKER SALAD ❦
Mary Lou Gustafson

1 box instant vanilla pudding   8 Granny Smith apples
1 c. milk   5 - 6 Snickers candy bars cut
8 oz. container Cool Whip   into bite size pieces

Mix pudding, milk, and Cool Whip. Blend well. Add diced apples to mixture. Add cut up Snickers, chill thoroughly and serve. Best if made on day to be served.

❦ APPLESAUCE JELLO ❦
Shari Garder

3 c. applesauce   16 oz. 7 up
6 oz. jello

Heat applesauce in saucepan. Dissolve jello in heated applesauce. Add 7 up, stir. Put in bowl. Refrigerate to set.

❦ ASIAN-STYLE SPINACH SALAD ❦
(A Side Salad with a Flair)
Jody Manning

Salad:

Baby spinach, pre-washed
Almond slices
1 sm. can mandarin oranges

Sugar snap peas, washed (and blanched, if desired)

Combine spinach, almond slices, mandarin oranges, and sugar snap peas.

Asian Dressing:

Juice of 1 lime
1 tsp. Tabasco or other hot
  pepper sauce
1 tsp. soy sauce

1 tsp. seasoned rice wine
  vinegar
⅓ c. olive oil
2 T. brown sugar

Combine lime juice, Tabasco, soy sauce, rice wine vinegar, olive oil and brown sugar. Dress salad just before serving.

❦ AUNT CLARA'S MACARONI SALAD ❦
Nancy Shinrock

Macaroni Salad:

½ c. macaroni, elbow or shell
2 hard boiled eggs, chopped
¼ c. chopped green pepper
½ c. celery, chopped

2 green onions, chopped
3 radishes, diced
4 oz. mild Cheddar cheese,
  cubed

Boil macaroni. Rinse in cold water. Mix all ingredients.

Dressing:

⅛ c. sour cream
¼ c. mayonnaise
1 tsp. white vinegar

½ tsp. regular mustard
Salt and pepper to taste

Mix all ingredients. Pour over macaroni mixture and mix well.

121822-12

❦ BETTY SALAD ❦
Heidi Meyer

1 c. oil
¾ c. sugar
⅓ c. ketchup
¼ c. vinegar
1 T. Worcestershire sauce

1 med. onion, grated
Salad greens
2 hard boiled eggs, diced
Bacon bits

Mix oil, sugar, ketchup, vinegar, Worcestershire sauce, and grated onion to make dressing. Refrigerate dressing at least 3-4 hours. Mix salad greens, eggs, and bacon bits in a bowl. Add desired amount of dressing.

❦ BROCCOLI APPLE SALAD ❦
Mary Lou Gustafson

1 bunch broccoli
2 Fuji apples

Kraft Cole Slaw dressing
Slivered almonds, optional

Break washed broccoli into bite size pieces. Cut washed apples into bite size pieces. Add dressing as needed right before serving and top with slivered almonds if desired.

❦ BROCCOLI DELIGHT SALAD ❦
Rose Roberts
Brandy Miller

Salad:

1 bunch broccoli, diced
1 med. onion, finely chopped
   or 1 T. dry minced onion
12 slices bacon, fried and
   crumbled

1 c. sunflower seeds
¼ c. celery, diced
½ c. raisins, if desired (or
   cranberries)
Grated carrots, if desired

Mix broccoli, onion, bacon, sunflower seeds, celery, raisins and carrots (if using) in a large bowl.

Dressing:

½ c. Miracle Whip
2 T. sweet cider vinegar

½ c. sugar
French fried onions

(continued)

Mix Miracle Whip, vinegar and sugar. Pour over salad immediately before serving. Top with French fried onions.

❦ BROCCOLI GRAPE SALAD ❦
Heidi Meyer

Salad:

2 stalks broccoli flowerets, cut into sm. bite sized pieces
1 - 2 bunches green onion, chopped
2 lg. stems celery, cut fine

1 (2 oz.) pkg. slivered almonds
2 c. green grapes, cut in half
6 - 8 slices cooked bacon, crumbled
1½ c. raisins

Mix all salad ingredients in a large bowl.

Dressing:

1 c. mayonnaise

¾ c. sugar

Mix mayonnaise and sugar to make dressing. Stir desired amount of dressing into salad mixture.

❦ BROCCOLI SALAD ❦
Randi VenHuizen

1 c. mayonnaise
½ c. sugar
2 T. vinegar
4 c. broccoli, finely chopped
½ c. raisins

1 c. roasted sunflower seeds
¼ c. chopped green onions
8 slices cooked bacon, drained and chopped

For dressing mix mayonnaise, sugar and vinegar. Mix remaining ingredients in large bowl, add dressing and mix well.

121822-12

❦ BROCCOLI SLAW ❦
Judy Egr

⅓ c. vegetable oil
⅓ c. olive oil
½ c. sugar
⅓ c. white wine vinegar
2 pkgs. beef flavor ramen
    noodles

1 pkg. broccoli slaw
½ c. sunflower seeds
½ c. sliced almonds
½ c. chopped green onions

Mix dressing the night before: Combine vegetable oil, olive oil, sugar, vinegar and the flavor package from the ramen noodles. Before serving combine broccoli slaw, seeds, nuts, green onions and broken up ramen noodles. Add dressing. I have made this without making the dressing the night before and it is still very good.

❦ CABBAGE SALAD ❦
Cheyrle Badtke

Salad:

8 T. slivered almonds
8 T. sesame seeds
1 bag shredded cabbage

8 green onions, chopped fine
1 pkg. ramen noodles,
    uncooked

Toast almonds and sesame seeds. Mix cabbage and onions in a large bowl. Just before serving, add sesame seeds, almonds and crushed up ramen noodles (uncooked) to cabbage and onion mixture.

Dressing:

4 T. sugar
1 tsp. pepper
2 tsp. Accent

2 tsp. salt
1 c. oil
6 T. rice vinegar

Mix all dressing ingredients and pour on salad just before serving.

❦ CALICO SALAD ❦
Ruth Manning

1 (14 oz.) can green beans
1 (14 oz.) can yellow wax
  beans
1 (14 oz.) can corn
Optional: add a can of
  garbanzo beans or black
  beans

½ c. red peppers, cubed
½ c. green peppers, cubed
1 red onion, sliced into thin
  rings.

Drain canned vegetables. Combine canned vegetables, peppers and red onion.

Dressing:

¾ c. sugar
1 c. cider vinegar
⅓ c. canola oil

1 tsp. salt
1 tsp pepper

Add dressing and marinate overnight for best taste. Keeps in refrigerator for 3 weeks. Stir often.

❦ CARMEL APPLE SALAD ❦
(W.W.)
Connie Walther

1 (20 oz.) can crushed
  pineapple, in own juice
1 sm. pkg. sugar-free
  butterscotch instant pudding
1 (8 oz.) fat free Cool Whip

3 c. chopped apples
1 c. miniature marshmallows
½ - 1 oz. chopped salted
  peanuts

Mix pineapple with juice and pudding. Add Cool Whip. Mix apples, marshmallows, and nuts. Combine all ingredients and chill. Makes 12 servings (⅔ c.=2 points).

❦ CHICKEN SALAD ❦
Shari Garder

2 pkgs. boneless chicken
  breasts
1 head lettuce
Grapes, use as many as you
  like
24 oz. Hellmann's mayonnaise

24 oz. sour cream
2 pkgs. bacon, fried crisp and
  crumbled
5 oz. bag chopped pecans
1 lg. box raisins (opt.)

Slice raw chicken into bite-size pieces; cut away any extra fat. Boil 1 package of chicken at a time for 5 minutes. Drain chicken pieces and rinse with fresh tap water. Clean, chop and shred lettuce. Clean grapes then cut in half. In large salad bowl, mix mayonnaise and sour cream. Stir in chicken next. As you put chicken in bowl; tear and squish pieces with your fingers. The chicken is then more tender to eat. Add bacon, pecans, and raisins; mix thoroughly. Keep refrigerated until ready to serve. Add lettuce immediately before serving to prevent sogginess. You can get everything ready the night before and mix together right before serving. Note: This salad is great served with croissants.

❦ CHILLED CORN SALAD ❦
Anne Yarger

2 cans corn niblets, drained
  well
1 c. mayonnaise
⅓ c. sliced green onion

⅓ c. chopped green pepper
Cheddar cheese
Crushed Chili-Cheese Fritos or
  plain Fritos

Mix corn, mayonnaise, onion and pepper. Top with cheese and crushed chips. Refrigerate.

❦ CHINESE SALAD ❦
Paula Foster

Nut Mixture:

¼ c. butter or margarine
1 pkg. crushed ramen noodles
  (do not use flavor packet)

4 T. sunflower seeds
1 c. slivered almonds

(continued)

In a sauce pan, brown butter, ramen noodles, sunflower seeds and slivered almonds until golden brown. Let this cool and store in a covered container.

Dressing:

¼ c. sugar   ¼ c. vinegar
½ c. vegetable oil   1 T. soy sauce

In another sauce pan, bring sugar, oil, vinegar and soy sauce to a boil. Stir constantly until the sugar is dissolved. Let this cool and place in another covered container and put in the refrigerator. This can be kept up to a week.

Cabbage:

1 med. head Chinese cabbage   1 bunch green onions, chopped

Chop the cabbage and green onion. In a large bowl, combine the nut mixture and dressing with the cabbage and onion. This serves 10 to 15 people.

❦ CHINESE SLAW SALAD ❦
(Family picnic favorite)
Connie Walther

Salad:

1½ bags (16 oz.) cole slaw mix   1 c. slivered almonds
5 - 6 green onions, sliced   1 c. salted sunflower seeds
2 pkg. ramen noodles, broken   ½ c. oleo (margarine or butter)
   up

Toss slaw mix and onions in large bowl. Sauté noodles and nuts in melted butter. Cool. Add to mixture.

Dressing:

1 c. salad oil   2 T. soy sauce
1 c. sugar   ½ c. cider vinegar

Shake dressing ingredients well. Pour ½ to ⅔ of dressing mixture over cole slaw mixture. Stir well. May add more dressing with left-overs, if it gets dry. Makes a large salad.

121822-12

❦ COLE SLAW ❦
Randi VenHuizen

1 c. mayonnaise
½ tsp. wine vinegar
¼ tsp. Worcestershire sauce
¼ tsp. seasoning salt
¼ tsp. celery seed

⅛ tsp. ground mustard
Dash marjoram and oregano
1 T. honey
Cole slaw vegetables (cabbage, carrots)

Mix all ingredients together for dressing except vegetables. Mix dressing well with vegetables. Refrigerate before serving to blend flavors.

❦ COLESLAW ❦
Dayla Miller

1 c. mayonnaise
1 tsp. sugar
1 tsp. vinegar
1 T. milk

1 tsp. salt and pepper
1 head cabbage, chopped
½ c. onion, chopped
1 apple, cored and diced

Mix mayonnaise, sugar, vinegar, milk, salt and pepper (I put in jar or shaker) and pour over cabbage, onion and apple. Chill and serve. May need to add extra liquid mixture depending upon how much cabbage is used.

❦ COOL CUCUMBER PASTA SALAD ❦
Susan Lueders
Lisa Lueders

1 (8 oz.) pkg. rotini pasta
1 T. vegetable oil
2 med. cucumbers, thinly sliced
1 med. onion, thinly sliced
Optional: fresh diced tomatoes, sliced green peppers

1½ c. sugar
1 c. water
¾ c. vinegar
1 T. prepared mustard
1 T. dried parsley flakes
1 tsp. salt
1 tsp. pepper
½ tsp. garlic salt

(continued)

Cook pasta, drain and rinse in cold water. Place in large bowl; stir in oil, cucumber, onion, tomatoes and green peppers. Combine remaining ingredients; pour over salad and toss. Cover and chill 3-4 hours, stirring occasionally. Makes 8-10 servings.

❦ CORN SALAD ❦
Pauline Shaffer

1 can white sweet corn	1 c. shredded Cheddar cheese
1 can yellow sweet corn	½ - ¾ c. mayonnaise
1 green pepper	Salt and pepper to taste
1 red pepper	½ bag Chile Cheese Fritos

Drain cans of corn. Chop green and red peppers. Mix together corn and peppers. Add cheese, mayonnaise, salt and pepper. Just before serving, add ½ bag of Fritos, crushed.

❦ COTTAGE CHEESE AND JELLO ❦
Lynda McGraw

1 sm. cottage cheese, small curd	1 (8 oz.) can crushed pineapple, drained (save juice)
1 lg. lime jello	1 c. chopped celery
4 - 6 T. Best Foods mayonnaise (no other kind of mayonnaise)	½ c. walnuts, if desired

Allow 3 cups liquid for jello, including juice from pineapple. Combine all ingredients. Put in refrigerator to set. Serve on top of lettuce leaf if desired or in small cup at side of plate.

❦ CRANBERRY JELLO SALAD ❦
Randi VenHuizen

2 (3 oz.) pkgs. raspberry jello	2½ c. of hot water
1 (3 oz.) pkg. orange jello	1½ c. chopped nuts, divided
16 oz. can whole cranberries	8 oz. cream cheese
16 oz. can of crushed pineapple, drained, reserving the juice	

(continued)

121822-12

Mix all packages of jello, cranberries, pineapple and water well, reserving some of the nuts for later. Chill in a 9 x 13-inch pan. Mix cream cheese with reserved pineapple juice. Spread over jello. Sprinkle with leftover nuts. Cut in squares. Serve on lettuce leaf.

❦ CREAMY CAULIFLOWER LETTUCE SALAD ❦
Karen Anderson

1 head cauliflower	¼ c. grated Parmesan cheese
¾ c. Miracle Whip dressing	¼ c. sugar
½ c. ranch dressing	6 c. romaine lettuce
¼ c. chopped red onion	
6 oz. turkey bacon, cooked and crumbled	

Cut cauliflower into pieces. Mix dressings, onion, bacon, cheese and sugar in large bowl. Add remaining ingredients; mix lightly.

❦ CRUNCHY BROCCOLI SALAD ❦
Lisa Rieff

½ c. vegetable oil	1 pkg. ramen noodles
½ c. sugar	4 T. butter
¼ c. red wine vinegar	1 c. chopped walnuts
1½ tsp. soy sauce	1 bag romaine lettuce
Salt and pepper to taste	2 green onions, sliced
1 head broccoli	Grape tomatoes, small handful

Mix vegetable oil, sugar, red wine vinegar, soy sauce, salt and pepper in a blender or food processor to make dressing. Chop broccoli into bite size chunks. Marinate broccoli in the dressing for several hours. Break ramen noodles apart. Melt butter in pan and brown noodles and walnuts. Lay out on paper towels to drain. Assemble salad with lettuce, green onions, tomatoes, walnuts and noodles. Pour dressing and broccoli on top and toss.

❦ DEANO'S MACARONI SALAD ❦
Debra Gillespie

Shell macaroni, vary amount
  by size needed
Cucumbers
Carrots
Green peppers
Tomatoes
Radishes
Miracle Whip salad dressing
Salt and pepper to taste

Bring water to a boil in sauce pan; add a pinch of salt and shell macaroni. Cook macaroni until tender, approximately 10 minutes. Place macaroni in drainer and let cold water run over it until it cools, then drain macaroni again. Pour macaroni into large bowl. Clean and cut vegetables into small pieces. Combine vegetables with macaroni. Spoon a generous amount of Miracle Whip and salt and pepper to taste into the macaroni and vegetables. Stir well to blend all ingredients. Best to refrigerate one hour or more before serving. This recipe can be adjusted according to the number of people you will be serving. The vegetables stated in the recipe are my favorites, but you may use fewer or add other vegetables of your choosing.

❦ EASY GRAPE NUTTY COLESLAW ❦
Kathy Christiansen

Bag coleslaw mix or pre-
  shredded cabbage
¾ c. dried cranberries
4 T. chopped green onion
6 T. crumbled blue cheese
1½ c. poppyseed dressing
¼ c. Grape Nuts cereal

Toss first five ingredients together. Add grape nuts just before serving. TIP: if you want leftovers, add grape nuts only to the portion you are going to eat now, as they get soggy at some point.

❦ FIELD GREENS SALAD ❦
Shari Garder

Vinaigrette:

¼ c. sugar
¼ c. rice vinegar
1 T. black pepper
½ c. salad oil

(continued)

121822-12

On stove, over low heat, stir sugar, vinegar, and pepper until sugar is dissolved. Remove from heat and whisk in salad oil. Set aside.

Salad:

2 T. butter
2 T. sugar
½ c. chopped pecans
Equivalent of 1 lg. head -
  mixed lettuces, spinach, etc.

¼ c. sliced green onions
12 diced strawberries

Heat oven to 400°. Melt butter and blend in sugar. Toss in chopped pecans until coated. Roast in shallow pan for approximately 10 minutes. Cool. Toss lettuces, cooled pecans, onions, strawberries and vinaigrette. 6-8 servings.

❦ FRESH CRANBERRY SALAD ❦
Barb Haskins

1 bag fresh cranberries
1 can crushed pineapple,
  drained
1¼ c. sugar

1 c. or so chopped walnuts
1½ c. miniature marshmallows
8 oz. refrigerated whipped
  topping

Clean cranberries and chop fairly fine (use a chopper, not a blender). Add the pineapple, sugar, walnuts and miniature marshmallows. Put in a sealed container and refrigerate over night or longer. When ready to serve, stir in whipped topping, as much as needed. Keeps in the refrigerator for a couple of weeks or more. Serves 8 to 10.

❦ FROG EYE SALAD ❦
Connie Walther

8 oz. Acini De Pepe pasta
1 (15 oz.) can crushed
  pineapple
1 (15 oz.) can pineapple tidbits
½ c. sugar
1 T. flour
2 (11 oz.) cans mandarin
  oranges, drained

1 c. colored marshmallows
½ c. chopped maraschino
  cherries
1 (8 oz.) Cool Whip
Whole maraschino cherries,
  drained, for garnish

(continued)

Cook, drain and rinse pasta. Drain both pineapples and reserve juices. Blend sugar, flour and 1 c. reserved pineapple juice together and cook until thick. Cool slightly and add cooked pasta. Cool. Add fruit, marshmallows and chopped cherries and fold in whipped topping. Garnish with cherries.

❦ FROZEN CUCUMBER SALAD ❦
Julie Concannon

2 qt. sliced unpeeled sm. cucumbers	1 T. salt
2 med. onions, sliced (about 4 c.)	1 c. vinegar
	1¼ c. sugar

Combine cucumbers, onions and salt. Let mixture soak for 3 hours. In a saucepan, warm the vinegar and sugar; stir to dissolve sugar. Drain cucumbers and add to vinegar mixture. Ladle into plastic freezer containers and freeze. When ready to use, defrost and serve chilled. 1½ quarts. This is a great use of summer garden cucumbers and then you can enjoy them all winter long!

❦ GERMAN CUCUMBER SALAD ❦
(Gurkensalat)
Jody Manning

1 lg. cucumber	¼ c. sour cream
½ tsp. salt	1 T. chopped fresh parsley leaves
1 T. sugar	
1 T. white wine vinegar	

Peel cucumber, leaving some of the green rind. Slice very thinly. Mix salt and sugar into vinegar and marinate cucumber in this mixture for 30 minutes. Drain off liquid, mix in sour cream and serve sprinkled with parsley.

121822-12

❦ GERMAN POTATO SALAD ❦
Nancy Shinrock

1 c. diced bacon, cooked and
   set aside
1 c. chopped onion
1 c. chopped celery
3 T. flour
Salt

Black pepper
⅔ c. sugar
⅔ c. vinegar
1½ c. water
8 c. boiled potatoes, peeled and
   chopped

Brown onion and celery in ¼ c. bacon grease. Stir in flour, salt, pepper, sugar, vinegar, and water and then bring all to a boil. Pour over potatoes. Bake 30 minutes at 350°. Stir in diced bacon.

❦ GRAMMA BETTY'S MACARONI SALAD ❦
Shawn Lorenzen

1 lb. spiral macaroni, cooked
   and drained
1 green pepper, diced
4 - 5 carrots, grated
1 onion, chopped
1 can Spam, chopped

1 can sweetened condensed
   milk
¾ c. sugar
¼ c. white vinegar
2 c. Miracle Whip

Mix all ingredients. Let set overnight. Salt and pepper to taste.

❦ GRAPE NUT SALAD ❦
Cheyrle Badtke

¾ c. Grape Nuts
2 bananas, sliced
2 oranges, cut up

½ c. sugar
1½ c. whipped cream or Cool
   Whip

Put Grape Nuts in a bowl, slice bananas and cut up oranges on top. Put sugar on top, set in refrigerator. Just before serving, stir in 1 to 1½ cups whipped cream or Cool Whip. The juice from the oranges and sugar keep the bananas from turning brown.

❧ LOU ANN'S RED JELLO ❧
Debra Gillespie

1 (16 oz.) can crushed pineapple	1 (3 oz.) pkg. raspberry jello
¾ c. white sugar	1 can cherry pie filling
1 T. cornstarch	3 or 4 bananas, sliced
	½ c. walnuts, chopped

In saucepan combine pineapple (do not drain), sugar and cornstarch. Cook until it boils hard for 1 minute. Add jello and mix well. Let cool some and then stir in pie filling. Pour into pretty glass bowl. Allow to set up partially then stir in bananas and nuts. Refrigerate several hours before serving.

❧ LOVE THAT SALAD! ❧
Marilyn Thomsen
Ruth Manning

12-25-12
good.

Salad:

2 c. shredded red cabbage	¾ c. chopped celery
1 c. frozen small peas (thawed and drained)	1 lg. red apple, unpeeled and cut up
1 can sliced water chestnuts	¼ tsp. salt
¼ c. sliced green onion	

Mix all salad ingredients.

Dressing:

½ c. sour cream	1 c. shredded sharp Cheddar cheese
½ c. mayonnaise	1 c. chopped pecans
1 tsp. sugar	

Within 1 hour of serving, mix sour cream, mayonnaise and sugar together and add to vegetable mixture. Just before serving, add cheese and pecans.

❦ MAGGIE'S FRUIT SALAD ❦
Dayla Miller

1 can peach pie filling
1 can pineapple chunks, drained

2 sm. or 1 lg. can mandarin oranges, drained
1 sm. bag frozen strawberries

Combine all and let set 1 hour or overnight.

❦ MANDARIN ORANGE SALAD ❦
Heidi Meyer

Salad:

½ c. slivered almonds
2 T. sugar
1 stalk romaine lettuce
1 c. celery, finely chopped

4 green onions, chopped
1 (11 oz.) can mandarin oranges, drained

Place almonds and 2 T. sugar in a frying pan. Stir constantly over medium heat to caramelize the almonds. Remove to foil, cool, and break apart. Mix lettuce, celery, onions, mandarin oranges, and caramelized almonds in a salad bowl.

Dressing:

¼ c. oil
2 T. sugar

2 T. vinegar
1 pinch salt

Stir together oil, sugar, vinegar, and salt to make dressing. Add desired amount of dressing to salad.

❦ MUSHROOM SALAD ❦
Marjorie Keiser

1 lb. fresh mushrooms, sliced
12 oz. shredded Swiss cheese
1 bunch green onions, sliced, including some green tops (I use onion powder if I don't have fresh onions)

½ c. oil
¼ c. wine vinegar
1½- 2 T. Cavander's Greek spice (found in spice section of grocery store)

(continued)

Toss the mushrooms, Swiss cheese and green onions together. Shake together the oil, vinegar and Greek spice and pour over mushroom mixture shortly before serving. People often think the cheese is noodles.

❦ ORANGE ASPIC SALAD ❦
Heidi Meyer

2 sm. pkgs. orange jello or 1
  lg. pkg.
2 c. boiling water

1 sm. can frozen orange juice
1¼ c. cold water
1 sm. can crushed pineapple

Dissolve jello in boiling water. Add frozen orange juice and dissolve. Add cold water. Add crushed pineapple. Refrigerate.

❦ ORANGE TAPIOCA SALAD ❦
Pat Brewer

3 c. water
3 oz. box tapioca pudding
  (cook and serve variety)
3 oz. box vanilla pudding
  (cook and serve variety)

3 oz. box orange jello
8 oz. Cool Whip
Lg. can mandarin oranges,
  well drained
2 c. small marshmallows

Put water in saucepan, bring to boil and add tapioca pudding, vanilla pudding and orange jello. Boil for 3 minutes. Mix well. Let cool completely. Fold in Cool Whip, mandarin oranges and marshmallows. Refrigerate at least 4 hours. Can be made the night before serving.

❦ ORIENTAL SALAD ❦
Shari Garder

Dressing:

½ c. salad oil
6 T. red wine vinegar
¼ c. sugar

Chicken flavor packet from
  soup

Combine all ingredients and mix well. Chill.

(continued)

121822-12

Salad:

1 pkg. broccoli slaw
1 bunch green onion, sliced
3 boneless chicken breasts,
   grilled and cut up

½ oz. sesame seeds
1 pkg. slivered almonds
1 pkg. ramen soup mix,
   chicken flavor

Mix slaw, onion, and chicken in large bowl. Toss with dressing. Chill. Toast sesame seeds, almonds, and noodles (dry and broken) until light brown at 300° for 10 minutes. Add toasted ingredients just before serving.

❦ PEA AND PEANUT SALAD ❦
Rose Roberts

2 boxes frozen baby peas,
   thawed
1 (8 oz.) sour cream
2 c. chopped celery
1 - 2 T. green onion, chopped

2 tsp. Beaumonde seasoning
1 lb. bacon, cooked, drained
   and crumbled
1 c. dry roasted peanuts

Mix peas, sour cream, celery, green onion and seasoning. Add bacon and peanuts when ready to eat.

❦ PEA SALAD ❦
Christie Klos

1 (10 oz.) pkg. frozen peas
3 hard boiled eggs, chopped
4 green onions, chopped
¾ c. mayonnaise

2 oz. pimento
½ c. celery, chopped
½ c. shredded Cheddar cheese
½ tsp. salad seasoning

Mix all ingredients and let stand 24 hours.

❦ POPPY SEED DRESSING ❦
Lisa Rieff

1 c. sugar
1½ tsp. dry mustard
1¼ tsp. salt
½ tsp. onion powder

⅔ c. red wine vinegar
1½ c. vegetable oil
1 T. poppy seeds

(continued)

In blender or food processor, combine sugar, mustard, salt, onion powder and vinegar. Drizzle in oil while mixing until blended. Stir in poppy seeds. Refrigerate at least one hour before using. Keeps for 7-10 days in refrigerator.

❦ PRETZEL SALAD ❦
Brenda Mac

2½ c. crushed pretzels
¾ c. melted butter
3 T. sugar
8 oz. cream cheese
½ c. sugar

3 c. Cool Whip
2 (3 oz.) pkgs. strawberry jello
2 c. boiling water
2 (10 oz.) pkgs. frozen strawberries

Mix crushed pretzels, butter and 3 tablespoons sugar and press into 9 x 13-inch pan. Bake 10 minutes at 350°. Blend cream cheese and ½ cup sugar; add in Cool Whip. Spread over cooled pretzel crust. Dissolve jello with water and add strawberries. Pour over Cool Whip mixture-- make sure edges are sealed with Cool Whip mixture before gently adding jello mixture. Place in refrigerator for 4-6 hours before serving.

❦ QUICK SALAD ❦
Jill Hild

1 (16 oz.) container small curd cottage cheese
1 can fruit cocktail or crushed pineapple

1 pt. whipped topping
1 (3 oz.) pkg. lemon jello (or other flavor)

Combine cottage cheese, fruit and whipped topping. Sprinkle jello over the top, mix well. Refrigerate until set.

❦ RASPBERRY APPLESAUCE SALAD ❦
Jill Hild

2 sm. pkgs. raspberry jello
2¼ c. water
1 box frozen raspberries

¼ c. lemon juice
2 c. applesauce
Cool Whip

(continued)

121822-12

Dissolve jello in boiling water. Add raspberries and lemon juice, allow to thicken. Stir in applesauce. Frost with Cool Whip.

❦ RASPBERRY CRANBERRY JELLO SALAD ❦
Kathy Christiansen

2 lg. pkgs. raspberry jello
4 c. water
1 lg. can crushed pineapple
2 (16 oz.) cans whole cranberry sauce
⅔ - 1 c. chopped walnuts

Dissolve jello into 4 cups boiling water, add undrained pineapple and undrained cranberry sauce; mix well. Chill until partially set, then add walnuts and pour into 9 x 13-inch dish or jello mold. Chill until set. This recipe can be easily halved and made in a 9 x 9-inch pan. Optional: Top with whipped topping and a few extra chopped nuts before serving.

❦ RED AND WHITE JELLO SALAD ❦
Shirley Schuchard

2 pkgs. cherry jello
2 c. boiling water
1 pkg. frozen strawberries, partially thawed
4 bananas, mashed
1 sm. can pineapple, undrained
1 pt. sour cream
1 c. cashews

This recipe needs to be prepared and served on the same day. Combine jello and water. Add strawberries, bananas and pineapple. Put 4 cups of mixture in glass bowl. Refrigerate until set. Frost with sour cream and cashews. Pour remaining jello mixture on top and refrigerate. Sometimes I just slice the bananas rather than mashing.

❦ "RED HOTS" SALAD ❦
Mary Lou Gustafson

1 (20 oz.) can crushed pineapple
1 (6 - 9 oz.) pkg. Red Hots candy (movie candy box size works well)
1 (8 oz.) container Cool Whip
1 (10 oz.) bag mini marshmallows

(continued)

About 24 hours before serving, mix crushed pineapple (with juice) into bowl with the Red Hots. Stir occasionally. Shortly before serving mix in Cool Whip and marshmallows. This is a Pastor Brad and office favorite!

❦ ROTINI SALAD ❦
Cathy Aden

8 oz. rotini pasta, cooked and
  drained
½ c. chopped green pepper
¼ onion, chopped
2 grated carrots

½ c. evaporated milk
½ pt. mayonnaise
½ c. vinegar
¾ c. sugar
1 tsp. salt

Cool cooked, drained pasta. Mix in pepper, onion and carrots. Mix together evaporated milk, mayonnaise, vinegar, sugar and salt. Stir into pasta mixture. Let sit overnight.

❦ SHIRLEY'S PASTA SALAD ❦
Dayla Miller

1½ c. sugar
1 c. vinegar
½ c. oil
1 tsp. Accent
Salt and pepper to taste
1 tsp. garlic powder

1 pkg. mostaccioli, cooked
  according to pkg. directions
1 sm. onion, chopped
1 green pepper, chopped
Cucumber, chopped, if desired
1 T. parsley

Bring sugar and vinegar to boil in small pan until sugar is dissolved. Add remaining ingredients together in large bowl. Chill and serve.

❦ SNICKER APPLE SALAD ❦
Anne Yarger

1 (8 oz.) pkg. cream cheese
1 (7 oz.) jar marshmallow
  creme

1 (8 oz.) container Cool Whip
5 chopped apples
6 chopped Snickers bars

Mix cream cheese and marshmallow creme well with mixer. Stir in Cool Whip. Add apples and Snickers bars and refrigerate before serving.

121822-12

❦ SPINACH SALAD ❦
Lisa Meyer

9 oz. bag spinach
3 T. almond slices
½ c. Craisins
¼ sm. red onion, chopped

½ c. feta cheese crumbles
Poppyseed dressing (my favorite is Paul Newman's brand)

Tear spinach into smaller pieces. Mix all ingredients with spinach and pour dressing over it.

❦ STEAKHOUSE SALAD ❦
Marilyn Thomsen

Salad:

1 lb. macaroni
1 lg. green pepper, chopped

1 onion, chopped fine
4 carrots, shredded

Cook macaroni. Drain. Add green pepper, onion and carrots.

Dressing:

1 can condensed milk
1 c. vinegar
1 c. sugar

2 c. mayonnaise
1 tsp. salt
¼ tsp. pepper

Blend in separate container the condensed milk, vinegar, sugar, mayonnaise, salt and pepper. Toss dressing in salad. You may want to use ⅔ or ¾ of the dressing. Chill well, at least four hours, before serving.

❦ STRAWBERRY ORANGE PASTA SALAD ❦
Julie Concannon

2 c. farfalle (bow-tie pasta), uncooked
⅓ c. creamy poppyseed dressing
¼ c. mayonnaise

¼ c. sliced green onions, or more to taste
1 can (11 oz.) mandarin oranges, drained
1 c. sliced strawberries

Cook pasta as directed on package; drain. Cool. Mix dressing and mayonnaise in medium bowl. Add pasta and onions; toss to coat. Gently

(continued)

stir in mandarin oranges and strawberries. Serve immediately or cover and refrigerate until ready to serve. 4 servings, 1 cup each.

❦ STRAWBERRY PUDDING SALAD ❦
Mary Lou Gustafson

3 c. water
1 lg. box strawberry jello
1 sm. box vanilla tapioca
  pudding
1 sm. box vanilla pudding

10 oz. frozen strawberries
  (partially thawed)
1 (20 oz.) can crushed
  pineapple (drained)
1 (9 oz.) carton Cool Whip

In large sauce pan bring water to a boil. Add the jello, tapioca pudding and vanilla pudding. Cook for 5 minutes - DO NOT BOIL. Cool this mixture. Add partially thawed strawberries, drained pineapple and Cool Whip to the cooled ingredients. Mix and chill.

❦ STRAWBERRY/CRANBERRY JELLO SALAD ❦
Randi VenHuizen

1 lg. pkg. strawberry jello
1 pkg. frozen strawberries (the
  kind in the square box)
1 can whole cranberries

1 can crushed pineapple
1 smashed banana
1½ pt. sour cream

Make jello according to directions eliminating ½ cup of liquid. Thaw the frozen strawberries and then combine all of the fruit together including juices. Add the jello to the fruit mixture. Pour ½ of the jello-fruit mixture into a 9 x 13-inch pan. Place in refrigerator until the jello sets. Keep the remaining fruit out of the refrigerator. After ½ of the jello-fruit mixture sets, spread the sour cream over the mixture. Pour the remaining jello-fruit mixture over the sour cream. Place the pan back in the refrigerator until the entire dish sets. This is easy to do the night before. It is also easier than it looks and it tastes incredible.

121822-12

❦ SUNSHINE SALAD ❦
Connie Walther

2 (11 oz.) cans mandarin oranges
2 pkgs. sugar free orange jello, or 1 lemon & 1 orange jello
2 c. boiling water (include juice from mandarin oranges)

2 (6 oz.) cans frozen orange juice

Drain oranges and add water to make 2 cups liquid. Boil juice and water mixture and dissolve jello. Add frozen, undiluted orange juice to jello, stir until juice is thawed. Add oranges. Chill until set.

❦ SWEET BROCCOLI SALAD ❦
Debra Gillespie

Salad:

1 bunch broccoli, washed and diced
1 c. white raisins
1 c. sunflower seeds

10 strips bacon, fried crisp and crumbled
¼ c. red onion

In large bowl combine all salad ingredients. Toss well.

Salad Dressing:

½ c. Miracle Whip
3 to 4 T. sugar

1 T. white vinegar

Combine Miracle Whip, sugar and vinegar. Pour over salad and stir until well blended.

❦ TACO PASTA SALAD ❦
Deb Schuchard

2 c. pasta
1 can kidney beans
2 Roma tomatoes
1 c. salsa
2 c. French dressing

1 pkg. taco seasoning
½ onion, diced
1 cucumber, diced
1 lb. Cheddar cheese, diced

(continued)

Boil pasta according to package directions, drain and cool. Drain kidney beans and rinse. Dice tomatoes. Combine salsa and dressing with ½ package taco seasoning. Mix all ingredients together. Taste and if you want more of a taco flavor, add more taco seasoning. Chill 1 hour and serve. Enjoy.

❦ TACO SALAD ❦
Randi VenHuizen

1 lb. cooked ground beef,
  drain the fat
1 can kidney beans
2 - 3 chopped tomatoes
1 can black olives
2 avocados, chopped
Head of iceberg lettuce, torn

1 lb. grated Cheddar cheese
Tortilla chips
2 c. mayonnaise
1 bottle green taco sauce
½ tsp. lemon juice
½ tsp. vinegar

Mix together in large bowl the hamburger meat, kidney beans, chopped tomatoes, black olives, avocado, lettuce, cheese and tortilla chips. Mix together the mayonnaise, taco sauce, lemon juice and vinegar. Mix with other ingredients.

❦ THREE BEAN SALAD ❦
Rose Roberts

1 can green beans
1 can wax beans
1 can kidney beans
1 sm. onion, chopped
1 green pepper, cut into sm.
  pieces

½ c. celery, diced
¾ c. sugar
⅔ c. vinegar
⅓ c. oil
Salt and pepper to taste

Drain green, wax and kidney beans. Mix all ingredients and let stand overnight in the refrigerator. You can use another type of beans such as black beans instead of the green or wax beans if desired.

❦ TORTELLINI SALAD ❦

Rose Roberts
Carol Jorgensen (LOL cookbook 1989)

1 (7 oz.) pkg. cheese tortellini
1 c. fresh broccoli florets
½ c. finely chopped parsley
Red pepper to taste
6 oz. jar marinated artichokes,
  undrained
2 green onions, chopped
2½ tsp. fresh basil or ¼ tsp.
  dried basil

½ tsp. garlic powder
Sliced ripe olives and whole
  for garnish
½ c. prepared light Italian
  dressing
Pepperoni slices*
5 - 6 cherry tomatoes
Parmesan cheese

Cook tortellini as package directs. Drain; rinse in cold water. Combine tortellini, broccoli, parsley, red pepper, artichokes, onions, basil, garlic powder, sliced olives, Italian dressing and pepperoni slices. Cover and refrigerate 4 to 6 hours. Garnish with tomato, cheese and whole olives. If refrigerating overnight, wait and add broccoli with tomatoes and cheese to prevent discoloration. *Chopped Canadian bacon or chopped ham can be substituted for the pepperoni slices if desired.

❦ TURKEY SALAD ❦

Shawn Lorenzen

¾ c. cooked turkey, diced
7 oz. shell macaroni, cooked
  and drained
1 c. diced celery
1 c. grated carrots
1 jar sliced green olives
1 bag sliced or slivered
  almonds

1½ c. Miracle Whip
2 tsp. yellow mustard
2 tsp. sugar
1 tsp. lemon juice
½ tsp. onion salt

Mix all ingredients together.

❦ UNDER THE SEA SALAD ❦
Shirley Schuchard

1 c. pineapple juice
3 oz. cream cheese, softened
2 sm. pkgs. lime jello, divided
16 marshmallows

1 pkg. Dream Whip
1 cup nuts, chopped
Pineapple juice, enough to
    prepare 2nd lime jello

Bring to boil 1 c. pineapple juice. Add the softened cream cheese (cut up), 1 package lime jello and marshmallows. Heat until melted. Cool until slightly thickened. Fold in Dream Whip and nuts. Pour into mold. Chill until set. Prepare second package of lime jello using pineapple juice instead of water. Pour over top to make clear green layer.

❦ WALDORF COLESLAW ❦
Nancy Shinrock

1 c. dairy sour cream
1 T. sugar
1 tsp. lemon juice
½ tsp. salt
1 red apple, chopped and
    placed in lemon juice

6 c. shredded cabbage
20 oz. can pineapple chunks,
    drained
1 c. red grapes
⅓ c. chopped walnuts

Mix sour cream, sugar, lemon juice, and salt. Drain apples. Combine apples, cabbage, pineapple, grapes, and walnuts. Stir in sour cream mixture.

❦ WHIPPED JELLO ❦
Rose Roberts
May Monsoon
Inez Baldwin

3 sm. boxes lime jello
3 c. boiling water
3 c. cold water (use pineapple
    juice to make up the total
    amt. needed)

1 c. crushed pineapple,
    drained
1 c. cottage cheese (1 c. grated
    cheese can be used instead)
1 c. Cool Whip

Dissolve jello in the boiling water. Add cold water/pineapple juice. Let set until it thickens. Add the crushed pineapple, cottage cheese and Cool Whip. Set overnight.

121822-12

SOUP

❧ BAKED STEW ❧
Lisa Meyer

3 lg. potatoes, peeled and
  cubed
6 carrots, cut in chunks
1 c. celery, chopped
2 lb. can diced tomatoes
3 T. tapioca
2 lbs. stew meat, cut up and
  browned

1 med. onion, chopped
1½ tsp. salt
¼ c. quick cook barley
1 tsp. Accent
Beef broth (I usually use 3-4
  sm. cans)

Mix all ingredients together and bake in covered casserole or roaster
pan at 250° for 5 hours.

❧ BARBEQUE CHILI ❧
Connie Walther
Rachel Ray

1½ lb. lean ground beef or
  stew beef
2 med. onions, chopped
1 can beer
1 jar chili sauce

1 can chopped tomatoes with
  lime and cilantro
2 c. vegetable juice
1 - 2 cans chili beans
1 T. brown sugar

Brown beef and onion. Drain. Add remaining ingredients. Stir well
and simmer for 30 minutes. You can also make this in a crock pot.
Serve with corn bread and salad. Works well to use left-overs on pasta.

🍎 BASQUE POTATO SOUP 🍎
Pauline Shaffer

1 lb. Italian sausage
½ c. chopped onion
2 (16 oz.) cans tomatoes
4 c. cubed potatoes
¼ c. fresh parsley
1 c. chopped celery
3 T. celery tops

1½ c. water
1 (12 oz.) can tomato juice
2 beef bouillon cubes
2 bay leaves
¾ tsp. dried leaf thyme
Salt and pepper to taste
1 T. lemon juice

If using link sausage, take off the casing. Brown sausage in Dutch oven. Pour off excess grease. Add remaining ingredients and simmer for 45 minutes. Good served with crusty bread.

🍎 BUTTERNUT SQUASH SOUP 🍎
Rose Roberts

1 butternut squash, peeled
2 T. unsalted butter
1 onion, chopped
3 - 4 stalks celery, chopped

6 c. chicken stock or use
  Knorr Leek Soup
Nutmeg
Salt and pepper

Cut squash into 1-inch chunks. In large pot melt butter. Add onion and celery and cook until translucent, about 8 minutes. Add squash and stock. Bring to a simmer and cook until squash is tender. Remove squash chunks with slotted spoon and place in a blender and purée. Return blended squash to pot. Stir and season with nutmeg, salt and pepper as desired.

🍎 CAMPFIRE STEW 🍎
Judy Egr

2 lbs. ground beef
Minced onion
2 cans vegetarian vegetable
  soup

Grands biscuits

Cook hamburger and drain. Add onion and soup. Add ½ can of water for each can of soup. Stir until bubbly. Serve over Grands biscuits. Sounds lame, but it is really good and easy!

❦ CAPE COD FISH CHOWDER ❦
Harry Naasz

1 lg. onion, chopped
4 T. butter
3 potatoes, diced
2 tsp. salt
¼ tsp. pepper

2 c. water
1 pkg. haddock or cod
1 can corn
1 tall can evaporated milk

Sauté onion in butter, add potatoes, salt, pepper and water. Bring to a full boil, reduce heat, cover and simmer for 15 minutes. Place fish on top of potatoes. Cover and simmer for another 15 minutes. Stir in corn and milk. Heat just to boiling.

❦ CHEATER CHILI ❦
Lisa Rieff

1 ¼ lb. ground beef
15 oz. can whole tomatoes
15 oz. can Hormel Chili with beans
15 oz. can Hormel Chili, no beans

16 oz. jar Pace picante sauce (mild to hot depending on your taste)

Cook and drain ground beef. Pour tomatoes with juice from the can into stockpot or crockpot. Pull the tomatoes apart with your fingers so they are small but still chunky. Add beef and remaining ingredients and mix. Heat and serve. Makes about 5-6 servings.

❦ CHEDDAR CHOWDER ❦
Amy Kragnes

2 cans chicken broth
4 baking potatoes, peeled and diced
1 onion, chopped
1 c. shredded carrots
1 green and 1 red pepper, seeded and chopped

¼ c. butter
⅓ c. flour
1 pt. half and half
1 ½ c. milk
16 oz. shredded sharp Cheddar cheese
⅛ - ¼ tsp. hot sauce

Combine broth, potatoes, onion, carrots, and peppers in large soup pot. Bring to a boil, reduce heat and simmer for 15 minutes. Melt butter

(continued)

in large saucepan; add flour and stir until smooth. Cook for 1 minute, stirring constantly. Gradually add half and half and milk; cook over medium heat and stir constantly until mixture thickens. Combine with vegetable mixture; add cheese and hot sauce and cook just until thoroughly blended; do not boil. Serves 6-8.

❧ CHEESE TORTELLINI SOUP WITH CANNELLONI AND SPINACH ❧
Ruth Manning

2 T. olive oil
½ onion, diced
4 cloves garlic, minced
1 T. fresh thyme, chopped
¼ tsp. dried crushed red pepper
6 c. chicken broth

8 oz. pkg. cheese tortellini
9 oz. fresh spinach leaves, about 5 c.
1 (15 oz.) can cannelloni beans, rinsed and drained
½ c. Parmesan cheese

Heat oil in large pot over medium high heat; add the onion, garlic, thyme and red pepper flakes. Sauté until the onion softens and the flavors meld together, about 3 minutes. Add the chicken broth, raise the heat to high and bring to a boil. Stir in the tortellini and cook for 4 minutes. Reduce heat to simmer and add the spinach and cannelloni beans. Continue to simmer until the spinach has wilted and the pasta is tender, about 1 minute. Ladle soup into bowls. Serve with Parmesan cheese on the side.

❧ CHICKEN ENCHILADA SOUP ❧
Karen Anderson

1 can fat free refried beans
1 can chicken broth
1 can black beans, rinsed and drained
1 can Mexicorn, drained

1 can Rotel tomatoes
1 - 2 lb. chicken, cooked; cubed or shredded
Shredded cheese
Crunchy tortilla strips

Combine all ingredients except shredded cheese and tortilla strips in a pan. Bring to a boil and then simmer at least 20 minutes. Garnish with shredded cheese and crunchy tortilla strips. Makes 7 cups. Best if you let it sit in the refrigerator overnight.

🦃 CHICKEN NOODLE SOUP 🦃
Karen Anderson

2 - 3 chicken breasts
3 c. water
3 chicken bouillon cubes
1 tsp. salt

1½ c. dry noodles
1 (10 oz.) can cream of
  chicken soup
1 (10 oz.) can water

Cook chicken breasts. In a 2 quart saucepan combine 3 cups water, bouillon and salt. Bring to boil. Add dry noodles. Reduce heat to low; stir occasionally until noodles are swelled. In another pan; mix soup and chicken, gradually adding 10 ounces of water. Stir until smooth. Add to broth and noodles. Simmer ½ to 1 hour.

🦃 CHICKEN RICE SOUP 🦃
Shari Garder

1 lb. chicken breasts
2 qt. water
½ c. celery
½ c. onion
1 c. regular rice
1 stick margarine

1 c. flour
½ gallon milk
¼ c. chicken paste (or 15
  chicken cubes)
Pepper to taste

This is a three pan project. In pan one boil 1 lb. chicken breasts until done. Cut up into bite size pieces. In large pot combine water, celery and onion, cook until tender. Add rice, cooking until ¾ done. In a large pan melt margarine. Stir in flour. Slowly add milk, whip with whisk. Pour into large pot and simmer. Add chicken paste, cut up chicken, and pepper. Serve.

❦ COMFORTING CHICKEN NOODLE SOUP ❦
Julie Concannon

2 qt. water
8 chicken bouillon cubes
6½ c. uncooked wide egg
  noodles
2 cans (10¾ oz. each)
  condensed cream of chicken
  soup, undiluted

3 c. cubed cooked chicken
1 c. sour cream
Minced fresh parsley

In a large saucepan, bring water and bouillon to a boil. Add noodles; cook, uncovered, until tender, about 10 minutes. Do not drain. Add soup and chicken; heat through. Remove from the heat; stir in the sour cream. Sprinkle with minced parsley. 10-12 servings (about 2½ quarts). This is best prepared and eaten right away. If it sits on the stove for a long period of time, it thickens greatly. It is good leftover, but will be very, very thick. I have also prepared this with 98% fat free cream of chicken soup, undiluted, and light sour cream and have liked it just as much.

❦ CORN CRAB CHOWDER ❦
Debra Gillespie
Robin Price (Debra's daughter)

2 T. butter
2 T. olive oil
1 onion, diced
4 cloves fresh garlic, diced
6 sprigs fresh thyme, leaves
  only, chopped
6 c. vegetable stock
1 c. celery, diced
1 c. carrots, diced

¼ c. flour to coat vegetables
½ c. mushrooms, diced
16 oz. pkg. frozen corn
1 lg. can jumbo crab meat
2 c. heavy cream
3 red potatoes, diced
1 can diced green chilies
¼ c. parsley leaves, chopped
Salt and pepper to taste

Heat butter and olive oil in soup pot. Add onion, garlic and thyme and sauté 8 to 10 minutes. Pour vegetable stock into pot, then coat celery and carrots with flour and place in pot. Add mushrooms, corn and crab meat. Bring to boil. Add cream and potatoes and bring to boil again until potatoes are softened. Add chilies, parsley, salt and pepper. Let

(continued)

121822-12

simmer 15 minutes. Turn heat off and let soup rest a few hours. Heat again to serve. Serves 6-8.

❦ CREAM OF BROCCOLI SOUP WITH WHITE WINE ❦
Rose Roberts

1 head broccoli, stem and all
  (peel the stem)
2 carrots, peeled
2 stalks celery
1 med. potato, peeled
1 med. yellow cooking onion,
  peeled
4 T. butter

1 c. white wine (leftovers are
  fine)
6 c. chicken or vegetable stock
1 T. dried oregano
1 tsp. dried thyme
Salt and freshly ground black
  pepper
1 pt. half and half (optional)

Roughly chop broccoli, carrots, celery, potato and onion. In your largest pot over medium heat, add butter and vegetables and cook for approximately 15 minutes or until veggies start to show signs of browning. Stir occasionally. Add wine to pot, reduce heat to low and let simmer for five minutes. Add stock, oregano and thyme. Cover with a lid and simmer for 30 minutes. Allow soup to cool, then purée in a blender or food processor. Be forewarned, if you attempt to purée before the soup has cooled down, the top of the blender will blow and you will have a green kitchen. Season to taste with salt and pepper. To serve, add approximately 2 tablespoons of cream per serving and reheat to a gentle simmer. Adding the cream at the reheating stage, rather than during the initial preparation, extends the refrigerator life of the soup. 6-8 servings.

🍎 DANIEL'S FAVORITE CREAM OF POTATO SOUP 🍎
Julie Concannon

12 c. cubed potatoes
4 c. rough chopped carrots
  (bite size)
12 slices bacon, cooked and
  crumbled, reserve drippings
1½ c. chopped onion
2 c. chopped celery

3 tsp. salt
½ tsp. pepper
6 c. whole milk
6 c. half and half
Shredded sharp Cheddar
  cheese

Cook potatoes and carrots in boiling water until ALMOST tender in a very large stock pot. Sauté bacon until crisp, drain and crumble. Sauté onion and celery in 2 tablespoons reserved bacon fat. Combine all ingredients EXCEPT Cheddar cheese. Simmer 30 minutes. DO NOT BOIL. Top individual servings with cheese. I like to prepare this the day before I plan to serve it. After it is prepared, I let it cool and then refrigerate. Before serving, I warm it back up being careful to not let it boil. I just think the flavors are even better when done this way. Leftovers are fantastic! 24 (1 cup) servings.

🍎 EASY BROCCOLI CHEESE SOUP 🍎
Susan Lueders

8 c. water
4 - 6 chicken bouillon cubes
6 potatoes, peeled and cubed
2 carrots, peeled and sliced
1 onion, diced

3 cloves garlic, minced
1 (16 oz.) bag frozen broccoli
2 cans cream of chicken soup
2 lbs. Velveeta cheese, cubed

In large pot with water and bouillon cubes, cook vegetables until tender. Reduce heat to simmer. Add cream of chicken soup and Velveeta cheese. Simmer until cheese melts and soup is heated throughout. Additions to the soup can include 2 cups diced ham. Frozen broccoli and cauliflower can also be used.

121822-12

❦ FRENCH ONION SOUP ❦
Connie Walther

1 lb. sweet onions, sliced thin
¼ c. margarine
½ tsp. dry mustard
2 tsp. flour
4 c. beef stock or consomme'
½ c. white wine
French bread, sliced
Shredded Parmesan cheese
Shredded Swiss cheese

Sauté onions in margarine for 2-3 minutes. Add mustard, flour, beef stock and wine. Pour into individual dishes and top with a slice of bread, ¼ c. grated Parmesan cheese and Swiss cheese. Broil a few minutes until slightly brown and bubbly.

❦ GARDEN CHEESE SOUP ❦
Lynnette Nore

1 c. raw potatoes (¼-inch cubes)
½ c. chopped onion
½ c. chopped celery
2 c. California blend frozen broccoli, carrots and cauliflower
14 oz. chicken broth
1 can cream of mushroom soup
½ lb. cubed Velveeta cheese

Cook the potatoes, onions, celery, California blend, chicken broth and mushroom soup until potatoes are cooked. Add ½ pound cubed Velveeta cheese. Keep heat on low and watch so cheese doesn't burn.

❦ HAMBURGER SOUP ❦
Randi VenHuizen

1 lb. lean ground beef
1 lg. chopped onion
2 cloves of garlic
1 c. chopped celery
1 (16 oz.) can tomatoes, cut up
1 c. pared potatoes with skin on
1 c. coarsely chopped cabbage
1 c. sliced carrots
1 c. diced zucchini
1 can beef broth
2 beef bouillon cubes
1 tsp. salt
½ tsp. pepper
½ tsp. oregano
¼ tsp. sage
1 c. water

(continued)

Brown ground beef with onion and garlic. Drain fat. Add all other ingredients. Simmer for 55 minutes or until vegetables are cooked.

❦ HEARTY CHIPOTLE CHICKEN SOUP ❦
Karen Armitage
Taste of Home

1 lg. onion, chopped
1 T. canola oil
4 garlic cloves, minced
4 c. reduced-sodium chicken broth
2 (15 oz.) cans pinto beans, rinsed and drained
2 (14.5 oz.) cans fire-roasted diced tomatoes, undrained
3 c. frozen corn

2 chipotle peppers in adobo sauce, seeded and minced
2 tsp. adobo sauce
1 tsp. ground cumin
¼ tsp. pepper
2 c. cubed cooked chicken breast
½ c. fat-free sour cream
¼ c. minced fresh cilantro

In a Dutch oven, sauté onion in oil until tender. Add garlic; cook 1 minute longer. Add the broth, beans, tomatoes, corn, chipotle peppers, adobo sauce, cumin and pepper. Bring to a boil. Reduce heat; simmer, uncovered, for 20 minutes. Stir in chicken; heat through. Garnish each serving with sour cream; sprinkle with cilantro.

❦ HEARTY ITALIAN SOUP ❦
Julie Concannon

1 lb. mild bulk Italian pork sausage
½ c. chopped green pepper
½ c. chopped onion
28 oz. can diced tomatoes
2 (8 oz.) cans tomato sauce
16 oz. water

1 T. instant chicken bouillon or 3 cubes
½ tsp. garlic powder
¾ c. small shaped macaroni, such as rings or shells
Shredded Cheddar cheese

In a large saucepan, brown sausage, green pepper and onion; drain. Stir in tomatoes, tomato sauce, water, chicken bouillon and garlic powder. Cover; simmer 15 minutes. Stir in macaroni, cover and simmer 10-12 minutes or until macaroni is tender. Top individual servings with cheese. 6 (1⅓ cup) servings. I make this in the crock pot occasionally but I do not add the macaroni until about 1 hour before serving.

121822-12

❦ LEEK AND POTATO SOUP ❦
Marilyn Thomsen

2 - 3 leeks, washed and
   chopped
1 onion, chopped
1 - 2 garlic cloves, minced
1 - 2 T. olive oil
7 - 10 potatoes, chopped

Chicken stock
1 tsp. thyme
Milk or half and half
Instant potatoes
Salt and pepper to taste

Sauté leeks, onion and garlic in olive oil until just starting to brown. Add potatoes and chicken stock to barely cover, approximately 4 cups. Cook until potatoes are done. Mash potatoes and add thyme and milk to desired creaminess. Add instant potato to desired consistency. Add salt and pepper to taste. I usually add part of the salt with the leeks and again with the potatoes and just adjust at this point. Serve with favorite toppings like bacon bits, Cheddar cheese, chives or green onions.

❦ MINESTRONE SOUP ❦
Rose Roberts
Mildred Nuetzman

1 clove garlic, minced
1 c. celery, chopped
1 c. onion, chopped
2 T. cooking oil
2 c. tomatoes
2 qt. canned chicken stock
1½ c. water
1 c. chopped cabbage
1 c. frozen peas
1 c. diced carrots
2 sm. zucchini, sliced

1 tsp. Worcestershire sauce
1 tsp. soy sauce
1 bay leaf
¼ tsp. thyme
1 tsp. marjoram
½ tsp. pepper
1½ tsp. salt
1 (10 oz.) pkg. frozen baby
   lima beans
1 can red beans
1 c. spiral macaroni

Cook garlic, celery and onion in oil in a large kettle. Stir in tomatoes, chicken stock, water, cabbage, peas, carrots, zucchini, Worcestershire sauce, soy sauce, bay leaf, thyme, marjoram, pepper and salt. Bring to a boil, cover and simmer for 1 hour. Add beans and macaroni and cook 15 minutes longer. Remove bay leaf before serving. Leftover roast beef is also good in the soup. This is the recipe I use at preschool when we make Stone Soup. Don't forget to add the stone.

❦ MOM'S BEEFY VEGETABLE SOUP ❦

Julie Concannon

1½ lbs. boneless beef chuck cut into bite sized pieces
2 med. onions, lg. chopped (3½ - 4 c.)
3 celery stalks, sliced
Salt and pepper to taste
1 (28 oz.) can petite diced tomatoes
4 cans reduced sodium beef broth
4 c. water
⅓ c. reduced sodium soy sauce
¼ tsp. dried thyme leaves
½ tsp. salt
1 lb. carrots, sliced
4 c. pared, cubed potatoes
2 cans green beans, drained
½ tsp. Tabasco sauce

Brown beef, onions, celery with some salt and pepper in large stock pot sprayed with nonstick spray. Add remaining ingredients to stock pot, bring to a boil and then reduce heat and cook all day on medium to medium low heat. This makes too much to fit in my crock pot! 24 (1 cup) servings. I generally purchase 2 pounds beef chuck, trim it very well and end up with about 1½ pounds to use in the recipe.

❦ NO LONGER RUTH'S WHITE CHILI ❦

Amy Kragnes

1 T. olive oil
1 sm. onion, chopped
1 - 2 cloves garlic, minced
1 chopped jalapeño pepper, no seeds, or any mild pepper
½ - 1 tsp. cumin, to taste
1 tsp. oregano
¼ tsp. cayenne pepper
2 cans white kidney beans (or great northern)
2 c. chopped, cooked chicken breasts
2 cans chicken broth
1 c. water
3 c. grated Colby Jack cheese, divided

Heat oil in soup pot. Add onion and sauté 3 or 4 minutes, or until translucent. Stir in garlic, peppers, cumin, oregano, and cayenne pepper and sauté 2 minutes. Add beans, chicken, broth, and water and bring to boil. Reduce heat and let simmer 20 minutes. Add 2 c. cheese and stir until it melts. Season with salt and pepper to taste. Serve chili with remaining cheese. This was originally Ruth Manning's recipe from the 1997 cookbook, but this is milder and more like soup.

❦ POTATO & HAM CHOWDER ❦
Dayla Miller

1 (5 oz.) pkg. scalloped
  potatoes
1 c. cooked diced ham
4 c. chicken broth
1 c. diced celery

½ c. diced onion
½ tsp. pepper
2 c. half and half
⅓ c. flour

Mix potatoes, sauce packet from potatoes, ham, broth, celery, onion and pepper in crock pot. Cook on low 7 hours. Mix half and half and flour, gradually stir into chowder until well blended. Cover and cook on low for 1 hour until thickened and vegetables are tender. Stir occasionally.

❦ SAUSAGE CORN CHOWDER ❦
Kathy Christiansen

1 lb. bulk pork sausage (i.e.,
  Jimmy Dean's)
1 c. chopped onion
4 c. cubed peeled potatoes (½-
  inch cubes)
2 c. water
1 tsp. salt

½ tsp. dried marjoram
⅛ tsp. pepper
1 can (15¼ oz.) whole kernel
  corn, drained
1 can (14¾ oz.) cream-style
  corn
1 can (12 oz.) evaporated milk

In a Dutch oven or soup kettle, cook sausage and onion over medium heat until meat is no longer pink; drain. Add the potatoes, water, salt, marjoram and pepper. Bring to a boil. Reduce heat; cover and simmer for 15 minutes or until potatoes are just tender. Add the corn, cream-style corn and milk; heat through.

❦ SEAFOOD CHOWDER ❦
Lisa Rieff
Pampered Chef

4-5 med. red potatoes (about 1 lb.)
1 T. butter
1 c. chopped onion
1 c. sliced carrots
1 c. sliced celery
1 c. diced red bell pepper
2 cans (6½ oz.) minced clams, drained, reserving juice for later
2 cans (14½ oz.) chicken broth
½ tsp. salt
¼ tsp. pepper
¾ c. flour
2 c. half and half
1 lb. bay scallops
1 lb. cooked med. shrimp, tails removed

Wash and cut potatoes into 1-inch cubes to measure 3 cups. Measure reserved clam juice. If it's not 1 cup, add a little water. Melt butter in large stockpot over medium heat. Add onion and cook 3 minutes. Add potatoes, carrots, celery, peppers, clam juice, broth, and seasonings. Bring to a boil, cover, reduce heat to light boil and cook 4-7 minutes until potatoes are tender. Meanwhile place flour in small bowl. Gradually whisk in half and half until smooth. Add clams, scallops and shrimp. Gradually add in flour mixture. Return to boil and stir constantly for 2 minutes as mixture thickens. Remove from heat and cover until ready to serve.

❦ SHORT CUT VEGETABLE BEEF SOUP ❦
Lynnette Nore

1 lb. lean ground beef
¼ c. chopped onion
4 c. water
2 tsp. beef bouillon granules
1 can (15 oz.) diced tomatoes
1 pkg. (10 oz.) frozen mixed vegetables, thawed
½ c. uncooked small pasta (orzo or acine de pepe)
Salt and ground black pepper to taste

Brown beef and onion in large skillet. Drain, place in large saucepan or Dutch oven. Stir in water, beef bouillon, tomatoes, mixed vegetables, salt and pepper and uncooked pasta; bring to boil. Reduce heat, simmer covered, 10 minutes or until vegetables are tender. 6 servings.

❦ SWEET POTATO SOUP WITH CURRIED CHEESE CRISPS ❦
Amy Kragnes

2 lbs. sweet potatoes
3 green onions, coarsely
  chopped
1 (14-oz.) can chicken broth,
  divided
1 c. whipping cream

1 tsp. curry powder, divided
¼ tsp. salt
¼ tsp. pepper
2 oz. (½ c.) white Cheddar
  cheese, shredded
Paprika

Preheat oven to 425°. Pierce potatoes in several places with knife. Cook 10 minutes in microwave or until tender, turning once. Halve potatoes lengthwise. Hold with oven mitt; scoop flesh into food processor. Add onions and half the broth. Process until smooth. Transfer potatoes, cream, and remaining broth to large saucepan. Cook over medium-high heat, stirring occasionally, until heated through. Stir in ¾ tsp. curry powder and salt and pepper. Meanwhile, for crisps, lightly coat baking sheet with cooking spray. In small bowl toss cheese and ¼ tsp. curry powder. Evenly divide in 8 mounds, 2 inches apart, on baking sheet; flatten slightly. Bake 4 to 5 minutes, until melted and beginning to brown. Cool slightly; remove with metal spatula. Sprinkle with paprika. Makes 4 large servings; but it's a rich soup and is better in smaller servings as a side dish.

❦ TACO SOUP ❦
Pauline Shaffer

1 lb. ground beef
1 pkg. dry taco seasoning
1 pkg. dry ranch dressing
1 (15 oz.) can pinto beans
1 (15 oz.) can mild Mexican
  beans

1 (15 oz.) can stewed tomatoes
1 (15 oz.) can Mexican stewed
  tomatoes
1 (15 oz.) can corn

Brown ground beef with taco seasoning and ranch dressing in Dutch oven. Add beans, tomatoes and corn. Cook 1 hour. Serve with toppings of Cheddar cheese, sour cream and taco chips.

❦ V-8 VEGETABLE BEEF SOUP ❦
Kathy Christiansen
Sharon Christiansen

48 oz. tomato-vegetable juice cocktail (V-8 juice)

1 lb. browned and drained ground beef (can do the night before)

2 (16 oz.) pkgs. frozen mixed vegetables

Italian seasoning or basil, oregano, thyme (whatever is your preference)

Place all ingredients into pot or Dutch oven. Simmer for 30 minutes. When using crock pot, cook 1 hour on high, then lower heat to low and simmer 6-8 hours.

❦ WEST AFRICAN PEANUT SOUP ❦
Amy Kragnes

1 T. olive oil

1 onion, chopped (1 c.)

1 carrot, peeled and chopped

1 - 2 tsp. fresh ginger, peeled, minced OR

¼ tsp. ground ginger

¼ tsp. cayenne pepper

1 sweet potato, peeled and chopped (1 c.)

2½ c. water, divided

½ c. tomato sauce or juice

¼ tsp. salt

¼ tsp. pepper

½ c. creamy peanut butter

5 green onions, chopped

1 packet concentrated chicken broth (optional)

Heat olive oil in large saucepan. Stir in onions and carrots and cook, stirring often, until onions are soft, about 3 minutes. Add ginger and cayenne; cook 1 minute. Add sweet potato, 2 c. water, tomato sauce, salt, and pepper. Bring to a boil; reduce heat and simmer, stirring often, until potatoes are soft (about 20 minutes). Let cool slightly. Ladle soup into a food processor. Add peanut butter. Cover and process until smooth. Return to saucepan, add remaining ½ c. water. Add the concentrated chicken broth if desired, although then it will no longer be a vegetarian soup. Heat over low heat. Serve topped with green onions.

Slow Cooker Cooking

SLOW COOKER COOKING

❦ AU JUS SANDWICHES ❦
(Open Faced)
Connie Walther

3 - 5 lb. beef rump roast
¼ c. soy sauce
3 cloves garlic, minced
2 cans beef broth or 1 can
  broth and 1 can beer

Hoagie buns or French loaf,
  sliced
2 lg. onions, sliced
Provolone or Swiss cheese

Place roast in slow cooker with soy sauce, garlic and broth. Cook on low 8 hours. Slice meat very thin and serve on toasted hoagie buns or french loaf. Add onions and sliced/or grated cheese. Can serve with small individual au jus bowls, on the side.

❦ AUNT MARILYN'S BURRITOS ❦
Shawn Lorenzen

1 pork roast
1 beef roast
2 onions, chopped
1 (4 oz.) can chopped chili
  peppers

2 T. flour
2 tsp. cumin
Dash garlic powder

Cook both roasts, save the juice. Cool and shred. Sauté onions and peppers. Add flour, cumin and garlic powder to the roast juices. Mix all together and heat slowly, stirring occasionally.

❦ AUNT MARILYN'S TACOS ❦
Shawn Lorenzen

3 lbs. hamburger
6 (8 oz.) cans tomato sauce

6 green peppers
4 (or more) hot chili peppers

Combine all ingredients and cook several hours until not juicy, stirring occasionally.

❧ CHICKEN AND DUMPLINGS ❧
Lisa Rieff

4 - 5 chicken breasts
Salt and pepper
Chicken broth flavor boost
1 can cream of chicken soup
1 can cream of celery soup
3½ c. chicken broth
2 T. butter

½ c. carrots, chopped
½ c. celery, chopped
½ c. onion, chopped
1 pkg. powdered chicken
gravy
10 oz. can refrigerated biscuits

Salt and pepper chicken breasts and put in 6 quart crockpot. Add broth flavor boost, soups, broth, butter and vegetables. Cook on low 7-8 hours. Remove lid and shred chicken using a fork. Add some powdered chicken gravy, as little or as much as you want for thickness. Add biscuits after cutting each one into 6-8 pieces. Cook another hour.

❧ CHICKEN TACOS ❧
Kathy Christiansen
Sisters of the Cloth

2 lbs. boneless skinless chicken
breasts
1 envelope taco seasoning
1 can chicken broth

Taco shells or tortillas
Taco fixings: lettuce, cheese,
chopped tomatoes, sour
cream, guacamole, etc.

Put chicken breasts in crock pot. Sprinkle taco seasoning on, then add 1 can chicken broth. Cook on low for 8-10 hours. Shred chicken before serving. This is great in chicken tacos or can also be used for enchiladas.

❧ CHICKEN TORTILLA SOUP ❧
Judy Egr

4 boneless chicken breast
halves
2 (15 oz.) cans black beans,
undrained
2 (15 oz.) cans Mexican stewed
tomatoes or Rotel tomatoes

1 c. salsa
4 oz. can chopped green chilies
14½ oz. can tomato sauce
Tortilla chips
2 c. grated cheese, your choice

Combine all ingredients except chips and cheese in large crockpot. Cover and cook on low 8 hours. Just before serving, remove chicken

(continued)

121822-12

breasts and slice into bite size pieces. Stir into soup. To serve, put chips in each individual soup bowl. Ladle soup over chips. Top with cheese.

❧ CHILI ❧
Julie Concannon

2 lbs. 85/15 ground beef, browned and drained
2 (28 oz.) cans petite diced tomatoes

2 (8 oz.) cans tomato sauce
16 oz. water
Carroll Shelby's Chili Kit

Combine the ground beef, tomatoes, tomato sauce and water in crock pot. Add large spice packet and salt packet from chili kit (I do not use the mesa or cayenne packets but go ahead if you want!). Cook in crock pot on low all day and serve. We like to put Fritos in the bottom of individual bowls, top with chili and then shredded Cheddar cheese. Paul and I also like our chili with beans, the kids do not, so we add some drained red kidney beans to our bowls.

❧ CHILI ❧
Paula Foster

1 lb. hamburger or chili meat
1 (15.5 oz.) can red beans
1 (15.5 oz.) can chili beans
1 (15.5 oz.) can pinto beans
1 green pepper, diced
1 red pepper, diced
1 sm. onion, diced
¼ c. chili powder

1 T. cumin
1 tsp. cayenne powder
1 T. oregano
2 cans tomato sauce or 1 can tomato sauce and 2 c. fresh/ frozen tomatoes
2 tsp. garlic powder

Brown hamburger, drain grease. Add all other ingredients into crock pot. If you use fresh or frozen tomatoes, you might want to add a tablespoon of tomato paste if you like your chili less soupy. Cook on low for 5 to 6 hours or high 3 to 4 hours. Serve with shredded Cheddar cheese, sour cream, crackers, chopped onions, whatever the crowd likes!

❦ CLAUDE'S CHILI ❦
Claude Hall

1 lb. (73%) ground beef
1 med. onion, chopped
1 T. sugar
1 T. flour
3 T. chili powder

1 (16 oz.) can of Bush's hot
chili beans
1 (16 oz.) can of Hunt's whole
tomatoes
2 c. water

Fry hamburger and onion in frying pan. Add sugar, flour and chili powder to hamburger. Combine beans and tomatoes in crockpot. Mash them with a potato masher. Mix hamburger and onion into the crock pot. Stir in 2 c. water. Cook on high about an hour and then on low for an hour or so.

❦ COLA BBQ BEEF ❦
Kathy Christiansen

Chuck roast (2½ - 3 lbs.)
1 med. onion, chopped
¾ c. cola (NOT DIET)
¼ c. Worcestershire sauce
1 T. apple cider vinegar
2 cloves garlic, minced or
crushed

1 tsp. beef bouillon granules
½ tsp. dry mustard
½ - 1 tsp. chili powder
¼ - ½ tsp. ground red pepper
½ c. ketchup
2 T. butter or margarine
6 hamburger buns

Combine roast and chopped onion in slow cooker. Combine cola, Worcestershire, vinegar, garlic, bouillon, mustard, chili powder and red pepper; reserve ½ cup in refrigerator. Pour remaining mixture over roast and onion. Cover, cook on high 6 hours or until roast is very tender; drain and shred roast. Keep warm. Combine reserved ½ cup cola mixture, ketchup and butter in a small saucepan; cook mixture over medium heat, stirring constantly, just until thoroughly heated. Pour over shredded roast, stirring gently. Spoon onto buns and serve.

121822-12

🦃 CRANBERRY PORK TENDERLOIN 🦃
Julie Concannon

1 pork tenderloin (1 lb.)	1 T. brown sugar
1 can (16 oz.) whole-berry cranberry sauce	1 tsp. ground mustard
	¼ - ½ tsp. ground cloves
½ c. orange juice	2 T. cornstarch
¼ c. sugar	3 T. cold water

Place the tenderloin in a slow cooker. Combine the cranberry sauce, orange juice, sugars, mustard and cloves; pour over pork. Cover and cook on low for 5-6 hours or until a meat thermometer reads 160°. Remove pork and keep warm. In a small saucepan, combine cornstarch and cold water until smooth; stir in cranberry mixture. Bring to a boil; cook and stir for 2 minutes or until thickened. Serve with pork. 4 servings.

🦃 CROCK POT DRESSING 🦃
Cheyrle Badtke

1 c. butter or margarine	1 tsp. salt
½ c. chopped onion	1 tsp. sage
2 c. chopped celery	½ tsp. pepper
13 - 14 c. dried bread crumbs	½ tsp. baking powder
2 well beaten eggs	3½ - 4½ c. broth
1 tsp. poultry seasoning	

Melt butter and sauté onion and celery. Pour over bread crumbs. Add eggs, poultry seasoning, salt, sage, pepper and baking powder. Pour on broth. Grease crock pot and pack dressing lightly in pot and cover. Cook on high 45 minutes or on low 4-8 hours. I cook it on high for 30 minutes then low for 4-5 hours. This makes a light and moist dressing.

❦ CROCKPOT BEEF STEW ❦
Susan Lueders
Jean Brummett

2 lbs. stew beef
5 carrots, peeled and sliced
1 lg. onion, diced
3 stalks celery, sliced
5 potatoes, peeled and cubed

2 bay leaves
1 (28 oz.) can tomatoes
½ c. quick-cooking tapioca
Salt and pepper to taste

Mix together, cover and cook on low for 12 hours.

❦ CROCKPOT DIP ❦
Pat Brewer

1 lb. Jimmy Dean hot sausage
3 (8 oz.) pkgs. cream cheese
1 can Rotel
1 lg. can green chilies
1 sm. bag frozen corn

½ tsp. chili powder
Cilantro to taste
Salt and pepper to taste
Bag of Fritos or tortilla chips

Cook sausage and put in crock pot. Melt cream cheese in crockpot and add Rotel, green chilies and corn. Add chili powder, cilantro if desired, and salt and pepper to taste. Serve with Fritos or tortilla chips.

❦ CROCKPOT MINESTRONE ❦
Susan Lueders

1 lb. beef stew meat
6 c. water
1 (28 oz.) can diced tomatoes, with liquid
1 beef bouillon cube
1 med. onion, chopped
2 T. minced dried parsley
2 tsp. salt

1½ tsp. ground thyme
½ tsp. pepper
1 med. zucchini, thinly sliced
2 c. finely chopped cabbage
1 can (16 oz.) garbanzo beans, drained
1 c. uncooked small elbow macaroni

Combine stew meat, water, tomatoes, bouillon cube, onion, parsley, salt, thyme and pepper in slow cooker. Cover and cook on low for 7-9 hours or until meat is tender. Add zucchini, cabbage, beans and macaroni; cover and cook on high for 35 to 45 minutes or more.

121822-12

❦ EASY SLOW-COOKER A.1. SWISS STEAK ❦
Julie Concannon

2 lbs. boneless beef chuck eye
    roast, cut into 1-inch pieces
¼ c. A.1. Original Steak Sauce
1 onion, sliced

1 can (14½ oz.) diced
    tomatoes, undrained
2 T. flour
¼ c. water

Toss meat with steak sauce; place in slow cooker. Top with onions and tomatoes; cover with lid. Cook on low 9-10 hours (or high 4-5 hours). Mix flour and water. Stir into meat mixture; cook, covered, 5 minutes or until sauce is thickened, stirring occasionally. 6-8 servings.

❦ FRENCH DIP SANDWICHES ❦
Heidi Meyer

Chuck roast
1 pkg. Lipton onion soup mix
2 cubes beef bouillon

2½ c. water
French rolls

Place chuck roast in bottom of crock pot. Sprinkle onion soup mix on top. Add bouillon cubes and water. Cook on high approximately 10 hours. Shred meat and serve on French rolls.

❦ FRENCH DIP SANDWICHES ❦
Kathy Christiansen

Beef roast (2 - 3 lbs.)
1 can French onion soup

Hard or crusty sandwich rolls

Place roast in crock pot. Top with soup and ½ can water. Cook all day on low. Shred meat and serve on hard rolls. Remaining juices in crock pot are great for dipping.

❦ MANY MEALS POT ROAST ❦
Julie Concannon

4 lbs. boneless beef chuck roast
½ tsp. salt
¼ tsp. ground black pepper
2 T. vegetable oil
1 lg. onion, chopped (about 1 c.)
1 lg. carrot, chopped (about ⅔ c.)
⅔ c. chopped celery
2 cans (14.5 oz. each) Hunt's diced tomatoes with basil, garlic & oregano
1 can (14 oz.) beef broth

Season both sides of roast with salt and pepper. Heat oil in large saucepan over medium-high heat 1 minute. Add roast; cook 5 minutes on each side, or until browned on both sides. Remove from pan and put in crock pot; cover to keep warm. Reduce heat to medium. Add onion, carrot and celery to same pan; cook 5 minutes, or until onion is tender, stirring frequently. Add tomatoes with their liquid and broth; stir in all the browned bits from bottom of pan. Bring to a boil over high heat. Carefully pour over roast in crock pot. Cover. Cook on high for about 4 hours and then reduce heat to low and continue cooking for about 3-4 more hours. Remove beef and let stand a few minutes before serving. I serve the remaining broth with mashed potatoes and cooked carrots. This is a Hunt's recipe and it calls for the leftovers from this recipe to be used with their recipes for Pulled Barbecue Beef Sandwiches and Tuscan-Style Penne Pasta. I have not ever made those recipes but they can be found on Hunt's web site. We enjoy eating the pot roast as leftovers for a few days! Serves 4-6 with plenty of leftovers.

❦ NO PEEP STEW ❦
Randi VenHuizen

2 lbs. good lean beef stew meat
3 stalks of celery
5 med. carrots
1 lg. onion
3 - 4 potatoes with skin on
Salt and pepper to taste
46 oz. spicy V8 juice

Cut up meat and all vegetables and put in crockpot. Season with salt and pepper. Pour V8 juice over and mix. Cook 5-6 hours on high or 10-12 hours on low.

121822-12

❦ PORK CHOP, SAUERKRAUT, APPLES AND SWEET POTATOES ❦
Sandy Hall

1 T. extra virgin olive oil
4 boneless pork chops
  (important to be boneless
  and at least 1-inch thick)
2 med. sweet potatoes, peeled
  and sliced approximately ½-
  inch thick
1 med. onion, sliced

2 apples, peeled and sliced
1 T. brown sugar
½ tsp. ground nutmeg
¼ tsp. salt
Black pepper to taste
½ of a 32 oz. jar sauerkraut
  with some of the juice

Heat skillet over medium-high heat with extra virgin olive oil. Brown pork chops on each side. Layer the following items in a 3 to 4 quart crock pot: Sweet potato slices, onion slices, and then apple slices. Top apples with brown sugar, nutmeg, salt and pepper. Top with pork chops and cover all with the sauerkraut. Cook on low for about 5 hours.

❦ PORK LOIN WITH SAUERKRAUT ❦
(Quick and Easy Pork Loin)
Sandy Hall

2 T. mustard: whatever kind
  you have available. I use
  Dijon.
1 (4 lb.) boneless pork loin
  roast
1 apple, chopped

1 onion, chopped
1 (16 oz.) jar sauerkraut with
  juice
1½ c. chicken broth
Salt and pepper to taste

Rub mustard all over the pork loin. Layer apple and onion in the crockpot. Put pork loin on top. Cover with the sauerkraut and juice. Salt and pepper to taste. Add the chicken broth. Cook on low 6 to 8 hours.

❦ POT ROAST ❦
Shirley Schuchard

3 lb. chuck roast
½ c. ketchup
1 c. water
¼ c. wine

1 tsp. Worcestershire sauce
3 tsp. cornstarch
1 brown gravy packet
2 tsp. Dijon mustard

(continued)

Put roast in crock pot. Combine the ketchup, water, wine, Worcestershire, cornstarch, gravy packet and Dijon mustard and pour over roast in crock pot. Cook on low for about 5-6 hours. Can put potatoes and carrots on top if desired.

❦ POTATO SOUP ❦
Lisa Rieff

6 lg. potatoes, peeled and cubed
1 onion, chopped
4 c. chicken broth
3 garlic cloves, minced

¼ c. butter
2½ tsp. salt
1 tsp. pepper
1 c. cream
1 c. shredded Cheddar cheese

Place potatoes, onion, chicken broth, garlic, butter, salt and pepper in a 6 quart crockpot. Cook on low for 7-8 hours or high for 4 hours. Remove lid and mash potatoes using a hand masher or back side of spoon. Leave as chunky as you want. Stir in cream and cheese. You can garnish with crumbled bacon, extra cheese and chives or green onions if desired.

❦ ROAST WITH GRAVY ❦
Lisa Rieff
Southern Living

1 boneless chuck roast approx. 2.5 lbs.
¾ tsp. pepper
1 can (14½ oz.) low-sodium beef broth
1 can cream of mushroom soup

1 envelope (1.0 oz.) onion soup mix
2 T. cornstarch
2 T. water

Place roast in a 5 or 6 qt. slow cooker. Sprinkle with pepper. Add broth and both soups. Cook on high for 1 hour then turn to low and continue to cook additional 7 hours. Remove roast to serving plate. In small bowl whisk together cornstarch and water. Add to juice in slow cooker. Cook on high a couple minutes while juices thicken, whisking often.

❦ 238

❦ SHERRIED CRAB MEAT ❦
Paula Foster

13 oz. crab meat, canned or
   frozen
3 T. butter
¼ c. cooking sherry
¼ c. light cream
1 egg, beaten
1 can (10 oz.) cream of
   mushroom or golden
   mushroom soup

½ tsp. Worcestershire sauce
2 green onions with tops,
   finely chopped
Salt and pepper to taste

Make sure all cartilage or shells are removed from the crab meat.
Break the crab meat into pieces and place in crock pot. Add all other
ingredients. Stir gently to mix. Cover and cook on high for 1 hour,
then turn on low and cook for 4 to 6 hours. Serve this over toast,
noodles or rice.

❦ SLOW COOKER JAMBALAYA ❦
Deb Lund

1 lb. boneless, skinless chicken
   breasts, cut in cubes
½ lb. andouille sausage, diced
1 (28 oz.) can diced tomatoes
1 med. onion, chopped
1 green bell pepper, seeded
   and chopped
1 stalk celery, chopped
1 c. chicken broth

2 tsp. dried oregano
2 tsp. Cajun or Creole
   seasoning
1 tsp. hot sauce
2 bay leaves
½ tsp. dried thyme
1 lb. frozen peeled and cooked
   shrimp, thawed
2 c. cooked rice

In slow cooker, combine chicken, sausage, tomatoes, onion, green
pepper, celery, and chicken broth. Stir in seasonings. Cover, and cook
on low for 7 hours, or on high for 3 hours. Stir in thawed shrimp and
cook until heated through, about 5 minutes. Discard bay leaves and
serve over rice.

❧ SLOW COOKER POT ROAST ❧
Nancy Shinrock

1 T. oil
3 - 3½ lb. boneless beef pot
  roast
4 carrots, sliced
4 med. potatoes, cut in 1-inch
  chunks

1 envelope onion soup mix
¾ c. water
¼ c. water
2 T. flour

In large skillet, heat oil and brown roast. In slow cooker, arrange vegetables and place roast on top. Combine soup mix with ¾ c. water and add to slow cooker. Cook covered on low 8-10 hours or high 4-6 hours. Remove roast and vegetables. To thicken gravy, stir in ¼ c. water blended with 2 T. flour. Cook on high until thickened.

❧ WHITE CHICKEN CHILI ❧
Brian Vandeventer

4 - 6 chicken breasts, cooked
  and diced
4 cans great northern beans
1 can diced tomato with green
  chilies

1 can chicken broth
2 c. Pepper Jack cheese,
  shredded
16 oz. sour cream

Combine the chicken, beans, tomatoes and broth in a crock pot on low overnight. Drain the beans for a thicker chili. Add cheese and sour cream one hour prior to serving. Add a little black pepper and onion powder for a little more zing.

121822-12

Sweets & Treats

SWEETS AND TREATS

BARS AND COOKIES

❦ 3 LAYER GOOD BARS ❦
Lisa Rieff

First Layer:

1 c. light Karo syrup
1 c. brown sugar
1½ c. peanut butter

2 c. Rice Krispies
2 c. Cornflakes

Melt Karo syrup, brown sugar and peanut butter together in large stock pot over medium heat until smooth, stirring often. Remove from heat and add Rice Krispies and Cornflakes, stirring to coat. Spread into a 9 x 13-inch pan.

Second Layer:

½ c. butter
6 T. vanilla instant pudding powder

2 c. powdered sugar
3 T. milk

Melt butter. Stir in pudding mix, powdered sugar and milk. Spread over first layer. Let sit until firm consistency is evident.

Third Layer:

6 oz. chocolate chips

6 T. butter

Melt the chocolate chips and butter together over medium heat, stirring often. Spread over second layer. This is one of our favorite recipes. You can omit the middle layer and just do the Rice Krispies layer with the chocolate. You can also double the bottom layer if you want them REALLY thick. We refer to the double thick ones as "two ton Bars" because the pan is so heavy when you are done!!

❧ ALMOND POPPY SEED BARS ❧
Karen Armitage

Bars:

3 eggs
2¼ c. sugar
1½ c. milk
1 c. vegetable oil
1½ tsp. almond extract
1½ tsp. vanilla

1½ tsp. butter flavoring
3 c. flour
4½ tsp. poppy seeds
1½ tsp. baking powder
1½ tsp. salt

Beat eggs, sugar, milk, oil, almond extract, vanilla and butter flavoring. Combine the flour, poppy seeds, baking powder and salt; add to the egg mixture and mix just until combined. Spread into a greased 15 x 10 x 1-inch jelly roll pan. Bake at 350° for 20 minutes or until toothpick comes out clean. Cool on a wire rack.

Frosting:

⅓ c. butter or margarine,
  melted

3 c. powdered sugar
3 T. milk

Combine frosting ingredients. Beat until smooth. Frost cooled bars.

❧ BANANA BARS ❧
Shirley Schuchard

Bars:

2 c. flour
1 tsp. baking soda
¼ tsp. salt
½ c. oleo (margarine)
1½ c. sugar

2 eggs
1 c. sour cream
3 ripe bananas
1 tsp. vanilla

Mix flour, baking soda and salt. Set aside. Cream oleo and sugar. Add eggs and sour cream, mixing well. Add mashed bananas, vanilla and flour mixture. Bake in jellyroll pan at 350° for 25 minutes.

(continued)

Cream Cheese Icing:

1 (3 oz.) pkg. cream cheese, softened
½ c. butter or oleo

1 tsp. vanilla
2 c. powdered sugar, sifted

Cream together cream cheese and butter. Add vanilla and sifted powdered sugar, beating until mixture is smooth. Spread icing over cooled bars.

❦ BUTTER PECAN TURTLE COOKIES ❦
Pauline Shaffer

Crust:

2 c. flour
½ c. butter

1 c. brown sugar
1½ c. whole pecan halves

Mix flour, butter and brown sugar with mixer for 2 to 3 minutes until well mixed. Pat in ungreased 9 x 13-inch pan. Lay pecan halves evenly on crust.

Caramel Layer:

⅔ c. butter
½ c. brown sugar

1½ c. milk chocolate chips

Cook butter and brown sugar until entire surface of mixture begins to boil. Boil one minute, stirring constantly. Pour over crust and pecans. Bake at 350° for 18-22 minutes. Remove from oven and cover with milk chocolate chips. Let melt and swirl over caramel mixture.

❦ CARAMEL LAYERED CHOCOLATE BARS ❦
Debra Gillespie

⅔ c. evaporated milk, divided
50 (14 oz. pkg.) light caramels
1 pkg. German chocolate cake mix

¾ c. butter, melted
1 c. chopped nuts
1 c. (6 oz. pkg.) chocolate chips

(continued)

Combine ⅓ c. milk and caramels in a saucepan and cook over low heat, stirring until smooth. Set aside. Combine cake mix, butter, remaining ⅓ c. milk and nuts. Mix with spoon until dough holds together. May need to add a few drops of milk if mixture is too dry. Press half of dough into well greased brownie pan and bake 6 minutes at 350 °. Sprinkle chocolate chips over crust. Spread with caramel mixture. Crumble remaining dough over top of caramel. Bake 15 to 18 minutes. Cool slightly, then chill about 30 minutes. Cut into small bars. Freezes well.

❦ CARAMEL WALNUT DREAM BARS ❦
Shirley Schuchard

1 box yellow cake mix
3 T. soft butter
2 eggs
14 oz. sweetened condensed
  milk

1 tsp. vanilla
½ c. walnuts
½ c. finely ground toffee bits

Preheat oven to 350°. Prepare cake pan with cooking spray. Combine cake mix, butter and 1 egg in bowl until crumbly. Press in bottom of pan. In another bowl, combine sweetened condensed milk, egg, vanilla, walnuts and toffee. Pour over cake mix in pan. Bake 35 minutes.

❦ CHEWY BROWNIES ❦
Heidi Meyer

2¼ c. sugar
⅔ c. cocoa
1¼ c. flour
1 tsp. baking powder

1 tsp. salt
¾ c. soft butter
4 eggs, beaten

Mix all ingredients in a bowl. Spray a 9 x 13-inch pan with Pam. Add mixture and spread to fill pan evenly. Bake at 350° 40-45 minutes.

❦ CHOCOLATE CHIP COOKIE BARS ❦
Shari Garder

2 T. butter, softened
2 T. oil
1 c. firmly packed dark brown sugar
1 lg. egg
½ c. unsweetened applesauce
1 tsp. vanilla

1½ c. flour
1 tsp. baking powder
½ tsp. baking soda
½ tsp. salt
2 c. oatmeal
1 c. semisweet chocolate chips
2 T. sugar

In large bowl, mix on medium speed; butter, oil, and brown sugar until smooth. Beat in egg, applesauce, and vanilla until well blended. In another bowl, mix flour, baking powder, baking soda, and salt; stir or beat into butter mixture until smooth. Stir in oatmeal and chocolate chips. Spread dough evenly in a lightly oiled 8-inch square baking pan. Sprinkle top with sugar if desired. Bake at 350° for 15 minutes or until pale golden brown. Let cool about 10 minutes, then cut.

❦ CHOCOLATE MINT BROWNIES ❦
Amy Kragnes

Brownies:

9 x 13-inch pan of brownies
2 c. powdered sugar
½ c. butter, softened

2 T. milk
½ tsp. peppermint extract
Green food coloring

Prepare any brownie recipe or mix and let cool. Mix powdered sugar, butter, milk, peppermint extract and food coloring together until smooth and spread over brownies.

Glaze:

1 c. milk chocolate chips

6 T. butter

Melt chocolate chips and butter in microwave 60 seconds, stir to blend, spread thinly over the frosting with a light touch. Refrigerate to set.

❦ CRANBERRY HOOTY CREEK COOKIES ❦
Ruth Manning

1 c. softened butter	1 c. oatmeal
⅔ c. brown sugar	1 tsp. baking soda
⅔ c. white sugar	1 tsp. salt
2 eggs	1 c. white chocolate chips
1 tsp. vanilla	1 c. dried cranberries
2 ¼ c. flour	1 c. chopped pecans

Beat together butter, sugars, eggs and vanilla until fluffy. Add remaining ingredients and blend well. Drop by heaping teaspoons onto greased cookie sheet. Bake at 350° for 8-10 minutes, or until edges start to brown. Cool on cookie sheet. Remove to wire rack. Makes about 3 dozen.

❦ CREAMY STRAWBERRY LEMON SQUARES ❦
Shirley Schuchard

1 ½ c. finely crushed graham crackers	3 c. cold milk, divided
½ c. sugar, divided	2 pkgs. (4 serving size) lemon flavor instant pudding and pie filling
6 T. butter, softened	
2 pkgs. (8 oz. each) cream cheese	1 container (8 oz.) frozen strawberry whipped topping

Mix graham crackers, ¼ cup sugar and butter until blended. Press firmly into bottom of 13 x 9-inch baking pan to form crust. Set aside. Beat cream cheese, ¼ cup sugar and ¼ cup milk in medium bowl with wire whisk; spread over crust. Pour remaining milk into large bowl, add pudding mixes. Beat with wire whisk 2 minutes. Pour over cream cheese layer in pan. Let stand 5 minutes until thickened. Cover with whipped topping. Refrigerate 4 hours covered with plastic wrap. Cut into 24 squares.

121822-12

❦ DEVILS FOOD COOKIES ❦
Randi VenHuizen

1 box devils food cake mix
   (without pudding)
2 eggs, slightly beaten

1 T. water
½ c. shortening
Powdered sugar

Stir together all ingredients except powdered sugar. Shape into balls approximately the size of a small walnut. Roll in the powdered sugar. Place on greased baking sheet. Bake 8-10 minutes at 375°.

❦ DOUBLE CHOCOLATE CHIP COOKIES ❦
Connie Walther

½ c. oil
2 eggs
1 box chocolate cake mix

5 oz. chocolate chips (optional: vanilla or peanut butter chips)

Mix oil and eggs, add to cake mix. Add chips. Drop by spoonfuls (batter will be stiff) onto cookie sheet. Bake at 350° for 10-15 minutes. Makes 4 dozen.

❦ DOUBLE MINT SQUARES ❦
Laura Armitage

Batter:

¾ c. mint chocolate chips
¾ c. butter
1 c. sugar
3 lg. eggs
½ tsp. vanilla

½ tsp. mint extract
1⅓ c. all-purpose flour
1 tsp. baking powder
8 drops green liquid food
   coloring

Preheat oven to 350°. Line a 9-inch baking pan with foil, letting ends extend above pan on 2 sides. Coat foil with nonstick spray. Melt ¾ cup mint chocolate chips as package directs. Cool slightly. Melt butter in a medium saucepan. Remove from heat, whisk in sugar. Stir in eggs, vanilla, and mint extract, then mix in flour and baking powder until just blended. Add 1¾ cups batter to the melted chocolate; stir until blended. Spread evenly in the pan. Stir green food color into remaining

(continued)

batter until evenly tinted. Carefully pour over chocolate batter, then gently spread into an even layer. Bake 30-35 minutes or until lightly brown on top and a wooden toothpick inserted in center comes out with moist crumbs attached. Cool in pan on a wire rack. Prepare glaze.

Glaze:

¾ c. mint chocolate chips
2 T. stick butter
1 T. light corn syrup

¼ c. crushed red and white striped candy canes (about 2)

Melt mint chocolate chips and butter in a small saucepan over low heat or in a bowl in the microwave. Stir in corn syrup until blended. Cool 5 minutes or until no longer hot, but still spreadable. Spread over brownie. Sprinkle with crushed candy. Chill until firm. Lift foil by ends onto cutting board. Best to cut into 36 squares.

❦ EASY BARS ❦
Heidi Meyer

¼ lb. butter
1½ c. crushed graham
  crackers
1 sm. pkg. chocolate chips

1 sm. pkg. butterscotch chips
1 c. coconut
1 can sweetened condensed milk

Melt butter in 9 x 13-inch pan. Add graham crackers to butter, stir and press into bottom of pan. Sprinkle chocolate chips and butterscotch chips on top. Sprinkle coconut on top of chips. Drizzle condensed milk on top to cover coconut. Bake at 350° for 25-30 minutes.

❦ EASY LEMONADE DESSERT ❦
Kathy Christiansen

60 crushed Ritz crackers
¼ c. powdered sugar
½ c. butter, softened
1 can sweetened condensed milk

1 (6 oz.) pink frozen lemonade, lightly thawed
1 (8 - 9 oz.) container frozen whipped topping, thawed

Mix crackers, sugar and butter in food processor until combined. Press ¾ of this mixture into a 9 x 13-inch pan. In a large bowl, mix milk, lemonade and thawed frozen whipped topping (may add a little red

(continued)

❦ 248

121822-12

food coloring to make mixture more pink). Spread lemonade mixture over crumb mixture. Sprinkle remaining crumbs on top and chill.

❦ FAVORITE CHOCOLATE BROWNIES ❦
Jackie Combes

Brownies:

2 c. flour
2 c. sugar
1 tsp. baking soda
½ tsp. salt
1 c. butter

¼ c. cocoa
1 c. water
½ c. buttermilk
2 eggs
2 tsp. vanilla extract

Preheat oven to 350°. Grease a 10 x 15-inch rimmed pan or 9 x 13-inch pan (for more cake like brownies) and set aside. Sift together the flour, sugar, baking soda and salt. In a medium saucepan, melt the butter. Add the cocoa and water and stir well to combine. When the mixture starts boiling, remove from heat, pour over dry ingredients and stir. Add the buttermilk, eggs and vanilla. Mix well. Pour into the pan and bake for 18-20 minutes, 25 if baked in a 9 x 13-inch pan. During the last 10 minutes of baking, make the frosting.

Frosting:

½ c. butter
5 T. cocoa
6 T. buttermilk

1 lb. (4¼ c.) powdered sugar
1 tsp. vanilla extract
½ c. chopped nuts

In a saucepan, melt the butter. Add the cocoa and buttermilk and stir. Remove from heat and add powdered sugar and vanilla. Beat until smooth. Fold in nuts. Carefully pour over brownies while still hot.

❧ FROSTED BANANA BARS ❧
Susan Lueders
Jean Brummett

Bars:

½ c. butter or margarine,
   softened
2 c. sugar
3 eggs
1½ c. mashed ripe bananas
   (about 3 med.)

1 tsp. vanilla
2 c. flour
1 tsp. baking soda
Pinch of salt

In a mixing bowl, cream butter and sugar. Beat in eggs, bananas and vanilla. Combine the flour, baking soda and salt; add to creamed mixture and mix well. Pour into greased 15 x 10 x 1-inch baking pan. Bake at 350° for 25 minutes. Cool.

Frosting:

½ c. butter, softened
1 (8 oz.) pkg. cream cheese,
   softened

4 c. powdered sugar
2 tsp. vanilla

Cream butter and cream cheese. Gradually add powdered sugar and vanilla. Beat well, spread over cooled bars. Makes 3 dozen bars.

❧ KELLOGG'S "K" BARS ❧
Karen Pickens

½ c. sugar
½ c. white corn syrup
¾ c. peanut butter

3½ c. Kellogg's "K" cereal
½ sm. pkg. chocolate chips
½ sm. pkg. butterscotch chips

Combine sugar and syrup in saucepan. Bring to a boil and add peanut butter and cereal. Press into 9 x 13-inch greased pan. Top with melted chocolate chips and butterscotch chips. Cut into squares and store in refrigerator.

121822-12

❦ LEMON COOKIES ❦
Pat Brewer

1 pkg. lemon cake mix
2 eggs
½ c. vegetable oil
¼ tsp. baking soda

Mix all ingredients and drop by teaspoonfuls on cookie sheet. Bake at 350° for 8-10 minutes or until done. Can frost with vanilla frosting. Chocolate or any cake mix may be used.

❦ LEMON DESSERT ❦
Randi VenHuizen

1 lemon cake mix
1 can lemon pie filling
4 eggs
Icing

Mix together lemon cake mix, lemon pie filling and 4 eggs. Pour onto greased cookie sheet. Bake at 350° for 25 to 30 minutes. Cool. Frost with any icing.

❦ LEMONY CRISPS ❦
Nancy Shinrock

1 pkg. lemon cake mix
⅓ c. oil
2 eggs
¼ c. sugar
1 c. powdered sugar
2 - 3 T. lemon juice
Yellow colored sugar

Heat oven to 375°. In large bowl, combine cake mix, oil, and eggs. Stir with spoon until thoroughly moistened. Shape dough into 1-inch balls. Place 2-inches apart on ungreased cookie sheets. Place sugar in shallow dish. Dip bottom of glass in sugar and flatten cookies to ¼-inch. Bake for 5-7 minutes or until edges are light golden brown. Cool 1 minute. Remove from cookie sheets. In small bowl, combine powdered sugar and lemon juice until smooth. Drizzle over cookies and sprinkle with colored sugar before icing sets. Makes about 4 dozen cookies.

❦ MIXED-UP BROWNIE DELIGHT ❦
Shari Garder

1 c. butter or margarine
4 squares (1 oz. each)
   unsweetened chocolate
2 c. sugar
4 eggs
2 tsp. vanilla
1½ c. flour

12 oz. caramels
⅛ c. creamy peanut butter
½ c. evaporated milk
½ c. white chocolate chips
½ c. milk chocolate chips
½ c. chopped walnuts
   (optional)

Melt butter and unsweetened chocolate squares in same pan (or carefully in microwave). Remove from heat. Stir in sugar. Add eggs, one at a time, beating after each addition. Add vanilla. Stir in flour and mix well. Pour ½ of the mixture into a greased 9 x 13-inch pan. Bake 6 minutes at 350°. While brownies are baking, melt the caramels, peanut butter, and evaporated milk (can carefully be done in microwave). Stir frequently until melted. Remove brownies from oven and pour caramel mixture over top. Sprinkle chips and nuts over top. Spoon remaining brownie mix over top to cover all. Bake additional 15 minutes. Allow to cool before cutting.

❦ MOCHA-TOFFEE CHOCOLATE COOKIES ❦
Julie Concannon

4 tsp. instant espresso coffee
   powder*
2 tsp. vanilla
1 box Betty Crocker Super
   Moist butter recipe chocolate
   cake mix

½ c. butter or margarine,
   softened
2 eggs
1 c. miniature semisweet
   chocolate chips
½ c. English toffee bits

Heat oven to 350°. In small bowl, stir together instant espresso coffee powder and vanilla until coffee is dissolved. In large bowl, mix cake mix, coffee mixture, butter and eggs with spoon until soft dough forms (this is very, very thick). Stir in chocolate chips and toffee bits. On ungreased cookie sheets, drop dough by scant teaspoonfuls about 2-inches apart. Bake 7 to 10 minutes or until surface appears dry. Cool 1 minute; remove from cookie sheets to cooling racks. Makes about 5 dozen cookies. *If you have trouble finding this locally, you can purchase through King Arthur Flour on line.

121822-12

❦ MOM'S LEMON BARS ❦
Kathy Christiansen
Ann Christiansen

Bars:

½ c. margarine
¼ c. powdered sugar
1 c. flour
2 T. flour, in addition to above
1 c. sugar

¼ tsp. baking powder
2 eggs, beaten
2 T. lemon juice
Grated rind of 1 lemon

Preheat oven to 350°. Cream together margarine, powdered sugar and flour then press into an 8-inch square pan. Bake 15-20 minutes. Sift together additional flour, sugar and baking powder. Add eggs, lemon juice and lemon rind. Place on baked crust and bake 25 minutes.

Icing:

2 c. powdered sugar
Lemon juice

Coffee cream

Mix icing ingredients. Frost bars when cool.

❦ MOM'S SUGAR COOKIES ❦
(from her sister, Esther Scheetz)
Kathy Christiansen
Ann Christiansen

¾ c. butter
¾ c. sugar
1 egg
½ tsp. vanilla

1½ tsp. baking powder
¼ tsp. salt
3 T. milk
2 c. flour

Mix ingredients in order given. Chill dough for several hours or overnight. Roll into small balls and flatten with bottom of glass or tenderizer hammer dipped in sugar. Bake at 350° for 10 to 12 minutes.

❦ MONSTER COOKIES ❦
Connie Walther

1 c. oleo (margarine)	6 lg. eggs
3 c. peanut butter	4 tsp. baking soda
1½ tsp. corn syrup	9 c. quick oats
1½ tsp. vanilla	1 (14 oz.) pkg. M & M candies
2½ c. packed brown sugar	1 (12 oz.) pkg. chocolate chips

Mix ingredients in order given. Place by ice cream scoop on cookie sheet covered with parchment paper. Bake at 350° for 10 minutes.

❦ OATMEAL CARAMEL BARS ❦
Kathy Christiansen
Sharon Abbey

32 caramels (approx. one bag)	½ tsp. soda
5 T. light cream or evaporated milk	¼ tsp. salt
	¾ c. butter, softened
1 c. flour	1 c. chocolate chips
1 c. quick oatmeal	½ c. chopped nuts
¾ c. brown sugar	

Melt caramels in cream in double boiler (or in microwave). Combine flour, oatmeal, brown sugar, soda and salt in large mixing bowl. Add in softened butter until mixture is crumbly. Press ½ the crumbs into 9 x 13-inch pan. Bake at 350° for 10 minutes. Remove, sprinkle with chocolate chips and nuts. Cover with caramel mixture and then sprinkle remaining crumbs and return to oven for 15 to 20 minutes. Cool slightly, cut into bars while warm.

121822-12

❦ OATY DOODLE COOKIES ❦
Deb Lund

2 c. rolled oats
1½ c. all-purpose flour
½ c. whole wheat flour
4 tsp. ground cinnamon
1 tsp. baking soda
½ tsp. cream of tartar
¼ tsp. salt
½ c. butter, softened
½ c. butter flavored
  shortening, softened
1½ c. sugar
2 eggs
1 tsp. vanilla
½ - ¾ c. raisins (optional)
⅓ - ½ c. sugar for rolling

Preheat oven to 400°. Line cookie sheets with parchment paper or foil; set aside. In a food processor process the oats until finely ground. In a medium bowl combine ground oats, flours, cinnamon, baking soda, cream of tartar, and salt; set aside. In a large mixing bowl beat butter and shortening with an electric mixer on medium to high speed for 30 seconds. Add 1½ cups sugar and beat until combined. Beat in eggs and vanilla. Beat or stir in flour mixture. Add raisins, if desired. Using a heaping teaspoon for each, roll dough into balls; roll in the ⅓ to ½ cup sugar. Place on prepared cookie sheets about 2-inches apart. Flatten to a little less than ½-inch thick. If desired, use your fingers to shape into hearts by shaping one end into a point and the other into two rounded shapes. Bake for 8 to 10 minutes or until set and lightly browned. Cool 1 minute on cookie sheet. Cool completely on wire racks. Makes about 60 cookies.

❦ PEAR CUSTARD BARS ❦
Dayla Miller

Bars:

½ c. butter or margarine,
  softened
⅓ c. sugar
¾ c. flour
¼ tsp. vanilla
⅔ c. chopped macadamia nuts

In mixing bowl cream butter and sugar. Beat in flour and vanilla until combined. Stir in nuts. Press into 8-inch square baking pan. Bake at 350° for 20 minutes or until lightly browned. Cool.

(continued)

Filling:

1 (8 oz.) pkg. cream cheese
½ c. sugar
1 egg
½ tsp. vanilla

1 can (15 oz.) pear halves, drained
½ tsp. sugar
½ tsp. cinnamon

In a mixing bowl beat cream cheese until smooth. Add sugar, egg and vanilla, mix well until combined. Pour over crust. Cut pears and arrange in a single layer over filling. Combine sugar and cinnamon; sprinkle over pears. Bake at 375° for 25-30 minutes, center will be soft set and will become firmer as it cools. Cover and refrigerate 2 hours before cutting. Store in refrigerator.

❦ PHILADELPHIA MARBLE BROWNIES ❦
Cheyrle Badtke

1 pkg. (9 x 13-inch size)
   brownie mix (and
   ingredients to prepare)
1 pkg. cream cheese, softened

½ c. sugar
1 egg
½ tsp. vanilla

Prepare brownie batter as directed on package. Spread into a greased 9 x 13-inch pan. Beat cream cheese with mixer until creamy. Add sugar, egg and vanilla. Mix well. Drop by tablespoonfuls over brownie batter. Swirl with a knife. Bake at 350° for 35 to 40 minutes or until cream cheese mixture is lightly browned. Cool before cutting to serve. Keep refrigerated.

❦ RHUBARB BARS ❦
Rose Roberts

3 c. rhubarb, cut up
1½ c. sugar
2 T. cornstarch
1 tsp. vanilla
1½ c. oatmeal

1½ c. flour
1 c. brown sugar
1 c. oleo (margarine)
½ tsp. baking soda
½ c. chopped nuts, optional

Mix the rhubarb, sugar, cornstarch and vanilla in saucepan and cook until thickened. Mix together the oatmeal, flour, brown sugar, oleo,

(continued)

baking soda and nuts (if using). Pat ¾ of oatmeal mixture in 9 x 13-inch baking pan. Top with rhubarb mixture and then top with the rest of the oatmeal mixture. Bake at 375° for 30 minutes.

❦ ROLO COOKIES ❦
Anne Yarger

2 ¼ c. flour
¾ c. cocoa
1 tsp. baking soda
1 c. sugar
1 c. packed brown sugar
1 c. butter, softened

2 tsp. vanilla
2 eggs
1 c. chopped nuts (your choice), divided
60 Rolo candies
4 T. sugar

Preheat oven to 375°. In small bowl, combine flour, cocoa, and soda; blend well. In large bowl, beat sugars and butter until fluffy. Add vanilla and eggs; beat well. Slowly add flour mixture; blend well. Stir in ½ cup nuts. For each cookie, with floured hands, shape about 1 tablespoon dough around Rolo candy, covering completely. In small bowl, combine ½ cup nuts and 4 tablespoons sugar. Press one side of each ball into nut mixture. Place, nut side up, on ungreased sheet. Bake 7 to 9 minutes. Cool slightly and remove from sheets. 60 cookies.

❦ SNOWBALL COOKIES ❦
Lynda McGraw

1 c. real butter
⅓ c. sugar
2 tsp. water
2 c. flour

2 tsp. vanilla
½ c. finely crushed pecans
2 c. powdered sugar

Mix butter, sugar, water, flour, vanilla and crushed pecans. Shape into medium balls. Bake at 325° for 10-15 minutes (bottoms should be light brown). Let cool a little. Roll in powdered sugar. Store one layer at a time.

❦ SOLO OATMEAL FRUIT BARS ❦
Lynnette Nore

1 pkg. yellow cake mix
2½ c. quick cooking oats
¾ c. softened butter or
  margarine
1 egg

2 cans Solo pastry filling (use
  any favorite: apricot,
  strawberry, blueberry, apple,
  pineapple, or cherry)

Preheat oven to 375°. Grease a 13 x 9 x 2-inch baking pan. Combine dry cake mix and oats. Add butter and egg and stir until crumbly. Put ½ of mixture in prepared pan. Press down lightly. Spread Solo filling over mixture in pan. Top with remaining oat mixture. Press down lightly. Bake at 375° for 22-26 minutes. Cool before cutting into squares.

❦ SOPPIA ❦
Connie Walther

Soppia:

2 pkg. crescent roll dough
1 c. butter
1 c. sugar

8 oz. cream cheese
1 tsp. vanilla

Pat 1 pkg. of crescents out in 9 x 13-inch baking dish. Mix butter, sugar, cream cheese and vanilla. Spread over dough. Put second layer of crescents on top of filling. Bake 350° for 30 minutes.

Topping:

¼ c. melted butter
1 tsp. cinnamon and 2 T.
  sugar

Pour butter over dish, sprinkle with cinnamon and sugar; bake 8 more minutes.

121822-12

CAKES AND FROSTING

❧ ALMOND CAKE ❧
Deb Lund

1 c. (2 sticks) butter, at room temperature
7 oz. (¾ c.) almond paste (*homemade or purchased)
2 c. sugar
6 eggs, separated

1½ c. flour
½ tsp. salt
2 tsp. baking powder
½ c. milk
1 T. almond extract
Powdered sugar

Preheat oven to 350°. Cream butter and almond paste thoroughly. Add sugar slowly and continue beating until light and fluffy. Beat in egg yolks one at a time. In a separate bowl, whisk together flour, salt and baking powder thoroughly. In a cup or small bowl, combine milk and almond extract. Add one-third of flour mixture to the butter mixture and stir gently but thoroughly; add one-third of milk mixture and stir gently but thoroughly. Continue to add flour mixture and milk alternately until all has been incorporated into the batter. Beat egg whites until stiff but not dry; gently fold into batter thoroughly. Spoon into well-greased, 10-cup tube pan (an angel food cake pan or Bundt pan) or in 2 loaf pans. Bake for about 50 to 55 minutes (slightly less for loaf pans), or until cake tests done with a toothpick. Cool in pan for 10 minutes. Loosen cake gently around rim and tube. Cool completely before removing from pan. Dust with powdered sugar and serve with strawberry-rhubarb sauce, raspberry sauce, any fruit sauce, or plain. Keeps well and freezes well, too. *See Deb's almond paste recipe in the Sweet Treats Section.

❧ BUTTER CREAM FROSTING ❧
Deb Lund

1½ c. butter, softened
½ c. margarine, softened
8 c. powdered sugar
2 tsp. vanilla extract

½ tsp. salt
6 oz. heavy cream or half and half

Beat butter and margarine until light and fluffy. Beat in powdered sugar. Add vanilla and salt, then gradually beat in cream or half and half. Beat until light and fluffy. Makes a large amount of frosting-- easily frosts a large cake or more. May halve the recipe.

❦ CARROT CAKE ❦
Dayla Miller

Cake:

1¼ c. oil	3 c. carrots, chopped
4 eggs	2 c. flour
2 c. sugar	1 tsp. soda
2 tsp. cinnamon	2 tsp. baking powder
1 tsp. salt	1 c. pecans

In blender add oil, eggs, sugar, cinnamon and salt. Blend a few seconds, gradually add carrots until grated. In large bowl combine flour, soda, baking powder and pecans, pour blender mixture into bowl, thoroughly mix together. Pour into oiled Bundt pan or angel food pan. Bake at 325° for 1 hour and 10 minutes. Cool and serve with rum sauce.

Rum Sauce:

1 c. sugar	3 tsp. rum flavoring
½ c. water	2 T. margarine or butter

Bring to boil sauce ingredients. Pour over cake slices.

❦ CHOCOLATE FROSTING ❦
Barb Haskins

6 T. butter	1½ c. sugar
6 T. milk	1 c. chocolate chips

Bring butter, milk and sugar to boil, stirring constantly (I use a wire whip). When a rolling boil starts, stir for 30 seconds and remove from heat. Stir in the chocolate chips until smooth. Can set pot in cold water as you stir to help thicken. Spread on cake, etc. and let set. Covers a 15 x 10-inch sheet or a large cake. Tip: if you boil too little, the frosting is too runny; too long boiling produces fudge. Enjoy!

121822-12

❦ CHOCOLATE KAHLUA CAKE ❦
Brenda Mac

1 fudge cake mix	4 eggs
1 sm. pkg. instant vanilla pudding	½ c. oil
1 pt. sour cream	¾ c. kahlua
	1½ c. chocolate chips

Beat cake mix, pudding mix, sour cream, eggs, oil and kahlua together with mixer for 10 minutes. Fold in chocolate chips. Pour in greased and floured bundt pan. Bake 50-60 minutes at 325° or until done. Let cool 10-15 minutes and turn upside down to remove from bundt pan. May top with Cool Whip when serving or drizzle a chocolate topping on top.

❦ CREME DE MENTHE CAKE ❦
Debra Gillespie

1 white cake mix (and ingredients to prepare)	1 can chocolate fudge topping
4 T. Creme De Menthe, divided	1 container Cool Whip

Prepare cake mix per package directions, adding 2 T. Creme De Menthe to the batter. Bake as usual. Allow cake to cool completely. Spread chocolate fudge over cake. Combine remaining 2 T. Creme De Menthe with Cool Whip and spread over chocolate fudge layer. Refrigerate until ready to serve.

❦ CREME-DE-MENTHE CAKE ❦
Lisa Meyer

1 box white cake mix (and ingredients to prepare)	½ c. Creme De Menthe
½ lg. (7 oz.) Hershey chocolate bar, grated	½ c. half and half
	Cool Whip

Prepare cake mix according to directions on box. Add grated Hershey chocolate bar to batter. Bake in 9 x 13-inch pan. Cool 30 minutes. Mix Creme De Menthe and half and half. Poke holes in cake with fork and pour creme de menthe mixture over cake. Refrigerate overnight and serve with Cool Whip.

❦ DELICATE WHITE CHOCOLATE CAKE ❦
Karen Pickens

1 white cake mix
1 (3.4 oz.) pkg. vanilla instant pudding and pie filling
4 lg. egg whites
1 c. water
½ c. vegetable oil
5 oz. finely chopped white chocolate
1 c. cherry preserves
8 drops red food coloring
2 c. whipping cream
2 T. powdered sugar
Maraschino cherries
1 oz. white chocolate shavings

Preheat oven to 350°. Grease and flour lightly the bottoms and sides of 3 (9-inch) round pans. Combine cake mix, pudding mix, egg whites, water and oil in a large mixing bowl. Beat at medium speed with electric mixer for 2 minutes. Fold in chopped white chocolate. Pour into prepared pans. Bake 18 to 20 minutes or until toothpick inserted in center comes out clean. Cool in pans 15 minutes. Invert onto cooling racks. Cool completely. Combine cherry preserves and food coloring, if desired. Stir to blend color. Beat whipping cream in a large bowl until soft peaks form. Add powdered sugar gradually. Beat until stiff peaks form. To assemble, place one cake layer on serving plate. Spread ½ c. cherry preserves over cake. Place second cake layer on top. Spread with remaining preserves. Place third cake layer on top. Frost sides and top with whipped cream. Decorate with maraschino cherries and white chocolate shavings. Refrigerate until ready to serve.

❦ LEMON-ORANGE CAKE ❦
Julie Concannon

1 box super moist white cake mix (and ingredients to prepare)
1¼ c. orange juice
Vegetable oil and egg whites called for on cake mix box
1 can (15¾ oz.) lemon pie filling
1 container whipped fluffy white frosting
Grated orange peel, if desired

Heat oven to 350° (325° for dark or nonstick pans). Make and cool cake as directed on box for two 8-inch or 9-inch round pans--EXCEPT use 1¼ cups of orange juice in place of the water. Cut each cake layer

(continued)

horizontally in half to make 2 layers. Fill layers with generous ½ cup pie filling. Frost side and top of cake with frosting. Garnish with orange peel if desired. Refrigerate about 1 hour or until chilled. Store covered in refrigerator. 16 servings. You can also garnish this with lemon and orange peel curled together.

❦ MILKY WAY CAKE ❦
Nancy Shinrock

6 Milky Way candy bars (or 13 miniature bars)	½ tsp. baking soda
¾ c. butter, divided	1¼ c. buttermilk
2 c. sugar	1 tsp. vanilla
4 eggs	1 c. chopped nutmeats, optional
2½ c. flour	Powdered sugar

Unwrap candy bars and place in saucepan with ¼ c. butter. Cook slowly over low heat, stirring frequently until candy is melted. Set aside to cool. Place remaining butter in large bowl and beat with electric mixer until creamy. Add sugar and beat until creamy. Add eggs and beat until all ingredients are well blended. In another bowl, combine flour and baking soda. To the butter mixture, add spoonfuls of flour mixture alternately with buttermilk. When all ingredients have been incorporated, add vanilla, reserved Milky Way mixture, and the nutmeats, if desired. Pour batter into a greased and floured Bundt pan. Bake at 350° for 1 hour and 20 minutes or until a toothpick comes out clean. Remove cake from pan and cool on wire rack. Dust with powdered sugar.

❦ MOON CAKE ❦
(Cream Puff Bars)
Karen Anderson

1 c. water	2 c. milk
½ c. butter	8 oz. soft cream cheese
1 c. flour	Cool Whip
4 eggs	Chocolate syrup
2 sm. boxes vanilla pudding	Chopped nuts, optional

Boil water and butter. Add flour and stir rapidly until mixture forms a ball. Take off burner and cool. Add eggs, beat after each one. Spread

(continued)

in 11 x 15-inch pan. Bake at 400° for 30 minutes. Mix pudding with milk (prepare according to directions on box). Add soft cream cheese. Spread over cake when cool and refrigerate 20 minutes. Spread Cool Whip over top of pudding. Drizzle with chocolate syrup and sprinkle with chopped nuts if desired.

❦ NORWEGIAN LINGONBERRY CAKE WITH STREUSEL TOPPING ❦
Ruth Manning

Cake:

2 c. flour	6 T. unsalted butter
⅔ c. sugar	1 egg
½ tsp. ground cardamom	¾ c. lingonberry preserves*
1 T. baking powder	

Preheat oven to 400°. Mix flour, sugar, cardamom and baking powder. Cut in butter with a pastry blender or with two knives. Beat the egg. Add to flour mixture and mix well. Spread the batter into a greased and floured 8 x 11-inch pan. Spread lingonberry preserves over batter. *Can be found in larger supermarkets, at IKEA or at Little Scandinavia in Elkhorn, NE. Raspberry preserves may be substituted if you can't find lingonberries.

Streusel Topping:

⅔ c. oatmeal	½ c. sugar
3 T. butter	½ tsp. vanilla

Blend topping ingredients and sprinkle over lingonberry preserves. Bake for 25 to 30 minutes or until golden. Cool in pan before serving.

121822-12

❦ OATMEAL CAKE ❦
Susan Lueders

Cake:

1 c. margarine	1 c. sugar
1 c. oatmeal	1½ c. flour
1¼ c. boiling water	1 tsp. baking soda
2 eggs	½ tsp. cinnamon
1 c. packed brown sugar	¼ tsp. salt

In mixing bowl combine margarine, oatmeal and boiling water. Let stand for 20 minutes. Add eggs, sugars, flour, baking soda, cinnamon, salt; mix well and pour into greased 9 x 13-inch baking dish. Bake at 350° for 30 minutes.

Topping:

1 c. packed brown sugar	1 c. chopped pecans
½ c. margarine	1 c. coconut
6 T. evaporated milk	1 tsp. vanilla

In saucepan, combine topping ingredients; boil for 10 minutes, stirring often. Pour hot topping over hot cake.

❦ RAW APPLE CAKE ❦
Debra Gillespie

Cake:

2 c. white sugar	8 med. sized apples
½ c. butter, softened	1 tsp. cinnamon
2 eggs	2 tsp. soda
2 c. flour	1 c. walnuts, chopped

Cream together white sugar and butter, then stir eggs into the creamed mixture. Add flour, apples, cinnamon, soda and walnuts, blending all ingredients together. Pour into 9 x 13-inch greased cake pan. Bake at 350° for 35-40 minutes. Allow cake to cool.

(continued)

Sauce:

2 T. corn starch
1 c. water
1 c. brown sugar

¼ c. butter
1 tsp. vanilla

In pan over medium heat, completely dissolve cornstarch in water, then stir in brown sugar and cook until thick. Add butter and vanilla last, stirring to blend with sauce (may double sauce ingredients for generous amount per serving). Spoon warm sauce over each piece of cake. Serves 12.

❦ RED WALDORF CHOCOLATE CAKE ❦
Paula Foster
In memory of Jackie Badtke

Cake:

½ c. shortening
1½ c. sugar
2 eggs
2 (2 oz.) bottles red food
  coloring
2 heaping T. cocoa

1 tsp. salt
2¼ c. flour
1 c. buttermilk
1 tsp. vanilla
1 tsp. soda dissolved in 1 T.
  vinegar

Preheat oven to 350°. Cream shortening and sugar together. Add eggs. Make a paste of the red food coloring and cocoa. Add this to the mixture. Put the salt in the flour. Add buttermilk and flour a cup at a time to the mixture. Add the vanilla. When all is thoroughly mixed, combine the soda and vinegar together and add the soda and vinegar mixture last as it is fizzing. Pour into two 5-inch round pans and bake 35 to 40 minutes or until toothpick comes out clean.

Frosting:

3 T. flour
1 c. milk
1 c. sugar

1 c. butter
1 tsp. vanilla

Heat the flour and milk until it becomes thick, stirring constantly. Once this is thick, take off the heat and let this mixture get COLD. If it is warm at all, it will ruin the frosting. Cream together the sugar, butter

(continued)

and vanilla until the sugar is dissolved. Once you are certain the flour milk mixture is cold, add to the mixture above, and beat the daylights out of it until it is like whip cream. Frost the cooled cake for a yummy 2 layer cake.

❦ SHELLY'S FROSTING RECIPE ❦
Rose Roberts

2 lb. pkg. powdered sugar
¾ c. Crisco shortening
½ c. water
1 tsp. Wilton clear butter
   flavor

1 tsp. salt
1 tsp. vanilla

Beat all ingredients on high for 5 minutes. Store in airtight container and refrigerate. It will last up to one month in the refrigerator. The frosting can also be frozen. Instead of using canned frosting for the preschool, we use this recipe.

❦ TEXAS SHEET CAKE ❦
Anne Yarger
Sherri Trout

Cake:

2 c. flour
2 c. sugar
½ tsp. salt
2 eggs
½ c. buttermilk

1 tsp. soda
2 sticks margarine
1 c. water
4 T. cocoa

Combine in large bowl, but do not mix: flour, sugar, salt, eggs, buttermilk, and soda. Bring margarine, water and cocoa to boil. Add all at once to flour mixture while hot and mix well. Pour into greased large pan. Bake at 350° for 20 to 25 minutes.

Frosting:

⅔ c. margarine
4 T. milk
3 T. cocoa

Powdered sugar
1 tsp. vanilla
1 c. nuts

(continued)

Bring margarine, milk and cocoa to a boil and add powered sugar until thick enough to spread. Add vanilla and nuts. Frost while cake is hot.

❦ TRIPLE CHOCOLATE CAKE ❦
Shari Garder

Cake:

1 ¾ c. milk
2 eggs
1 tsp. vanilla
1 pkg. chocolate cake mix

4 oz. pkg. instant chocolate
     pudding mix
12 oz. chocolate chips

In large bowl, combine milk, eggs, and vanilla. Add the cake mix, pudding mix and chocolate chips to the liquid mixture and blend well. Pour into greased 10-inch bundt pan. Bake at 350° for 50-55 minutes. Cool 15 minutes. Remove from pan.

Glaze:

2 T. cocoa
1 T. plus 2 tsp. water
1 T. oil

1 T. cornstarch
1 c. powdered sugar

Combine cocoa, water, oil, and cornstarch in a saucepan; cook over low heat until smooth. Add powdered sugar and mix well. Drizzle warm glaze over cooled cake.

❦ WHITE TEXAS SHEET CAKE ❦
Marilyn Thomsen

Cake:

1 c. butter or margarine
1 c. water
2 c. flour
2 c. sugar
2 eggs, beaten

½ c. sour cream (or ½ c. half
     and half plus 1 tsp. vinegar)
1 tsp. almond extract
1 tsp. salt
1 tsp. baking soda

Bring butter and water to a boil in a saucepan. Stir in flour, sugar, beaten eggs, sour cream, almond extract, salt and baking soda, and stir

(continued)

121822-12

until smooth. Pour into greased jelly roll pan. Bake 20 minutes at 375°
until golden brown. Cool 20 minutes before frosting. .

Frosting:

½ c. butter
¼ c. milk
4½ c. (1 lb.) powdered sugar

½ tsp. almond extract
Chopped pecans, if desired

Bring butter and milk to a boil in saucepan. Add powdered sugar and
almond extract. Pour over cake. Top with chopped pecans, if desired.

PIES

❦ "BISHOP'S" CHOCOLATE PIE ❦
Kathy Christiansen
Rita Bigelow

1 pkg. instant French vanilla
  pudding
1 pkg. instant chocolate fudge
  pudding
2 c. vanilla ice cream

2 c. cold milk
1 prepared graham cracker
  crust
Whipped cream
Chocolate shavings, if desired

In a large bowl beat both puddings, ice cream and milk on low speed
until creamy. Pour into the prepared graham cracker crust. Cool in
refrigerator until set. When set, top with whipped cream and serve.
May put chocolate shavings on top to be truly authentic Bishop's pie!

❦ BROWN BAG APPLE PIE ❦
Randi VenHuizen

Apple Filling:

7 c. apples
2 T. lemon juice
½ c. sugar
2 T. flour

¼ tsp. nutmeg or ½ tsp.
  cinnamon
2 - 3 dashes angostura bitters
9-inch pastry shell

Pare and core apples into chunks. Put in bowl and sprinkle with lemon
juice. In another bowl, combine sugar, flour, nutmeg or cinnamon and
bitters. Pour over apples, toss and spoon into pie shell.

(continued)

Topping:

½ c. sugar   1 stick butter
½ c. flour

Combine sugar and flour. Cut in butter. Sprinkle over apples. Slide pie into heavy paper bag (large enough to cover pie loosely). Fold open end over twice, staple closed. Place on cookie sheet. Bake at 425° for one hour.

❦ CHERRY PIE ❦
Julie Concannon

Two Crust Standard Pastry:

⅔ c. plus 2 T. shortening   4 - 5 T. very cold water (I put
2 c. all-purpose flour   in the freezer while I prep.)
1 tsp. salt

Cut shortening into flour and salt until particles are size of small peas. Sprinkle in water, 1 tablespoon at a time, tossing with fork until all flour is moistened and pastry almost cleans side of bowl. Gather pastry into two balls; shape one ball into flattened round on lightly floured surface. Roll pastry two inches larger than inverted pie plate with floured rolling pin. Roll flattened pastry onto rolling pin and ease into pie plate, pressing against bottom and side. Trim overhang ½-inch from rim of pie plate. Prepare cherry filling.

Cherry Filling:

1 ⅓ c. sugar   ¼ tsp. almond extract
½ c. all-purpose flour   2 T. butter
3 cans (14.5 oz. each) pitted
   red tart cherries, drained

Heat oven to 425°. Mix sugar and flour. Stir in cherries. Turn into pastry-lined pie plate; sprinkle with almond extract and dot with butter. Cover with top crust which has been rolled out just as bottom crust and trim overhang 1-inch from rim of plate. Cut a few slits in top crust to let steam escape during baking. Fold and roll top edge under lower edge, pressing on rim to seal; flute. Cover edge with 2 to 3-inch strip of foil to prevent excessive browning; remove foil during last 15 minutes of baking. Bake until crust is light golden brown and juice begins to bubble through slits in crust, 35 to 45 minutes. Cool and enjoy.

121822-12

❦ CHOCOLATE PIE ❦
Deb Schuchard

1 lg. chocolate bar
1 (8 oz.) Cool Whip

1 graham cracker crust
1 regular chocolate bar

In medium pan, melt large chocolate bar on low heat. Put Cool Whip in bowl. When chocolate is melted, fold into Cool Whip. Pour into pie crust. Refrigerate 2 hours. Take other chocolate bar and with carrot peeler, slice off parts of chocolate bar to go on top of pie. Enjoy.

❦ COCONUT TORTE ❦
Cheyrle Badtke

1 c. crushed graham crackers
½ c. chopped nuts
½ c. coconut (angel flake)
¼ tsp. salt

1 c. sugar
1 tsp. vanilla
4 egg whites, beaten until stiff
Ice cream

Mix graham crackers, chopped nuts, coconut, salt and sugar. Add vanilla and egg whites. Bake in an 8-inch pie tin for 30 minutes in a 300° or 350° oven. Cool, cut into wedges and serve with ice cream on top.

❦ EASY BLUEBERRY PIE ❦
Mary Lou Gustafson
From Donna Humphrey

1 c. sugar
2 T. corn starch
2 pt. fresh blueberries, divided
⅓ c. water

1 T. lemon juice
1 T. butter
9-inch baked pie shell
  (shortbread is best)

Mix sugar, cornstarch and one pint of blueberries and water in a sauce pan. Cook slowly, stirring, until thickened. It looks like a blueberry glaze as it thickens. Cook one minute more. Remove from heat and add lemon juice and butter. Place one pint of cleaned and well drained blueberries in the pie shell. Pour hot blueberry mixture over the fresh ones in the pie shell. Chill. Serve with whipped cream or ice cream. Enjoy!

❦ EASY PIE CRUST ❦
Deb Lund

1½ c. flour (I use ½ c. whole
  wheat pastry flour)
1 tsp. sugar

¾ tsp. salt
½ c. canola oil
2½ T. milk

Stir dry ingredients together in large pie plate (9½-inch or 10-inch).
Stir oil and milk together, and pour over dry ingredients in pie plate.
Stir together. Press into pie plate. Bake at 400° at least 10 minutes
until lightly browned, if baked crust desired. Or add pie filling and
bake. Makes one large, single crust.

❦ FRESH PUMPKIN PIE ❦
Rose Roberts

Fresh Pumpkin:

Pumpkin
Nonstick spray

¼ c. water

To fix fresh pumpkin, cut a pumpkin into strips, peel, remove seeds,
and cut into small pieces. Spray roaster pan with nonstick spray, place
pumpkin pieces in pan and add ¼ cup water. Bake for 2 hours at 375°.
Take from oven and put into blender and purée.

Pie Filling:

2 eggs
2 c. freshly prepared pumpkin
¼ c. white sugar
¼ c. brown sugar
¼ tsp. salt
1¼ tsp. cinnamon

1 tsp. ginger
¾ tsp. nutmeg
1 tsp. pumpkin spice
⅔ c. evaporated milk
9-inch pastry shell

Combine eggs and fresh pumpkin. Blend in sugars, salt and spices.
Add milk, mix well. Pour into 9-inch pastry shell. Bake at 400° for
50 minutes or until knife inserted halfway comes out clean.

❦ LAUREL'S FAVORITE APPLE PIE ❦

Julie Concannon

Two Crust Standard Pastry:

⅔ c. plus 2 T. shortening
2 c. all-purpose flour
1 tsp. salt

4 - 5 T. very cold water (I put in the freezer while I prep.)

Cut shortening into flour and salt until particles are size of small peas. Sprinkle in water, 1 tablespoon at a time, tossing with fork until all flour is moistened and pastry almost cleans side of bowl. Gather pastry into two balls; shape one ball into flattened round on lightly floured surface. Roll pastry two inches larger than inverted pie plate with floured rolling pin. Roll flattened pastry onto rolling pin and ease into pie plate, pressing against bottom and side. Trim overhang ½-inch from rim of pie plate. Prepare apple filling.

Fresh Apple Filling:

¾ c. sugar
¼ c. all-purpose flour
½ tsp. ground nutmeg
½ tsp. ground cinnamon
Dash salt

6 c. thinly sliced pared tart apples (about 6 med., I use Jonagold)
2 T. butter

Heat oven to 425°. Mix sugar, flour, nutmeg, cinnamon and salt. Stir in apples. Turn into pastry-lined pie plate; dot with butter. Cover with top crust which has been rolled out just as bottom crust and trim overhang 1-inch from rim of plate. Cut a few slits in top crust to let steam escape during baking. Fold and roll top edge under lower edge, pressing on rim to seal; flute. Cover edge with 2 to 3-inch strip of foil to prevent excessive browning; remove foil during last 15 minutes of baking. Bake until crust is light golden brown and juice begins to bubble through slits, 40-50 minutes. Cool and enjoy!

❦ MOM'S DELUXE CHOCOLATE PECAN PIE ❦
Brian Vandeventer

3 eggs
½ c. sugar
½ c. butter
1 c. dark Karo syrup
1 c. pecans

1 tsp. vanilla
½ tsp. salt
1 c. chocolate chips
Prepared pie crust

Beat eggs slightly, add sugar and butter. Cream until fluffy. Add all other ingredients and fold into egg mixture. Pour into prepared pie crust. Bake at 325° for 50 minutes. Makes one large pie.

❦ PIE CRUST ❦
Harry Naasz
From my Aunt Althea

4 c. flour
2 c. Crisco

1 c. 7 up pop or diet 7 up
A little salt

Combine all ingredients. Not sure how many crusts this makes and I never used 4 cups flour. This recipe is from my Aunt Althea who had 9 children and was the cook at Bowdle School in South Dakota. She baked a lot!

❦ SOUR CREAM RHUBARB PIE ❦
Kay Keiser

1 (9-inch) deep pie crust
3½ c. chopped rhubarb
1 egg, slightly beaten
1½ c. sugar

3 T. flour
½ tsp. salt
1 c. sour cream

Preheat oven to 425°. Place rhubarb in pie shell. Blend well egg, sugar, flour, salt and sour cream. Pour over rhubarb. Bake 15 minutes at 425°; then turn down to 350° for 30 to 35 minutes.

121822-12

❦ STRAWBERRY PIE ❦
Connie Walther

Crust:

1 c. flour

2 T. sugar

½ c. soft oleo (margarine)

1 qt. strawberries, sliced

Mix flour, sugar and oleo then pat crust into 9-inch pie pan. Prick well. Bake at 350° for 10 minutes. Cool. Arrange strawberries in cooled pie shell.

Glaze:

1¼ c. water

1 c. sugar

2 T. cornstarch

1 (3 oz.) sugar free strawberry jello

Whipped cream

Boil water, sugar and cornstarch until clear. Add strawberry jello. Pour cooled gelatin mixture over berries in crust. Chill. Top with whipped cream and a berry to serve.

SWEET TREATS

❦ ALMOND PASTE ❦
Deb Lund

1½ c. blanched almonds, finely ground, I use my little food processor

1½ c. powdered sugar

1 egg white

1½ tsp. almond extract

⅛ - ¼ tsp. salt

Grind the almonds. Add the sugar. Add the egg white and work the mixture vigorously. Use dough hook in mixer or food processor or knead by hand. Add almond extract and salt and process until smooth. Divide into ½ cup portions and keep refrigerated in airtight containers for 1 month or freeze up to 3 months. Yield 1½ cups.

❦ APPLE CRUMBLE ❦
Lisa Rieff

3 c. apples, peeled and
  chopped
½ c. sugar
¼ c. packed brown sugar
2 tsp. cinnamon

¼ c. butter, cut small
½ c. melted butter
1 pouch Betty Crocker
  oatmeal cookie mix
½ c. chopped pecans

In a large bowl toss together the apples, sugar, brown sugar and cinnamon. Stir in the cut butter. Spread into a lightly greased 8 x 8-inch pan. In the same bowl (not rinsed), melt the ½ cup butter and stir in the cookie mix. Sprinkle over the filling. Bake at 300° for 40 minutes. Remove and sprinkle the pecans on top. Bake an additional 15-20 minutes. Recipe can be doubled and baked in a 9 x 13-inch pan. The cooking time remains the same. Serve with cinnamon or vanilla bean ice cream.

❦ BAKED APPLES ❦
Julie Concannon

4 lg. unpeeled tart cooking
  apples (I like to use
  Jonagold)

2 - 4 T. packed brown sugar
4 tsp. butter
½ tsp. ground cinnamon

Heat oven to 375°. Core apples to within ½-inch of bottom. Peel 1-inch strip of skin from around middle of each apple, or peel upper half of each apple to prevent splitting. Place apples in ungreased glass baking dish. Place 1 teaspoon to 1 tablespoon sugar (I use 2 teaspoons packed brown sugar in each apple), 1 teaspoon butter and ⅛ teaspoon cinnamon in center of each apple. Pour water into baking dish until ¼-inch deep. Bake 30 to 40 minutes or until apples are tender when pierced with a fork. Time will vary depending on size and variety of apple. Spoon syrup in dish over apples several times during baking if desired. Although this is an excellent dessert it is also very good as a side dish with pork dishes or even breakfast dishes (which we usually enjoy for dinner instead).

❧ BLUEBERRY SURPRISE ❧
Debra Gillespie

½ c. butter, softened
¼ c. packed brown sugar
1 c. flour
½ c. pecans, chopped

½ gal. vanilla ice cream, softened
1 (21 oz.) can blueberry pie filling

Heat oven to 400°. Mix butter, sugar, flour, and pecans. Press evenly in bottom of ungreased 9 x 9 x 2-inch pan. Bake about 12 minutes until light brown, then crumble with spoon. Cool. Reserve 1 cup of crumbs. Press remaining crumbs evenly in bottom of pan. Pack ice cream on crumbs. Sprinkle reserved crumbs on top. Wrap tightly and place in freezer. Before serving: Heat the can of pie filling. Cut the ice cream base into 3-inch squares. Spoon on warm pie filling and serve immediately. Serves 9.

❧ BLUEBERRY-RHUBARB CRISP ❧
Karen Armitage

Topping:

1 c. pecan halves, chopped
2 c. old fashioned rolled oats
1 tsp. salt
1 c. light brown sugar

¾ c. flour
½ tsp. cinnamon
½ c. (1 stick) butter, cold and cubed

Mix pecans, oats, salt, sugar, flour and cinnamon. Cut in the cold butter. Set aside.

Filling:

1½ lbs. fresh or frozen blueberries
2 lbs. rhubarb, chopped, fresh or frozen

Juice of ½ lime
½ tsp. salt
1 c. sugar
⅔ c. flour

Preheat oven to 350° for frozen fruit or 375° for fresh. Toss blueberries, rhubarb, lime juice, salt, sugar and flour together until evenly mixed. Spread into a deep 9 x 13-inch pan. Sprinkle topping over filling. Bake 40-50 minutes until bubbling and browned for fresh. For frozen, bake for 25 minutes, then increase oven to 375° and bake another 30-40 minutes. Serve with vanilla ice cream.

❦ BUTTERFINGER CANDY BAR DESSERT ❦
Karen Anderson

2 c. graham cracker crumbs
1 c. soda cracker crumbs
1 stick butter, softened
2 pkgs. vanilla instant pudding
2 c. milk

4 c. vanilla ice cream, softened
8 oz. Cool Whip
3 Butterfinger candy bars, crushed

Combine crumbs and butter. Lightly grease a 9 x 13-inch pan. Press ⅔ of crumb mixture in bottom of pan. Combine instant pudding and milk. Blend in ice cream. Pour over crumbs. Place in freezer until ice cream is set. Spread Cool Whip on top. Mix crushed candy bars with saved crumb mixture and sprinkle over top of dessert.

❦ CARAMEL SAUCE ❦
Deb Lund

1 c. sugar
⅓ c. softened butter (must use butter)

½ c. cream or half and half (I use half and half)

Must have the butter and the half and half measured and ready to go, as the sugar cooks quickly. Melt the sugar, stirring often, in large, heavy kettle (2-3 qt. kettle) over high heat. I use a large metal whisk. When sugar becomes a rich amber color, add butter and stir carefully, as the mixture bubbles and creates steam. Add the half and half, stirring carefully. Remove from heat. Stir to make sure mixture is smooth. Cool for a few minutes, then pour into glass jar. Keep in refrigerator, and warm in microwave before using. Great on ice cream, and any dessert that asks for caramel.

❦ CARAMELS ❦
Dawn Burton

15 oz. condensed milk
½ c. half and half
1 c. light Karo syrup
2 c. sugar

1 c. whole milk
¼ c. butter
2 tsp. pure vanilla

(continued)

121822-12

Combine condensed milk, half and half, Karo, sugar, whole milk and butter in heavy pan and stir constantly to 245° on a candy thermometer or firm ball stage in cold water. Remove from heat and add vanilla. Pour into buttered 8-inch pan. Cool and cut into small pieces. Alternate choices: 1) Pour ½ caramel mixture into buttered pan and sprinkle with 1 c. pecans and then continue as above. 2) Remove caramel mixture from heat before the 245° temperature is reached and dip clean, dry apples with stick inserted into mixture and place on waxed paper covered pan or dip in nuts and then place on waxed paper.

❦ CATHEDRAL WINDOWS ❦
Brian Vandeventer
Marjorie Galloway

1 (6 oz.) pkg. chocolate chips	½ c. chopped nuts
1 T. butter	1 c. flaked coconut
1 egg, beaten	⅛ tsp. coconut flavoring
3 c. miniature marshmallows (colored)	¼ tsp. vanilla
	Coconut for rolling

Melt chocolate chips and butter. Slowly add egg and let cool to lukewarm. Fold in remaining ingredients except coconut for rolling. Turn out on waxed paper covered in additional coconut and form into a roll. Wrap roll in waxed paper or foil. Chill until time to slice and serve. May be frozen if desired.

❦ CHOCOLATE CLUSTERS ❦
Heidi Meyer

6 oz. chocolate chips	1 c. mini marshmallows
6 oz. butterscotch chips	7 oz. salted peanuts that have
½ c. peanut butter	been in the freezer

Melt chocolate chips, butterscotch chips, and peanut butter in a medium sauce pan on low. Remove from heat and stir in marshmallows and cold peanuts. Drop by teaspoonful in paper candy cups. Refrigerate.

❦ CHOCOLATE HAYSTACKS ❦
Cheyrle Badtke

4 squares semi-sweet chocolate
1 c. butterscotch chips
2 c. chow mein noodles

2 c. miniature marshmallows
½ c. cocktail peanuts

Microwave chocolate and butterscotch chips in a medium bowl on high for 2 to 3 minutes or until almost melted, stirring after 1½ minutes. Then stir until completely melted. Add noodles, marshmallows and peanuts and mix well until evenly coated. Drop mixture by tablespoons onto waxed paper or a baking sheet. Refrigerate 1 hour or until firm.

❦ CHOCOLATE MOUSSE ❦
Carol Novak

1 envelope unflavored gelatin
¼ c. cold water
⅓ c. boiling water
1 c. sugar (or Splenda for low carb recipe)
⅔ c. cocoa powder (I use Hershey's Special Dark Cocoa)

1 pt. cold whipping cream
2 tsp. vanilla extract
1 tsp. chocolate extract, optional

In a small bowl, sprinkle gelatin over cold water. Let stand 2 minutes to soften. Add boiling water and stir until gelatin is completely dissolved. Cool slightly. Mix sugar or Splenda and cocoa in mixer bowl. Add whipping cream and extracts. Beat at medium speed, scraping bottom of bowl occasionally, until mixture is stiff. Watch this closely. Do not over beat or you will have lumpy chocolate butter-- voice of experience! Pour in gelatin mixture and mix until well blended. Spoon into dessert dishes and cover. Store covered in refrigerator. You can also freeze them and enjoy a frozen dessert. Makes 8 servings. If you use Splenda, this dessert has approximately 5 grams of carbohydrates per serving.

121822-12

🍎 EASY APPLE CRISP 🍎
Karen Anderson

6 lg. Granny Smith apples	½ c. flour
8 graham crackers	1 tsp. cinnamon
¾ c. packed brown sugar	½ tsp. nutmeg
½ c. instant oats	½ c. butter, melted

Peel and slice apples, place in baking dish. Finely chop graham crackers. Combine crumbs, sugar, oats, flour and spices. Add melted butter; mix well. Spoon mixture over apples. Microwave on high 12-15 minutes or until apples are tender. Turn dish after 6 minutes. Allow to cool slightly. Serve with whipped cream or ice cream.

🍎 EASY FUDGE 🍎
Randi VenHuizen

1 stick butter	2 eggs
12 oz. pkg. semi-sweet chocolate chips	½ tsp. vanilla
1 lb. powdered sugar	Non-stick cooking spray

Melt butter and chocolate chips. In a large bowl, mix powdered sugar, eggs and vanilla. Add the melted chocolate, blend until smooth. Pour into pan (sprayed with non-stick cooking spray), chill.

🍎 EASY MICROWAVE PEANUT BRITTLE 🍎
Deb Lund

1 c. sugar	1 tsp. butter
½ c. light corn syrup	1 tsp. vanilla
1 generous c. raw peanuts	1 generous tsp. baking soda

Have a greased cookie sheet ready. In 2-quart glass bowl or Pyrex measuring bowl, combine sugar and syrup. Microwave on high for 3 minutes. Stir, and add peanuts. Microwave on high for 5-8 minutes, stirring every 2 minutes, until peanuts turn light brown, but are not burning! Add butter and vanilla and stir well. Add baking soda, and stir gently and quickly, until light and foamy. Pour mixture onto lightly greased cookie sheet. Let cool at least 30 minutes. When cool, break into pieces and store in tight container.

❦ EASY OREO TRUFFLES ❦
Shari Garder

8 oz. cream cheese, softened
1 pkg. Oreo cookies, finely crushed

2 pkgs. (8 squares each) semi-sweet chocolate, melted

Mix cream cheese and 3 c. of cookie crumbs until well blended. Shape into 48 (1-inch) balls. Dip in melted chocolate; place on waxed paper-covered baking sheet. Sprinkle with remaining cookie crumbs. Refrigerate 1 hour or until firm. Store in tightly covered container in refrigerator.

❦ FRUIT PIZZA ❦
Lisa Rieff

2 c. flour
1 c. butter, softened
1½ c. sugar, divided
8 oz. cream cheese, softened
1 tsp. vanilla

8 oz. Cool Whip, thawed
Fresh fruit such as:
   strawberries, pineapple, kiwi, blueberries and raspberries

Make a soft dough mixing together the flour, butter and ½ cup of the sugar. Spread into a greased pizza pan and bake at 350° for 20-25 minutes. Let cool. Combine the remaining 1 cup sugar with the cream cheese and vanilla. Fold in the Cool Whip. Spread over crust. Top with fruit. Refrigerate about 2 hours before serving.

❦ FUDGE TRUFFLE CHEESECAKE ❦
Julie Concannon

1½ c. vanilla wafer crumbs (about 45 wafers)
6 T. powdered sugar
⅓ c. unsweetened cocoa powder
⅓ c. butter, melted
3 (8 oz.) pkgs. cream cheese, softened
1 (14 oz.) can Eagle Brand sweetened condensed milk

12 oz. semi-sweet chocolate chips, melted
4 eggs
2 tsp. vanilla extract
¼ c. coffee-flavored liqueur, optional
Melted semi-sweet chocolate, optional

(continued)

121822-12

Preheat oven to 300°. Prepare chocolate crumb crust by combining the wafer crumbs, powdered sugar, unsweetened cocoa powder and melted butter in a bowl. Press firmly on bottom and ½-inch up side of 9-inch springform pan. Set aside. With mixer, beat cream cheese in large bowl until fluffy. Gradually beat in Eagle Brand until smooth. Add melted chocolate chips, eggs and vanilla; mix well. Stir in liqueur if desired. Pour into prepared pan. Bake 65-70 minutes or until center appears nearly set when shaken. Cool on wire rack for 2 hours. Chill in refrigerator for at least 4 hours. To serve, drizzle with additional melted chocolate if desired. Store leftovers covered in refrigerator. 16 servings.

❦ ICE CREAM DESSERT ❦
Shawn Lorenzen

¾ c. butter
1 c. brown sugar
6 c. rice chex

1 c. coconut
1 c. chopped nuts
½ gallon ice cream of choice

Bring butter and brown sugar to a boil. Pour over dry ingredients, mix well. Press ½ of the mixture into the bottom of a cake pan. Use ½ gallon of ice cream and cover bottom. Pour remaining ½ of topping onto ice cream and press down. Freeze.

❦ ICE CREAM YUMMY DESSERT ❦
Dayla Miller

2 c. crushed rice chex
1 c. coconut
⅔ c. brown sugar
1 c. chopped nuts

½ stick margarine or butter
½ gallon butter brickle or
    butter pecan ice cream,
    softened

Mix everything but ice cream and spread in a 13 x 9-inch pan. Bake at 250° for 25 minutes, stir occasionally. Reserve 1 cup for the top. Spread mixture evenly and add ½ gallon softened ice cream on top of mixture, top with reserved mixture and refreeze.

❦ JELLO CHEESECAKE ❦
Lynda McGraw

1 lg. box orange or any flavor jello
1 c. boiling water
1 can Pet or Carnation milk, chilled
1 lg. pkg. cream cheese
¾ c. sugar
2 tsp. vanilla
1 graham cracker crust

Mix jello and water together; set aside in refrigerator until syrupy. Beat Pet/Carnation milk until fluffy (takes a while). Mix cream cheese, sugar and vanilla together. Mix jello and Pet/Carnation milk together real well. Add cream cheese mixture. Pour all into a graham cracker crust. Chill until firm. Makes two 9-inch pies or 1 loaf pan.

❦ MICROWAVE APPLE CRISP ❦
Cheyrle Badtke

4 lg. Granny Smith apples, peeled, cored and sliced
½ c. butter, melted
¾ c. packed brown sugar
¾ c. quick cooking oats
½ c. flour
1 tsp. cinnamon
½ tsp. allspice

Spread the apples in an 8-inch square glass baking dish. A deep glass pie plate will also work. In a bowl, mix together the melted butter, brown sugar, oats, flour, cinnamon and allspice. Sprinkle topping evenly over apples. Cook on full power in the microwave for 10-12 minutes until apples can easily be pierced with a knife.

❦ MINI CHEESE CAKES ❦
Anne Yarger
Sherri Trout

Cup cake liners
3 (8-oz.) pkgs. cream cheese
⅔ c. sugar
3 eggs
1 tsp. vanilla
24 vanilla wafers
1 can cherry pie filling or blueberry pie filling

Line 2 muffin tins with cup cake liners. Mix cream cheese (at room temperature), sugar, eggs and vanilla. Put a vanilla wafer in each muffin cup and spoon in cheese mixture. Bake 15 minutes at 350°. When cooled, spoon pie filling over cake. Serves 24.

121822-12

❦ OVEN CARAMEL CORN ❦
Dawn Burton

2 c. brown sugar
2 sticks butter
½ c. Karo white corn syrup

1 tsp. salt
1 tsp. baking soda
7½ qt. popped popcorn

Cook sugar, butter, corn syrup and salt in a heavy pan for 5 minutes. Remove from heat and add soda. Pour over popcorn and stir well. Spread on cookie sheets. Bake at 200° for one hour, stirring every 15 minutes. Remove from oven. Let cool.

❦ PEANUT BRITTLE (MICROWAVE) ❦
Kathy Christiansen
Tami Watts-McPhail

1 c. sugar
½ c. white corn syrup
⅛ tsp. salt (don't add the salt
   if using salty peanuts)
2 T. butter

1 tsp. vanilla
1 c. raw peanuts (or you can
   use the salty ones with skins)
1 tsp. baking soda

In 1½-quart casserole or large bowl (able to go into microwave), stir together sugar, syrup, and salt. Cook 8 minutes at high, stirring well after 4 minutes. BE CAREFUL - GETS VERY HOT!! Stir in butter and vanilla. Cook 3 minutes longer on high. Add peanuts. Add baking soda and quickly stir until light and foamy. Immediately pour onto lightly greased baking sheet; spread out thin. When cool, break into small pieces. Store in airtight container.

❦ PEANUT BUTTER FUDGE ❦
Christie Klos

2 c. sugar
½ c. milk
1⅓ c. peanut butter

1 (7 oz.) jar marshmallow
creme

In saucepan bring sugar and milk to a boil. Boil for 3 minutes. Add peanut butter and marshmallow creme. Mix well. Quickly pour into a 8-inch square pan. Chill.

❦ PECAN CRUNCH ❦
Jackie Combes

9 c. corn chex
9 c. rice chex
8 oz. pecan pieces

2 sticks butter
1 c. brown sugar
1 c. white Karo syrup

Mix cereal and pecans and set aside. Combine butter, sugar, and syrup in a saucepan and cook over medium heat until melted. Once melted, turn heat up until mixture reaches a rolling boil. Boil for 90 seconds, stirring constantly. Pour over cereal and stir until cereal is well coated. Spread cereal mixture on two cookie sheets. Bake at 225° for 15 minutes. Stir and bake an additional 15 minutes. Spread on wax paper to cool. Stir occasionally so mixture does not stick to wax paper. Store in air tight container.

❦ POPCORN BALLS ❦
Dawn Burton

1 c. sugar
½ c. butter
½ c. white Karo corn syrup
¼ c. water

2 T. vinegar
1 tsp. vanilla
2 bags microwaved popped popcorn

Stir sugar, butter, corn syrup, water and vinegar in a saucepan, then boil until soft ball stage. Add vanilla and pour over popcorn in a large mixing bowl. Pour out onto cake pan. Can form balls with buttered hands or leave as loose clumps.

❦ SALTED PEANUT CHEWS ❦
Julie Concannon

Crust:

1½ c. all-purpose flour
⅔ c. firmly packed brown sugar
½ tsp. baking powder
½ tsp. salt
¼ tsp. baking soda

½ c. margarine or butter, softened
1 tsp. vanilla
2 egg yolks
3 c. miniature marshmallows

(continued)

121822-12

Heat oven to 350°. In large bowl, combine all crust ingredients except marshmallows at low speed until crumbly. Press firmly in bottom of ungreased 13 x 9-inch pan. Bake at 350° for 12 to 15 minutes or until light golden brown. Remove crust from oven. Immediately sprinkle with marshmallows. Return to oven, bake an additional 1-2 minutes or until marshmallows just begin to puff. Cool while preparing topping.

Topping:

⅔ c. corn syrup
¼ c. margarine or butter
2 tsp. vanilla
1 (10 oz.) pkg. peanut butter
  chips

2 c. crisp rice cereal
2 c. salted peanuts

In large saucepan, combine all topping ingredients except cereal and peanuts. Heat just until chips are melted and mixture is smooth, stirring constantly. Remove from heat; stir in cereal and peanuts. Immediately spoon warm topping over marshmallows; spread to cover. Refrigerate 45 minutes or until firm. Cut into bars. 36 bars. You can prepare these bars several days ahead; keep them covered and refrigerated. These bars also freeze well.

❦ SOUTHERN PRALINES ❦
Ruth Manning

1 c. granulated sugar
1 c. brown sugar
¾ c. half and half
¼ tsp. salt

2 T. butter
1 tsp. vanilla
1 c. chopped pecans

Butter sides of a heavy saucepan (2-quart size). Add sugars, half and half and salt to saucepan. Cook over low heat, stirring constantly until sugar is dissolved. Raise heat to medium and continue to cook, stirring constantly until mixture boils. Reduce heat and continue cooking to 234° on a candy thermometer. Remove from heat. Add butter and vanilla, but do not stir. Cool for 5 minutes, stir in nuts. Beat with wooden spoon until candy is no longer glossy and is thickened, about 2 to 3 minutes. Quickly spoon candy onto buttered baking sheets or waxed paper. If mixture becomes too thick to drop from a spoon, add a little hot water, no more than half a teaspoon at a time. Makes about 36 pralines.

❦ SUSIE'S BAKED RICE PUDDING ❦
Rose Roberts

3 c. cooked rice
1 c. evaporated milk
1 c. regular milk
Dash of salt

¼ c. sugar
4 eggs, beaten
2 tsp. vanilla
Nutmeg and cinnamon to taste

Combine all ingredients and bake for 45 minutes at 350°.

❦ SWEET CRISPIX MIX ❦
Dayla Miller

2 sticks margarine or butter
1½ c. brown sugar
⅓ c. light Karo syrup
1 tsp. vanilla

½ tsp. baking soda
1 box Crispix cereal
2 c. peanuts
1 bag M & M's

In medium pan combine margarine, brown sugar and Karo syrup. Bring to a boil for 3 minutes, remove from heat and add vanilla and baking soda. Empty Crispix into paper bag, add peanuts and pour liquid over cereal and shake bag. Microwave 2½ minutes, remove bag from microwave and shake, put back into microwave for another 2½ minutes. Pour onto wax paper to cool. Once cool, break up the pieces and put into bowl or Zip lock bag. Add M & M's. Enjoy!

❦ SWEET PARTY MIX ❦
Lisa Meyer

1 box Crispix cereal
1 lb. bag pretzel sticks
2 cans cocktail peanuts or a
   jar of dry roasted peanuts
2 c. brown sugar
½ c. white corn syrup

1 c. butter
1 tsp. salt
1 tsp. baking soda
⅛ tsp. cream of tartar
1 lg. bag plain M & Ms

Put the Crispix cereal, pretzels and peanuts in a paper grocery sack and mix. Mix the brown sugar, white corn syrup, butter and salt and boil for 3 minutes. Add baking soda and cream of tartar. Mix and pour the melted mixture over the ingredients in the grocery sack. Mix. Close the grocery sack and microwave for 2½ minutes. Shake it up or stir and microwave 2½ minutes more. Pour into a large bowl to cool. Stir

(continued)

121822-12

about every 15 minutes and, after about an hour, add the M & M's (they will melt or crack if you add them when it is too hot).

❦ TOFFEE ❦
Dawn Burton

1 c. butter
1 c. sugar
¼ c. water

Hershey bars or chocolate
chips
Pecans, if desired

Combine butter, sugar and water in a heavy pan and cook for 15 minutes on medium to medium high heat until amber in color, stirring constantly. Pour into pan and put pieces of Hershey bars or chocolate chips on top, spread with a knife. Put pecans on if desired. Break into pieces when cool.

❦ ZUPPA INGLESSE ❦
Mary Lou Gustafson

Prepared angel food cake
Amaretto liquor
2 sm. boxes instant French
vanilla pudding
2 c. half and half

1 c. real whipping cream,
whipped
English toffee chips
Nutmeg

Tear cake into small pieces in bowl. Sprinkle heavily with Amaretto. In another bowl mix pudding with half and half. Add ¼ cup Amaretto to pudding. Fold pudding into cake. Put in serving container (oblong dish or is very pretty in a footed glass bowl). Spread whipped cream over top. Sprinkle with toffee chips. Sprinkle nutmeg over all. Refrigerate. Serves 16.

Recipe Favorites

Vegetables & Side Dishes

VEGETABLES & SIDE DISHES

❧ BAKED LEMON PASTA ❧
Kathy Christiansen

1 lb. thin spaghetti
4 T. butter
2 T. olive oil
2 cloves garlic, minced
1 lemon, juiced and zested
2 c. sour cream
½ tsp. salt, or more to taste
Extra lemon juice
Plenty of grated Parmesan
    cheese
Chopped parsley

Preheat oven to 375°. Cook spaghetti until al dente. In a skillet, melt butter with olive oil over LOW HEAT. When butter is melted, add minced garlic. Squeeze lemon juice into the pan. Turn off heat. Add sour cream and stir mixture together. Add lemon zest and salt. Taste, then add more salt if necessary. Pour mixture over drained spaghetti and stir together, then pour spaghetti into an oven safe dish. Cover with foil and bake for 15 minutes. Remove foil and bake for an additional 7 to 10 minutes (don't bake too long or the pasta will dry out). When you remove it from the oven, squeeze a little more lemon juice over the top. Top generously with Parmesan cheese, then chopped parsley. Give it a final squeeze of lemon juice at the end.

❧ BAKED VEGGIE MEDLEY ❧
Brian Vandeventer

1 (10 oz. pkg.) frozen broccoli
1 (10 oz. pkg.) frozen
    cauliflower
1 (10 oz. pkg.) frozen green
    beans
1 (10 oz. pkg.) diced carrots
½ c. margarine
1 can cream of chicken soup
½ c. grated Cheddar cheese
Croutons

Cook vegetables separately and drain. Arrange in layers in a 9 x 13-inch glass baking dish. Melt margarine. Add soup and cheese, and pour over vegetables. Top with croutons and bake for 30 minutes at 350°. May substitute 2 cups canned vegetables for frozen beans and carrots.

❦ BARBEQUED GREEN BEANS ❦
Ruth Cooley

4 slices bacon
¼ c. onion, chopped
½ c. catsup

¼ c. brown sugar
1 T. Worcestershire sauce
2 cans green beans, drained

Dice bacon and brown in skillet along with onion. Add catsup, brown sugar and Worcestershire sauce. Simmer 2 minutes. Place green beans in 1½-quart casserole. Pour bacon mixture over the top of the beans, but do not stir. Bake at 350° for 20-30 minutes. Serves 6.

❦ BOURBON CORN PUDDING ❦
Randi VenHuizen

3 lg. eggs
1⅛ c. evaporated milk
2 cans cream style corn
2 cans corn kernels, drained
3 T. melted butter
3 T. brown sugar

3 T. cornstarch mixed with 3 T. water
¾ tsp. ground nutmeg
4½ T. bourbon (optional)
⅜ tsp. salt
⅜ tsp. pepper

Preheat oven to 350°. Grease a 2-quart baking dish with non stick cooking spray. Beat eggs and evaporated milk together in large bowl. Stir in all remaining ingredients and pour mixture into baking dish. Bake 45 minutes or until slightly browned and a knife inserted in center comes out clean. Serve hot.

❦ CALIFORNIA MIX CASSEROLE ❦
Jill Hild

½ c. onion, chopped
½ c. celery, chopped
½ stick butter
2 pkgs. frozen California mixed vegetables

1 can cream of chicken soup
1 (8 oz.) jar of Cheese Whiz
½ c. Minute Rice, uncooked

Sauté onion and celery in butter. Cook vegetables as directed. Combine the onion/celery mixture and vegetables with the remaining ingredients and blend well. Place in a greased 13 x 9-inch casserole. Bake 20 minutes at 325°.

121822-12

❦ CARROT SOUFFLÉ ❦
Valerie Florea

1½ lbs. carrots, chopped
½ c. butter
3 lg. eggs
¼ c. flour

1½ tsp. baking powder
1 c. sugar
¼ tsp. cinnamon

Preheat oven to 350°. Lightly grease 1½-quart soufflé dish. Cook carrots in water for 15 minutes or until tender. Drain. Combine carrots with butter, eggs, flour, baking powder, sugar and cinnamon and blend until smooth. Pour into prepared dish. Bake for one hour.

❦ CHEESY MACARONI CASSEROLE ❦
(Kid's Favorite Potluck Dish)
Connie Walther

1 (12 oz.) pkg. sm. shell pasta
1 c. cottage cheese, drained
1 can cream of chicken soup
2 T. margarine
½ c. milk
1 (16 oz.) jar Cheese Whiz or
  cheese pasta sauce

8 oz. Cheddar cheese,
  shredded
Spice to taste: black pepper,
  dry mustard, onion powder

Cook pasta until tender and drain. Add cottage cheese, soup, margarine and milk. Add cheese sauce and stir well. Place in greased 9 x 13-inch pan. Sprinkle with shredded cheddar. Bake at 350° for 25 minutes.

❦ CINNAMON ROASTED SWEET POTATOES ❦
Carol Novak

1½ lbs. sweet potatoes, peeled
  and cut into 1-inch chunks
6 unpeeled garlic cloves
3 T. olive oil
2 thyme branches

1 cinnamon stick, broken into
  pieces
1 tsp. salt
½ tsp. freshly ground black
  pepper

(continued)

Preheat oven to 425°. Put all the ingredients in a baking pan and toss to combine, then spread out in an even layer. Roast until the potatoes are tender and browned, 20-40 minutes. Serve hot or warm, along with the garlic cloves. For a savory taste, use a bay leaf and some smoked paprika instead of cinnamon.

❦ COPPER PENNIES ❦
Randi VenHuizen

2 lbs. sliced carrots
½ c. oil
½ tsp. prepared mustard
1 sm. green pepper, thinly
   sliced

¾ c. vinegar
1 onion, thinly sliced
1 c. sugar
1 can tomato soup, undiluted
Salt and pepper to taste

Cook carrots until firm, do not overcook. Add rest of the ingredients. Marinate in refrigerator several days. Serve cold.

❦ CORN AND MACARONI CASSEROLE ❦
Dayla Miller

1 can cream style corn
1 can whole kernel corn
1 c. macaroni, small rings or
   elbow
½ c. American cheese or
   Velveeta

½ c. melted butter
2 T. grated onion
Salt and pepper to taste

Mix together in a greased baking dish, stir through several times while baking. Bake at 350° for 1 hour.

❦ CORN CASSEROLE ❦
Shawn Lorenzen

1 can creamed corn
1 can whole corn, drained
1 c. cut up spaghetti (raw)
1 c. Velveeta cheese, cubed

½ c. butter, melted
¼ c. milk
2 T. minced onion

(continued)

121822-12

Mix all ingredients, bake at 375° for ½ hour with the lid on, ½ hour with the lid off.

❦ CORN CASSEROLE ❦
Lisa Rieff

1 box Jiffy cornbread/muffin mix
1 can cream style corn
1 can whole kernel corn with its liquid

1 egg
1 stick butter, room temperature, cut up
8 oz. sour cream, room temperature

Mix all ingredients and bake at 325° for 1 hour.

❦ COUSCOUS WITH MUSHROOMS ❦
Julie Concannon

1 ¼ c. water
2 T. butter
2 T. chicken bouillon granules or 2 chicken bouillon cubes
¼ tsp. salt

¼ tsp. pepper
1 c. uncooked couscous
1 can (7 oz.) mushroom stems and pieces, drained

In a large saucepan, bring the water, butter, bouillon, salt and pepper to a boil. Stir in couscous and mushrooms. Cover and remove from the heat; let stand for 5 minutes. Fluff with a fork. 4 servings.

❦ CRANBERRY GREEN BEANS ❦
Karen Armitage

1 ½ lbs. fresh green beans
2 T. olive oil
½ c. unsalted, roasted slivered almonds

¼ c. dried cranberries or craisins
Salt and pepper to taste

Bring a large pot of water to boil and add the green beans, cooking until tender or about 4-6 minutes. While beans are boiling, you can combine the olive oil, almonds and cranberries in a large bowl, tossing just enough to coat with olive oil. Drain beans and dry on paper towel, then toss with nuts and cranberries. Salt and pepper to taste.

❦ CREAMY ZUCCHINI CASSEROLE ❦
Kathy Christiansen

4 c. zucchini, sliced
1 stick butter or margarine
1 sm. to med. onion, chopped
1 cup sour cream

1 can cream of celery soup
1 box Pepperidge Farms
seasoned croutons, divided

Boil zucchini just until tender, drain (if using zucchini you had frozen, just thaw it and drain very well, I found no need to cook it). In a large skillet, melt butter. Add onion and sauté until tender. Remove from heat and stir in sour cream and soup (right out of the can). Stir in the drained zucchini and half of the croutons and mix until croutons are coated. Pour into buttered 3-quart baking dish. Top evenly with remaining croutons, cover with foil and bake at 350° for 35-40 minutes or until hot.

❦ FLAVOR BAKED BEANS ❦
Karen Pickens

2 (1 lb.) cans pork and beans
in tomato sauce, divided
¾ c. brown sugar

1 tsp. dry mustard
6 slices bacon, chopped
½ c. catsup

Empty one can of beans into 1 ½-quart casserole. Combine brown sugar and mustard and sprinkle half over beans. Top with the other can of beans and sprinkle with remaining brown sugar mixture. Add chopped bacon and catsup. Bake uncovered in a slow oven 325° for 2 hours. Makes 6-8 servings.

❦ FRUITED WILD RICE ❦
Ruth Manning

¾ c. wild rice
¼ c. butter (½ stick)
1 lg. onion, finely chopped
1 tsp. dried thyme
1 bay leaf
¾ c. long grain white rice
2 c. chicken stock

Salt and pepper to taste
¾ c. coarsely chopped dried
apricots
¾ c. cranberries
½ c. golden raisins
½ c. pecan pieces, toasted

(continued)

121822-12

Cover wild rice with hot water in a large bowl. Let soak for 30 minutes. Drain. Preheat oven to 350°. Melt butter in a large Dutch oven over low heat. Add onion, thyme and bay leaf. Cover and cook until onion is almost tender, stirring occasionally, about 15 minutes. Add wild rice, white rice and stock to onions. Season with salt and pepper. Bring to a boil. Cover and bake until liquid is absorbed, about 30 minutes. Mix apricots, cranberries, raisins and pecans into rice, discarding bay leaf. Transfer to ovenproof dish, cover and bake until fruit softens, about 15 minutes. Uncover and bake another 10 minutes. Yield: 6-8 servings.

❦ GREEK POTATOES ❦
Valerie Florea

8 lg. potatoes, peeled and cut
   into lg. wedges
4 cloves of garlic, minced
½ c. olive oil
1 c. water

1 T. dried oregano
1 lemon
Sea salt to taste, be generous
Black pepper to taste, be
   generous

Preheat oven to 425°. Spray 9 x 13-inch pan with cooking spray. Add all ingredients to pan. Bake for 40 minutes. The potatoes should be a nice golden brown. Give them a stir and add more salt, pepper and oregano. Bake another 30 minutes.

❦ GREEN BEAN & ALMOND RICE ❦
Kathy Christiansen
Sisters of the Cloth

2 c. beef broth
1 c. short grain brown rice
4 T. butter or margarine
¾ c. chopped red pepper

¾ c. chopped onion
10 oz. frozen French-style
   green beans
½ c. toasted slivered almonds

Boil broth in a small sauce pan with a tight fitting lid. Add rice, cover and bring back to a boil. Turn down heat and simmer for 1 hour or until done. Taste to determine how done you like it. In a microwave-safe bowl, combine butter, red pepper and onion. Cook on high power for 2 minutes or until vegetables are soft or sauté in a frying pan until onions are translucent and peppers are cooked. Cook green beans in lightly salted water as directed on package. Drain. Combine rice, onion mixture and green beans. Add almonds and serve.

❧ GUESS AGAIN CARROTS ❧
Ruth Manning

2 lbs. carrots
2 T. butter
1 med. onion, grated
8 oz. grated sharp Cheddar
cheese

½ tsp. salt
⅛ tsp. pepper
Optional: chopped green
pepper, bread crumbs,
melted butter

Peel, slice, and boil carrots until tender. Mash carrots well. Add butter, onion, cheese, salt and pepper and mix well. Place mixture in buttered casserole. If desired, top with green pepper and sprinkle with mixture of crumbs and melted butter. Bake 40 minutes at 350° or until bubbling.

❧ HERB ROASTED SQUASH ❧
Julie Concannon

1 med. zucchini, cut into ¼-
inch slices
1 yellow summer squash, cut
into ¼-inch slices
1 med. tomato, seeded and
chopped

½ c. chopped onion
1 tsp. dried parsley flakes
½ tsp. dried rosemary, crushed
¼ tsp. salt
¼ tsp. pepper
1 T. olive oil

In a large bowl, combine the zucchini, summer squash, tomato, onion, parsley, rosemary, salt and pepper. Drizzle with oil and toss to coat. Place vegetables in a single layer in a greased 15 x 10 x 1-inch baking pan. Bake, uncovered, at 450° for 10-15 minutes or until lightly browned and tender, stirring once. 4 servings.

❧ HERBED-PARMESAN CRISPS ❧
Julie Concannon

4 oz. Parmesan cheese, finely
shredded (about 1½ c.)
2 T. chives, fresh, minced

2 T. parsley, fresh, minced
¼ - ½ tsp. black pepper,
freshly ground

Preheat oven to 425°. Line two cookie sheets with parchment paper (or coat with cooking spray). Place scant tablespoons of cheese on prepared pans, about 1½ to 2-inches apart. Flatten out each pile of cheese into an oval shape; sprinkle with herbs and pepper (when I don't have the fresh herbs on hand I have sprinkled the cheese with

(continued)

Italian seasoning instead). Bake until cheese crisps turn golden and resemble lace cookies, about 5 to 6 minutes. Cool on pan until set and then remove to wire rack to cool completely. 12 servings, 2 cheese crisps per serving. Very good with salads, pasta dishes, soups.

❦ ITALIAN CORN ❦
Karen Anderson

1 can creamed corn
1 can plain corn, ½ drained
1 c. uncooked spaghetti, broken
1 c. Velveeta cheese, cubed or grated American cheese
1 green pepper, diced
½ c. melted butter
1 tsp. grated onion

Mix all ingredients together. Bake at 350° for 30 minutes.

❦ MICROWAVED SCALLOPED POTATOES ❦
Shari Garder

3 c. peeled and sliced potatoes
1 med. onion, diced
¾ c. powdered creamer
3 T. flour
1½ tsp. salt
½ tsp. pepper
1 c. shredded Cheddar cheese
3 T. margarine
1½ c. boiling water

Mix together potatoes, onions, creamer, flour, seasonings, and cheese. Dot with margarine. Pour boiling water over all. Stir. Bake at 350° for 1 hour or in microwave 25 to 30 minutes.

❦ NO NAME POTATOES ❦
Rose Roberts

1 (2 lb.) pkg. frozen hash browns
1 can cream of potato soup
1 can cream of celery soup
16 oz. sour cream
Salt and pepper to taste
Garlic powder to taste

(continued)

Combine ingredients together and pour into a 9 x 13-inch pan. Bake for 2 hours at 300°. Stir occasionally. This works well in the crock pot also.

❦ ONION ROASTED POTATOES ❦
Brian Vandeventer

2 lbs. red potatoes, cut into
  large chunks
⅓ c. olive oil
One envelope dry onion soup
  mix

One large onion sliced/
  chunked (but only for the
  onion lover)

Preheat oven to 425°. In a 13 x 9-inch baking or roasting pan, combine all ingredients. Bake, stirring occasionally, 35 minutes or until potatoes are tender and golden brown.

❦ OVEN FRIED POTATOES ❦
Deb Lund

Potatoes, scrubbed, and sliced
  into thick, long slices
Canola oil or olive oil

Onion salt or powder
Garlic salt or powder
Pepper

Preheat oven to 425°. Spray jelly roll pan with Pam. Place prepared potato slices in bowl or plastic bag. Add small amount of oil (varies according to number of potatoes) and seasonings to taste. Stir or shake, then spread out in prepared pan. Bake 20-30 minutes, stirring occasionally, until done.

❦ PIROGUES CASSEROLE ❦
Kathy Christiansen
Sharon Christiansen

1 lb. lasagna noodles
10 - 12 potatoes, cooked
¼ lb. Cheddar cheese, grated

2 onions, finely diced
2 sticks butter or margarine

Cook noodles according to the package. Mash potatoes, add cheese and beat with mixer. Sauté onions in butter until soft. Add ⅓ of onion and butter mixture to potato mixture. Salt to taste. Generously butter

(continued)

❦ 300

a 9 x 13-inch baking pan. Place layer of lasagna noodles in pan, then a layer of potato mixture. Repeat, ending with noodles. Pour remaining onions and butter over all. Cover with foil (optional). Bake at 350° until heated through, usually about 30 to 45 minutes.

❦ POTATO CASSEROLE ❦
Shari Garder

30 oz. frozen hash brown potatoes	1 onion, chopped
2 c. shredded Cheddar cheese	1 c. (2 sticks) butter, divided
16 oz. sour cream	3 c. crushed corn flakes
1 (10.75 oz.) can cream of mushroom soup	

Preheat over to 425°. Pour the hash browns into a lightly greased 9 x 13-inch baking dish. In a large bowl, combine cheese, sour cream, and soup. In a large skillet over medium heat, combine the onion with 1 stick of butter and sauté for 5 minutes. Add this to the soup mixture and spread over the potatoes. Arrange crushed corn flakes over the potato mixture. Melt 1 stick of butter and pour over corn flakes. Bake for 1 hour.

❦ RICE AND SOUR CREAM CASSEROLE ❦
Kathy Christiansen
Sisters of the Cloth

¾ lb. Monterey Jack cheese	3 c. cooked rice
3 c. sour cream	½ c. grated Cheddar cheese
1 can diced green chilies	

Preheat oven to 350°. Cut MontereyJack cheese in strips. Mix sour cream and chilies. Season with salt and pepper. In a 1½-quart casserole layer rice, sour cream mixture and cheese strips ending with rice on top. Bake for 30 minutes. During the last few minutes of baking, sprinkle Cheddar cheese on top and heat until cheese melts. This usually makes enough for an army so unless you eat like an army or intend on feeding one, half this recipe.

❦ RICH MASHED POTATOES ❦
Karen Armitage

5 lbs. potatoes, peeled and cut
5 T. butter, divided
1 pkg. (8 oz.) cream cheese
1 c. (8 oz.) sour cream
1 tsp. onion salt
¼ tsp. garlic powder
¼ tsp. pepper

Cook potatoes in boiling, salted water until very tender; drain well. Mash with 3 T. butter. Add the cream cheese, sour cream, onion salt, garlic powder, and pepper; mix well. Spread into a greased 9 x 13-inch baking dish. Melt remaining butter; drizzle over the top of potatoes. Cover and freeze for up to 1 month, OR, bake uncovered at 350° for 30-35 minutes or until heated through. Serves 12-14. Can also be frozen in individual or family-sized portions. Good with light sour cream and light cream cheese. Also, good with Yukon Gold potatoes, or unpeeled red potatoes.

❦ SAVORY BAKED BEANS ❦
Shari Garder

1 (16 - 18 oz.) can pork and
   beans
2 T. brown sugar
¼ tsp. dry mustard
1 to 2 T. molasses
¼ c. catsup
2 slices bacon, browned and
   crumbled or bacon bits

Combine ingredients. Bake in greased casserole in 350° oven. Bake covered for 20 minutes. Uncover and continue baking 20 minutes. Serves 4.

❦ SAVORY RICE WITH PEAS AND CARROTS ❦
Karen Pickens

2 cans (10½ oz.) condensed
   French onion soup
1 c. uncooked converted rice
1 T. olive oil
⅛ tsp. ground black pepper
1 c. frozen peas and carrots

Heat soup, rice, oil and black pepper in a 2-qt. saucepan over medium high heat to a boil. Reduce heat to low. Cover and cook for 15 minutes. Stir peas and carrots into saucepan. Cover and cook for 5 minutes or

(continued)

until rice is tender. Remove saucepan from heat and let stand for 5 minutes before serving. Makes 4 (1 c.) servings.

❦ SCALLOPED CHEESY POTATOES ❦
Julie Concannon

2 lbs. frozen shredded hash browns, thawed	¼ c. chopped onion
2 c. shredded Cheddar cheese	¾ c. butter, divided
16 oz. sour cream	1 tsp. salt
1 can cream of chicken soup	¼ tsp. pepper
	2 c. cornflakes cereal

Mix hash browns, cheese, sour cream, soup, onion, ½ cup butter (cubed), salt and pepper and put in a 9 x 13-inch baking dish. Crumble cornflakes and mix with teaspoon size butter pieces. Sprinkle on top of casserole. Bake at 350° for 45 minutes to 1 hour. Let set for a few minutes before serving. 12-18 servings.

❦ SCALLOPED CORN BAKE ❦
Valerie Florea

½ c. melted butter or margarine	1 c. sour cream
1 can cream style corn	2 eggs, beaten
1 can whole kernel corn, drained	1 (8 oz.) box corn muffin mix
	1 c. grated cheese

Mix melted butter with corn, sour cream, eggs and corn muffin mix. Pour into a 2-quart or 9 x 13-inch greased casserole dish. Sprinkle with grated cheese and bake 45 to 60 minutes at 350°.

❦ SCALLOPED CORN WITH CORN BREAD MIX ❦
Debra Gillespie
Joni Ham

1 qt. frozen corn OR 2 cans cream style corn
1 sm. pkg. Jiffy corn bread mix

1 stick melted butter
1 pt. sour cream

Blend all ingredients in bowl. Pour into greased casserole dish. Bake at 325° for 50 minutes.

❦ SPICY OVEN FRIED POTATOES ❦
Deb Lund

Potatoes, scrubbed, and sliced into long, thick slices
Canola or olive oil
Garlic salt or powder
Onion salt or powder

Cumin
Chili powder
Black Pepper
Seasoned salt
Paprika

Preheat oven to 425°. Spray large baking sheet with Pam. Place potatoes in plastic bag or large bowl. Add small amount of oil (depending on number of potatoes) and seasonings, to taste. Shake together or stir well, and spread out onto prepared pan. Bake 20-30 minutes or until done. You can experiment with the amount of seasonings according to desired spiciness. Very little oil or salt is necessary, which makes this a healthy side dish, too.

❦ SUPREME CORN CASSEROLE ❦
Leah Klos
Great Great Grandma Eleanor Ward

1 egg, beaten
½ c. milk
½ c. sweet pickle relish, drained

1 can cream of chicken soup
1 (15 oz.) can corn
1 T. butter
½ c. bread crumbs

Beat egg and milk. Add relish, soup and corn. Mix and pour into 2-quart baking dish. Melt butter and mix with bread crumbs. Top corn mixture with buttered crumbs. Bake 30 minutes at 350°.

❦ 304

121822-12

❦ SWEET POTATO CASSEROLE ❦
Debra Gillespie

Sweet Potatoes:

2 ¼ lbs. sweet potatoes, peeled and chopped	1 tsp. salt
1 c. half and half	2 tsp. vanilla
¾ c. brown sugar, packed	2 lg. eggs

Place potatoes in pan and cover with water. Bring to boil over medium heat and cook until very tender. Drain and cool slightly. Place potatoes in large bowl. Add half and half, brown sugar, salt and vanilla. Beat with electric mixer until smooth. Add eggs and beat well. Pour into greased 9 x 13-inch baking dish.

Topping:

1 ½ c. miniature marshmallows	2 T. butter, chilled
½ c. flour	½ c. pecans, chopped and toasted
¼ c. packed brown sugar	

Sprinkle marshmallows over top of casserole. Then combine flour, brown sugar and butter (cut into small pieces) and pecans. Spread this topping over marshmallows. Bake at 375° for 30 to 40 minutes until golden brown.

❦ SWEET POTATO CASSEROLE ❦
Paula Foster

2 (1 lb. 2 oz.) cans vacuum packed sweet potatoes	½ c. packed brown sugar
1 tsp. salt	½ c. orange juice
2 eggs	⅓ c. melted butter
	⅔ cup pecan halves

Mash sweet potatoes with the salt and then whip in the eggs. Spread the sweet potato mixture evenly into a greased 2-quart glass baking dish. Over medium heat, cook the sugar, orange juice and butter until the sugar is completely dissolved. Pour all but ½ cup of the syrup over the sweet potatoes. Arrange the pecans over the sweet potato mixture, and then pour the remaining syrup over the pecans. Bake in a 375° oven for 40 to 45 minutes.

❦ SWEET POTATO WITH CRUNCHY TOP ❦
Lynda McGraw

Sweet Potatoes:

3 c. mashed sweet potatoes or
   1 (2 lb. 8 oz.) can
1 c. sugar
½ tsp. salt

2 eggs
½ stick margarine (¼ c.)
1 tsp. vanilla

Mix all sweet potato ingredients and pour into greased dish.

Topping:

1 c. brown sugar
1 c. chopped pecans

⅓ c. flour
½ stick margarine (¼ c.)

Mix topping ingredients, sprinkle over sweet potato mixture. Bake at 350° for 35 minutes.

❦ SWEET POTATOES WITH CARAMELIZED APPLES ❦
Jody Manning

6 sweet potatoes (about 4 lbs.)
1 tsp. kosher salt
3 Granny Smith apples, peeled
   and cored
1 T. fresh lemon juice
8 T. (1 stick) plus 1 T.
   unsalted butter, divided

¼ c. plus 2 T. packed dark
   brown sugar, divided
¼ c. plus 2 T. heavy cream,
   divided
¼ c. Calvados (French apple
   brandy) or other brandy
¼ c. fresh orange juice

Preheat oven to 425°. Prick each potato several times with a fork or a paring knife. Bake the potatoes until tender when pierced with tip of a knife, 40 to 45 minutes. When cool enough to handle, peel and place the flesh in a medium bowl, add the salt, and mash. Meanwhile slice the apples into ¼-inch thick wedges and place in a medium bowl. Add the lemon juice and toss to combine. In a medium skillet, melt 3 T. butter over medium-high heat. Add 2 T. brown sugar and cook, stirring, until the sugar dissolves. Cook the apple slices in the butter and sugar in 3 or 4 batches, until golden and caramelized, about 1

(continued)

121822-12

minute on each side. As they finish cooking, transfer to a plate, and set aside. In a medium skillet, melt 3 T. butter over high heat. Add 2 T. brown sugar and cook until the sugar dissolves. Stir in ¼ c. cream and the Calvados, and cook until slightly thickened, about 1 minute. Remove from the heat and add to the sweet potatoes, mixing well to combine. Transfer mixture to a buttered 3-quart ovenproof casserole. Arrange the apple slices over the potatoes; set aside. In a medium skillet, melt the remaining 3 T. butter over medium heat. Add the remaining 2 T. brown sugar, and cook until dissolved. Add the remaining 2 T. cream and cook, stirring, for 30 seconds. Stir in orange juice and cook for 1 to 2 minutes, until thickened and dark brown. Pour over the apples and cover with aluminum foil. Bake until heated through, about 30 minutes. Remove from the oven and serve immediately or let stand at room temperature for up to 30 minutes before serving.

❦ TWICE BAKED POTATOES ❦
Shari Garder

6 med. unpeeled baked potatoes	1 lb. bacon, cooked and crumbled
2 onions, diced	3 c. sour cream
¼ tsp. salt	2 c. shredded mozzarella
¼ tsp. pepper	2 c. shredded Cheddar

Cut potatoes into 1-inch cubes. Place potatoes and onions in greased 9 x 13 x 2-inch pan. Sprinkle salt, pepper, and bacon over potatoes and onions. Top with sour cream and cheeses. Bake at 350°, uncovered, for 20 minutes or until cheese is melted.

❦ VEGETABLE CASSEROLE ❦
Christie Klos

1 (15 oz.) can French style green beans	¼ c. green pepper, diced
1 (15 oz.) can corn, drained	¼ c. onion, diced
½ c. sour cream	Ritz crackers
1 (15 oz.) can cream of celery soup	1 T. butter, melted

(continued)

Mix green beans, corn, sour cream, soup, green pepper and onions. Put in baking dish. Mix crushed Ritz crackers and melted butter. Top mixture. Bake 45 minutes at 350°.

❦ ZUCCHINI & TOMATO CASSEROLE ❦
Shirley Schuchard

2 med. zucchini, sliced
4 lg. tomatoes, peeled and sliced
1 lg. Bermuda onion, sliced
2 med. green peppers, sliced

8 oz. sliced Swiss cheese
Salt and pepper to taste
½ c. melted butter
2 c. seasoned croutons

Grease 9 x 13-inch casserole dish. Layer half of zucchini, tomato, onion, green pepper and cheese in dish. Repeat layers. Salt and pepper to taste. Pour melted butter on top of vegetables and cheese and then cover with seasoned croutons. Cover and bake at 325° for 45 minutes to one hour.

❦ ZUCCHINI CASSEROLE ❦
Shirley Schuchard

2 lbs. zucchini, sliced ⅜-inch thick (7 c.)
¼ c. onion, chopped
1 (10½ oz.) cream of chicken soup

1 c. sour cream
1 c. shredded carrots
¼ c. butter or margarine
2 c. herb seasoned stuffing

Combine all ingredients. Bake at 325° for about 30 minutes.

121822-12

INDEX OF RECIPES

APPETIZERS AND BEVERAGES

APPETIZERS

8 LAYER NACHO DIP	1
ARTICHOKE DIP	1
BACON WRAPPED WATER CHESTNUTS	1
BANG BANG SHRIMP	2
BLACK BEAN AND CORN SALSA	2
BUFFALO CHICKEN DIP	3
BUFFALO WING DIP	4
CHAMPP'S SEASONED SOUR CREAM	4
CHEESE BALL	4
CHICKEN ENCHILADA DIP	5
CHICKEN ROLL UPS	5
CILANTRO DIP	5
COCKTAIL SMOKIES	6
CUCUMBER SALSA	6
FESTIVE CRANBERRY BRIE	6
FIESTA BAKED CHEESE DIP	7
GRAMMA RUTH'S FRUIT PIZZA	7
GREEK HUMMUS DIP	8
HERBED CREAM CHEESE SPREAD	8
HOT CORN DIP	8
JANEEN'S DIP	9
MARDI GRAS DIP	9
MEXICAN DIP	9
MOM'S APPLE DIP	10
MOM'S CHEESE BALL	10
MOM'S OLIVE DIP	10
NACHO APPETIZER	10
OYSTER CRACKER APPETIZERS	11
PEACH SALSA	11
PIGS IN A BLANKET	11
POT STICKERS	12
PROSCIUTTO ARTICHOKE APPETIZERS	12
PUMPKIN APPLE DIP	13
PUMPKIN FLUFF DIP	13
RANCH PRETZELS	13
REUBEN DIP	13
ROASTED RED PEPPER DIP	14
ROTEL SALSA	14
SALSA	14
SANTA FE CHEESECAKE	14
SAUSAGE CHEESE BALLS	15
SAUSAGE CHEESE DIP	15
SAUSAGE STUFFED MUSHROOMS	15
SEASONED OYSTER CRACKERS	16
SHOEPEG CORN DIP	16
SHRIMP IN GARLIC SAKE SAUCE	16
SOUTHWESTERN CHICKEN DIP	17
SPINACH ARTICHOKE BREAD	17
SPINACH DIP	17
STUFFED CRESCENT ROLLS	18
TOMATO AND BASIL BRUSCHETTA	18
TOMATO AND BASIL SQUARES	18
TORTILLA WRAPS	19

BEVERAGES

CHAI	19
CRANBERRY PUNCH	19
FACE BOOK FRIENDS ROOT BEER FLOAT NIGHT	20
HOT BUTTERED RUM	20
MOJITO	21
MULLED CIDER PUNCH	21
ORANGE JUBILEE	21
TROPICAL PUNCH	22
WASSAIL	22

BREADS AND ROLLS

APRICOT-ORANGE CREAM SCONES	23
BLACK FOREST BREAD	23
BLUEBERRY CRUMBLE COFFEE CAKE	24
BLUEBERRY-BANANA BREAD	24
BREAD MACHINE CINNAMON ROLLS	25
CHERRY CHEESE DANISH	26
COCONUT PECAN RING	26
CRANBERRY ORANGE BREAD	27
DUMPLINGS "FOR SUNDAY"	27
EASY GOOEY CARAMEL ROLLS	27
EASY WHEAT BREAD IN A BAG	28
FROZEN BREAD CARAMEL ROLLS	28
FRY BREAD	29
HERB CHEESE BEER BREAD	29

KOLACHES FROM THE BREAD MACHINE	30
LITTLE TEXAS CORN BREAD	30
MOM'S BRAN MUFFINS	31
MONKEY BREAD	31
MY FAVORITE ROLLS	32
ORANGE ROLLS	32
PIZZA DOUGH	33
PLACHENDA/BLADGINDA/ PLATCHINTA	34
SCONES	34
SNICKERDOODLE BREAD	35
SOMETHING DIFFERENT SWEET ROLLS	36
STAY-SOFT CARAMEL ROLL SYRUP	36
SWEET CORN BREAD MUFFINS	37
ZUCCHINI BREAD	37

BREAKFAST AND BRUNCH

APPLE CINNAMON FRENCH TOAST	39
BAKED EGG BRUNCH	39
BANANA PANCAKES	40
BREAKFAST BAKE	40
BREAKFAST CASSEROLE	41
BREAKFAST HOT DISH	41
BREAKFAST PIE	42
BREAKFAST PIZZA	42
BROCCOLI, EGG AND HAM BAKE	42
BRUNCH FRUIT SALAD	43
BRUNCH PIZZA	43
CASSY'S QUICHE	44
CREME BRULEE FRENCH TOAST	45
CROISSANT STUFFED FRENCH TOAST	45
EGG CASSEROLE	46
FESTIVE FILLED FRENCH TOAST	46
FRENCH TOAST CASSEROLE WITH MAPLE SYRUP	47
FROZEN FRUIT CUPS	48
HAM AND EGG STUFF	48
HAM & CHEESE OMELET BREAD	48
HASHBROWN BREAKFAST CASSEROLE	49
IMPOSSIBLE BACON QUICHE	49
OMELETTE IN A BAG	50
OVEN BAKED EGG CASSEROLE	50
OVERNIGHT EGG CASSEROLE	50
PEACH FRENCH TOAST	51
QUICHE	51
SAUSAGE PIE	52
STUFFIN' EGG MUFFIN	52
WAKE UP BREAKFAST CASSEROLE	52

COOKING FOR A CROWD

BREAKFAST STRATA	55
CHICKEN ENCHILADA CASSEROLE	55
CHICKEN SALAD FOR 50	56
CITRUS PUNCH	56
EASY EGG BAKE	57
FANCY SAUERKRAUT	57
FRENCH TOAST CASSEROLE WITH FRUIT	58
HOT HAM SANDWICHES	59
MEAT LOAF MINIATURES	59
MORNING PECAN CASSEROLE	60
OVEN-BAKED FRENCH TOAST	60
PARTY SCRAMBLE	61
SCRAMBLED EGGS FOR 100	61
SEAFOOD CHOWDER	62
SLOPPY JOES	62
STUFFED MUSHROOMS	63
SWEDISH FRUIT SOUP	63
TASTEE SANDWICHES	64
TATER TOT CASSEROLE	64
WESTERN STYLE BEANS	65

GRANDMA'S / MOM'S RECIPES

AEBLESKIVER	67
APPLESAUCE PUFFS	67
ARABIAN SPICE CAKE	68
AUNT CORA'S POTATOES	68
BAKED APPLE PANCAKE	68
BARBECUE BURGERS	69
BBQ GREEN BEANS	69
BEEF BRISKET	70
BUTTER BALLS FOR HOMEMADE CHICKEN NOODLE SOUP	70
CHICKEN AND RICE CASSEROLE	71
CHICKEN CASSEROLE	71
CHIFFON SALAD	72
COCONUT FRUIT SALAD	72
CORN FRITTERS	72
CREAM CHEESE PARTY MINTS	73

DANISH DUMPLINGS FOR
   CHICKEN SOUP   73
DANISH PASTRIES   74
FLANK STEAK ROLL   75
FLEMISH POT ROAST   75
FRUIT SALAD   76
GRANDMA FERN'S MEAT
   LOAF   76
GRANDMA HAZEL'S APPLE
   COFFEE CAKE   77
GRANDMA'S BROWN SUGAR
   COOKIES   77
GRANDMA'S OLD FASHIONED
   SUGAR COOKIES   78
GRANDMA'S RED HOT SALAD   78
GRANDMA'S SUMMER
   SAUSAGE   79
GREEN BEAN CASSEROLE   79
HAM AND TOMATO QUICHE   79
HOT PUNCH   80
ICE CREAM DESSERT   80
KNOEPHLA SOUP   81
LEMON CAKE   81
LIME JELLO SALAD   82
MAKE AHEAD MASHED
   POTATOES   82
MEXICAN PINWHEELS   83
MINCE MEAT   83
MOM'S APPLE PUDDING WITH
   BUTTER SAUCE   84
MOM'S CHICKEN AND RICE   84
NORWEGIAN FLATBREAD   85
OLD-FASHIONED ROLLED
   MOLASSES COOKIES   85
ONION CASSEROLE   85
PEACH CAKE   86
PEANUT BUTTER FUDGE   86
PECAN SNOW BALLS   87
QUICK CAKE   87
RHUBARB UPSIDE DOWN
   CAKE   87
SAUERKRAUT IN JARS   88
SLOPPY JOES   88
SNICKERDOODLES   89
STRAWBERRY RHUBARB
   BAKE   89
TOOTIE FRUTIE SALAD   89
TWO DAY BUNS   90
VEGETABLE CHEESE
   CHOWDER   90
WESSON OIL DRESSING   91
WORLDS BEST CHOCOLATE
   CAKE   91
YOLK COOKIES   92

HEALTHY EATING

ANGEL FOOD PINEAPPLE
   ORANGE MUFFINS   93
ANGEL LUSH   93
APPLE COLESLAW   94
AVOCADO AND BLACK EYED
   PEA SALSA   94
BROCCOLI WILD RICE SOUP/MY
   LIGHTER VERSION   95
CARROT AND ZUCCHINI
   MUFFINS   95
CHEESY POTATO SOUP   96
CHICKEN ASPARAGUS ROLL-
   UPS   96
CHICKEN WITH BALSAMIC
   VINEGAR, ONIONS &
   THYME   97
COLORFUL BLACK BEAN
   SALAD   97
GLUTEN-FREE BROWNIES   98
GREEK PIZZA   98
MADE OVER CHICKEN
   TETRAZZINI   99
MAKEOVER ZUCCHINI
   SUPPER   100
MEXICAN CHICKEN CHILI   100
MEXICAN-STYLE BROWN RICE
   CASSEROLE   101
ONION-APPLE PORK CHOPS   101
ORANGE-CILANTRO BLACK
   BEAN SALAD   102
POTATO BAKE   102
PUMPKIN PIE TARTLETS   103
SEASONED TILAPIA FILLETS   103
SIZZLIN' CHICKEN SKEWERS   104
TILAPIA FLORENTINE   104
TILAPIA WITH CORN SALSA   105
WHITE BEAN DIP AND
   PARMESAN PITA CRISPS   105

HOLIDAY FAVORITES

BIRDS' NESTS WITH JELLY
   BEANS   107
BUNNY ROLLS   107
CANDY CANE CHEESECAKE   108
CHRISTMAS ROSE SWEET
   ROLLS   108
CORN CASSEROLE   109
CRANBERRY CAKE
   DESSERT   109
CRANBERRY FRUIT SALAD   110
CRANBERRY JELLO SALAD   110
CRANBERRY-ALMOND COFFEE
   CAKE   111

DARK PFEFFERNUSS	112
FANCY DEVILED EGGS	112
FESTIVE HOLIDAY BARK	113
FRUIT CAKE	113
GLUWEIN	113
GRAND MARNIER SWEET POTATOES	114
HALLOWEEN BARS	114
HALLOWEEN PIZZA	115
HOLLY CRACKLES	115
IRISH BEEF STEW	116
IRISH CHOCOLATE MINT DESSERT	116
IRISH SODA BREAD	117
JELLO SPRITZ COOKIES	118
LEFSE (NO POTATOES)	118
LIBBY'S PUMPKIN PIE	119
NORWEGIAN NUT COOKIES	119
PEPPERMINT DESSERT	119
PUMPKIN LAYER CAKE	120
SCANDINAVIAN SANDBAKKELS	120
SPARKLE POPCORN	121
SPOOKY CINNAMON ROLLS	121
SPRITZ COOKIES (CHRISTMAS TREES)	122
ST. PATRICK'S DAY CHEESE-CRUSTED BISCUITS	122
ST. PATRICK'S DAY SCALLOPED POTATOES	123
SWEET & SPICY MIXED NUTS	123
SWEET POTATO CASSEROLE	124
THANKSGIVING CRANBERRY COBBLER	124
WHITE PFEFFERNUSS	125

MAIN DISHES AND MEATS

BEEF

APRICOT MEAT LOAF	127
ASIAN BEEF NOODLES	127
B & G BURGERS (SLOPPY JOES)	128
BARBEQUE MEATBALLS	128
BEAN CASSEROLE	129
BEEF BURGUNDY	129
BEEF ENCHILADAS	130
BEEF, RICE AND BEAN ENCHILADAS	131
BEEF STROGANOFF	130
CABBAGE ROLLS CASSEROLE	131

CAVATINI PIZZA CASSEROLE	131
CHEESEBURGER PIE	132
CHUCKWAGON BEEF AND BEANS	132
CRUNCHY CHEESERONI CASSEROLE	133
EASY BEEF ENCHILADA'S	133
FARMERS DELIGHT	133
FOOLPROOF STANDING RIB ROAST	134
FOOTBALL STEW	134
FRENCH DIP SANDWICH	134
GERMAN PIZZA	135
HAMBURGER STROGANOFF	135
ITALIAN MEATBALL AND BISCUIT BAKE	136
ITALIAN MEATBALLS	136
JEANNE'S SLOPPY JOES	137
JOES TO GO	137
LASAGNE	137
MEAT LOAF	138, 139
MEAT LOAF CORDON BLEU	139
MEATBALL DINNERS	140
MEATBALLS	140
MONGOLIAN BEEF	141
NOAH'S FAVORITE BROCCOLI & BEEF STIR-FRY	141
NORWEGIAN MEATBALLS	142
PIKES PEAK ROAST	142
POPPIN' FRESH BARBECUES	143
PRIME RIB	143
QUICK SUPPER	143
ROUND STEAK	144
SEVEN-UP CASSEROLE	144
SIMPLIFIED LASAGNA	144
SLOPPY JOES	145
STIR-FRIED BEEF GYROS IN PITA POCKETS	145
STUFFED PEPPERS	146
STUFFED SHELLS	146
TACO HOT DISH	147
TACO PIE	147
TAMI'S MARINARA SAUCE	148
TAMI'S MEATBALLS	148
TATER TOT CASSEROLE	149
TATER TOT CASSEROLE	149
TEXAS HASH	149

MEATLESS

ANGEL HAIR WITH SUN-DRIED TOMATOES AND GOAT CHEESE	150
CHEESE SPREAD	150
EASY MANICOTTI	151
PESTO FOR PASTA	151

SUMMER DAY LUNCHEON 152
VEGETABLE FRITTATA 152

PORK

BACON EGG SALAD
  CROISSANTS 152
BAKED SPAGHETTI 153
BROWN SUGAR PORK CHOPS
  WITH ONIONS 153
CHEESE AND HAM-STUFFED
  LOAF 154
HAM AND SWISS QUICHE 154
PORK, CHICKEN, OR SALMON
  MARINADE 155
PORK CHOP CASSEROLE 155
PORK CHOPS MEXICALI 155
ROASTED PORK WITH APPLES
  AND POTATOES 156
SECRET INGREDIENT SAUCY
  CHOPS 156
SMOKED PORK LOIN 157
SMOTHERED PORK CHOPS 157
STROMBOLI (MAKES 2) 157
STUFFED ANAHEIM
  PEPPERS 158
SUMMER RIBS 158
THE BEST PORK CHOPS YOU
  WILL EVER TASTE 159

POULTRY

BRUSCHETTA AND CHEESE
  STUFFED CHICKEN
  BREASTS 159
BRUSCHETTA CHICKEN
  BAKE 160
CHICKEN A LA ORANGE 160
CHICKEN AND MUSHROOM
  PASTA 161
CHICKEN AND RICE 162
CHICKEN AND WILD RICE
  CASSEROLE 162
CHICKEN ARTICHOKE PASTA 163
CHICKEN & RICE 161
CHICKEN CACCIATORE 163
CHICKEN FINGERS 164
CHICKEN LASAGNA
  FLORENTINE 164
CHICKEN MARSALA 165
CHICKEN PICCATA 166
CHICKEN SOUVLAKI 166
CILANTRO CREAM CHICKEN 167
CREAMED CHICKEN
  CASSEROLE 168
FIREMAN'S CHICKEN 168

GRILLED CHICKEN KABOBS 169
GRILLED CHICKEN WITH
  PROSCIUTTO AND BASIL 169
GRILLED ORANGE CHICKEN WITH
  MANGO PEACH SALSA 170
ONE-PAN POTATOES AND
  CHICKEN TERIYAKI 170
ORANGE CHICKEN 171
OVEN-FRIED CHICKEN 171
PENNE GORGONZOLA WITH
  CHICKEN 172
PLUMP AND JUICY CHICKEN
  BREASTS 173
POPPYSEED CHICKEN 173
SESAME CHICKEN 174
SMOTHERED CHICKEN 174
SOUR CREAM CHICKEN
  ENCHILADAS 175
SWEET AND SOUR CHICKEN 175
TASTY ITALIAN CHICKEN 176
TERIYAKI CHICKEN 176
THAI GREEN CURRY WITH
  CHICKEN (OR SHRIMP) 177
TURGETTI 177
TURKEY PUFFS 178

SEAFOOD

BAKED SHRIMP AND FETA
  WITH PASTA 178
BEER BOILED SHRIMP 179
FISH TACOS 179
FRIED WALLEYE 180
GRILLED SHRIMP 180
SALMON SALAD 181
SEAFOOD ALFREDO 181
SHRIMP BROCCOLI
  ALFREDO 182
TILAPIA 182
TUNA NOODLE CASSEROLE 182

SALADS & SOUPS

SALAD

APPLE SALAD 185
APPLE SNICKER SALAD 185
APPLESAUCE JELLO 185
ASIAN-STYLE SPINACH
  SALAD 186
AUNT CLARA'S MACARONI
  SALAD 186
BETTY SALAD 187
BROCCOLI APPLE SALAD 187
BROCCOLI DELIGHT SALAD 187
BROCCOLI GRAPE SALAD 188

BROCCOLI SALAD 188
BROCCOLI SLAW 189
CABBAGE SALAD 189
CALICO SALAD 190
CARMEL APPLE SALAD 190
CHICKEN SALAD 191
CHILLED CORN SALAD 191
CHINESE SALAD 191
CHINESE SLAW SALAD 192
COLE SLAW 193
COLESLAW 193
COOL CUCUMBER PASTA
   SALAD 193
CORN SALAD 194
COTTAGE CHEESE AND
   JELLO 194
CRANBERRY JELLO SALAD 194
CREAMY CAULIFLOWER
   LETTUCE SALAD 195
CRUNCHY BROCCOLI SALAD 195
DEANO'S MACARONI SALAD 196
EASY GRAPE NUTTY
   COLESLAW 196
FIELD GREENS SALAD 196
FRESH CRANBERRY SALAD 197
FROG EYE SALAD 197
FROZEN CUCUMBER SALAD 198
GERMAN CUCUMBER SALAD 198
GERMAN POTATO SALAD 199
GRAMMA BETTY'S MACARONI
   SALAD 199
GRAPE NUT SALAD 199
LOU ANN'S RED JELLO 200
LOVE THAT SALAD! 200
MAGGIE'S FRUIT SALAD 201
MANDARIN ORANGE SALAD 201
MUSHROOM SALAD 201
ORANGE ASPIC SALAD 202
ORANGE TAPIOCA SALAD 202
ORIENTAL SALAD 202
PEA AND PEANUT SALAD 203
PEA SALAD 203
POPPY SEED DRESSING 203
PRETZEL SALAD 204
QUICK SALAD 204
RASPBERRY APPLESAUCE
   SALAD 204
RASPBERRY CRANBERRY
   JELLO SALAD 205
RED AND WHITE JELLO
   SALAD 205
"RED HOTS" SALAD 205
ROTINI SALAD 206
SHIRLEY'S PASTA SALAD 206
SNICKER APPLE SALAD 206

SPINACH SALAD 207
STEAKHOUSE SALAD 207
STRAWBERRY ORANGE PASTA
   SALAD 207
STRAWBERRY PUDDING
   SALAD 208
STRAWBERRY/CRANBERRY
   JELLO SALAD 208
SUNSHINE SALAD 209
SWEET BROCCOLI SALAD 209
TACO PASTA SALAD 209
TACO SALAD 210
THREE BEAN SALAD 210
TORTELLINI SALAD 211
TURKEY SALAD 211
UNDER THE SEA SALAD 212
WALDORF COLESLAW 212
WHIPPED JELLO 212

SOUP

BAKED STEW 213
BARBEQUE CHILI 213
BASQUE POTATO SOUP 214
BUTTERNUT SQUASH SOUP 214
CAMPFIRE STEW 214
CAPE COD FISH CHOWDER 215
CHEATER CHILI 215
CHEDDAR CHOWDER 215
CHEESE TORTELLINI SOUP WITH
   CANNELLONI AND
   SPINACH 216
CHICKEN ENCHILADA SOUP 216
CHICKEN NOODLE SOUP 217
CHICKEN RICE SOUP 217
COMFORTING CHICKEN
   NOODLE SOUP 218
CORN CRAB CHOWDER 218
CREAM OF BROCCOLI SOUP
   WITH WHITE WINE 219
DANIEL'S FAVORITE CREAM OF
   POTATO SOUP 220
EASY BROCCOLI CHEESE
   SOUP 220
FRENCH ONION SOUP 221
GARDEN CHEESE SOUP 221
HAMBURGER SOUP 221
HEARTY CHIPOTLE CHICKEN
   SOUP 222
HEARTY ITALIAN SOUP 222
LEEK AND POTATO SOUP 223
MINESTRONE SOUP 223
MOM'S BEEFY VEGETABLE
   SOUP 224
NO LONGER RUTH'S WHITE
   CHILI 224

121822-12

POTATO & HAM CHOWDER   225
SAUSAGE CORN CHOWDER   225
SEAFOOD CHOWDER   226
SHORT CUT VEGETABLE BEEF
   SOUP   226
SWEET POTATO SOUP WITH
   CURRIED CHEESE
   CRISPS   227
TACO SOUP   227
V-8 VEGETABLE BEEF SOUP   228
WEST AFRICAN PEANUT
   SOUP   228

SLOW COOKER COOKING

AU JUS SANDWICHES   229
AUNT MARILYN'S BURRITOS   229
AUNT MARILYN'S TACOS   229
CHICKEN AND DUMPLINGS   230
CHICKEN TACOS   230
CHICKEN TORTILLA SOUP   230
CHILI   231
CLAUDE'S CHILI   232
COLA BBQ BEEF   232
CRANBERRY PORK
   TENDERLOIN   233
CROCK POT DRESSING   233
CROCKPOT BEEF STEW   234
CROCKPOT DIP   234
CROCKPOT MINESTRONE   234
EASY SLOW-COOKER A.1.
   SWISS STEAK   235
FRENCH DIP SANDWICHES   235
MANY MEALS POT ROAST   236
NO PEEP STEW   236
PORK CHOP, SAUERKRAUT, APPLES
   AND SWEET POTATOES   237
PORK LOIN WITH
   SAUERKRAUT   237
POT ROAST   237
POTATO SOUP   238
ROAST WITH GRAVY   238
SHERRIED CRAB MEAT   239
SLOW COOKER JAMBALAYA   239
SLOW COOKER POT ROAST   240
WHITE CHICKEN CHILI   240

SWEETS AND TREATS

BARS AND COOKIES

3 LAYER GOOD BARS   241
ALMOND POPPY SEED BARS   242
BANANA BARS   242
BUTTER PECAN TURTLE
   COOKIES   243

CARAMEL LAYERED
   CHOCOLATE BARS   243
CARAMEL WALNUT DREAM
   BARS   244
CHEWY BROWNIES   244
CHOCOLATE CHIP COOKIE
   BARS   245
CHOCOLATE MINT
   BROWNIES   245
CRANBERRY HOOTY CREEK
   COOKIES   246
CREAMY STRAWBERRY LEMON
   SQUARES   246
DEVILS FOOD COOKIES   247
DOUBLE CHOCOLATE CHIP
   COOKIES   247
DOUBLE MINT SQUARES   247
EASY BARS   248
EASY LEMONADE DESSERT   248
FAVORITE CHOCOLATE
   BROWNIES   249
FROSTED BANANA BARS   250
KELLOGG'S "K" BARS   250
LEMON COOKIES   251
LEMON DESSERT   251
LEMONY CRISPS   251
MIXED-UP BROWNIE
   DELIGHT   252
MOCHA-TOFFEE CHOCOLATE
   COOKIES   252
MOM'S LEMON BARS   253
MOM'S SUGAR COOKIES   253
MONSTER COOKIES   254
OATMEAL CARAMEL BARS   254
OATY DOODLE COOKIES   255
PEAR CUSTARD BARS   255
PHILADELPHIA MARBLE
   BROWNIES   256
RHUBARB BARS   256
ROLO COOKIES   257
SNOWBALL COOKIES   257
SOLO OATMEAL FRUIT BARS   258
SOPPIA   258

CAKES AND FROSTING

ALMOND CAKE   259
BUTTER CREAM FROSTING   259
CARROT CAKE   260
CHOCOLATE FROSTING   260
CHOCOLATE KAHLUA CAKE   261
CREME DE MENTHE CAKE   261
CREME-DE-MENTHE CAKE   261
DELICATE WHITE CHOCOLATE
   CAKE   262
LEMON-ORANGE CAKE   262

MILKY WAY CAKE	263
MOON CAKE	263
NORWEGIAN LINGONBERRY CAKE WITH STREUSEL TOPPING	264
OATMEAL CAKE	265
RAW APPLE CAKE	265
RED WALDORF CHOCOLATE CAKE	266
SHELLY'S FROSTING RECIPE	267
TEXAS SHEET CAKE	267
TRIPLE CHOCOLATE CAKE	268
WHITE TEXAS SHEET CAKE	268

PIES

"BISHOP'S" CHOCOLATE PIE	269
BROWN BAG APPLE PIE	269
CHERRY PIE	270
CHOCOLATE PIE	271
COCONUT TORTE	271
EASY BLUEBERRY PIE	271
EASY PIE CRUST	272
FRESH PUMPKIN PIE	272
LAUREL'S FAVORITE APPLE PIE	273
MOM'S DELUXE CHOCOLATE PECAN PIE	274
PIE CRUST	274
SOUR CREAM RHUBARB PIE	274
STRAWBERRY PIE	275

SWEET TREATS

ALMOND PASTE	275
APPLE CRUMBLE	276
BAKED APPLES	276
BLUEBERRY SURPRISE	277
BLUEBERRY-RHUBARB CRISP	277
BUTTERFINGER CANDY BAR DESSERT	278
CARAMEL SAUCE	278
CARAMELS	278
CATHEDRAL WINDOWS	279
CHOCOLATE CLUSTERS	279
CHOCOLATE HAYSTACKS	280
CHOCOLATE MOUSSE	280
EASY APPLE CRISP	281
EASY FUDGE	281
EASY MICROWAVE PEANUT BRITTLE	281
EASY OREO TRUFFLES	282
FRUIT PIZZA	282
FUDGE TRUFFLE CHEESECAKE	282

ICE CREAM DESSERT	283
ICE CREAM YUMMY DESSERT	283
JELLO CHEESECAKE	284
MICROWAVE APPLE CRISP	284
MINI CHEESE CAKES	284
OVEN CARAMEL CORN	285
PEANUT BRITTLE (MICROWAVE)	285
PEANUT BUTTER FUDGE	285
PECAN CRUNCH	286
POPCORN BALLS	286
SALTED PEANUT CHEWS	286
SOUTHERN PRALINES	287
SUSIE'S BAKED RICE PUDDING	288
SWEET CRISPIX MIX	288
SWEET PARTY MIX	288
TOFFEE	289
ZUPPA INGLESSE	289

VEGETABLES & SIDE DISHES

BAKED LEMON PASTA	291
BAKED VEGGIE MEDLEY	291
BARBEQUED GREEN BEANS	292
BOURBON CORN PUDDING	292
CALIFORNIA MIX CASSEROLE	292
CARROT SOUFFLÉ	293
CHEESY MACARONI CASSEROLE	293
CINNAMON ROASTED SWEET POTATOES	293
COPPER PENNIES	294
CORN AND MACARONI CASSEROLE	294
CORN CASSEROLE	294, 295
COUSCOUS WITH MUSHROOMS	295
CRANBERRY GREEN BEANS	295
CREAMY ZUCCHINI CASSEROLE	296
FLAVOR BAKED BEANS	296
FRUITED WILD RICE	296
GREEK POTATOES	297
GREEN BEAN & ALMOND RICE	297
GUESS AGAIN CARROTS	298
HERB ROASTED SQUASH	298
HERBED-PARMESAN CRISPS	298
ITALIAN CORN	299
MICROWAVED SCALLOPED POTATOES	299
NO NAME POTATOES	299

121822-12

ONION ROASTED POTATOES	300
OVEN FRIED POTATOES	300
PIROGUES CASSEROLE	300
POTATO CASSEROLE	301
RICE AND SOUR CREAM CASSEROLE	301
RICH MASHED POTATOES	302
SAVORY BAKED BEANS	302
SAVORY RICE WITH PEAS AND CARROTS	302
SCALLOPED CHEESY POTATOES	303
SCALLOPED CORN BAKE	303
SCALLOPED CORN WITH CORN BREAD MIX	304
SPICY OVEN FRIED POTATOES	304
SUPREME CORN CASSEROLE	304
SWEET POTATO CASSEROLE	305
SWEET POTATO WITH CRUNCHY TOP	306
SWEET POTATOES WITH CARAMELIZED APPLES	306
TWICE BAKED POTATOES	307
VEGETABLE CASSEROLE	307
ZUCCHINI & TOMATO CASSEROLE	308
ZUCCHINI CASSEROLE	308

121822-12

How to Order

Get additional copies of this cookbook by returning an order form and your check or money order to:

Lord of Love Women of the ELCA
10405 Fort St.
Omaha, NE 68134
marylou@lord-of-love.org

- -

Please send me _____ copies of:
Taste and See that the Lord is good ~ Psalm 34:8
at **$18.00** plus **$5.00** for s/h per book.
Enclosed is my check or money order for $_____.

Mail Books To:

_____
Name

_____
Address

_____   _____   _____
City   State   Zip

- -

Please send me _____ copies of:
Taste and See that the Lord is good ~ Psalm 34:8
at **$18.00** plus **$5.00** for s/h per book.
Enclosed is my check or money order for $_____.

Mail Books To:

_____
Name

_____
Address

_____   _____   _____
City   State   Zip

121822-dl

PANTRY BASICS

A WELL-STOCKED PANTRY provides all the makings for a good meal. With the right ingredients, you can quickly create a variety of satisfying, delicious meals for family or guests. Keeping these items in stock also means avoiding extra trips to the grocery store, saving you time and money. Although everyone's pantry is different, there are basic items you should always have. Add other items according to your family's needs. For example, while some families consider chips, cereals and snacks as must-haves, others can't be without feta cheese and imported olives. Use these basic pantry suggestions as a handy reference list when creating your grocery list. Don't forget refrigerated items like milk, eggs, cheese and butter.

STAPLES

Baker's chocolate
Baking powder
Baking soda
Barbeque sauce
Bread crumbs (plain or seasoned)
Chocolate chips
Cocoa powder
Cornmeal
Cornstarch
Crackers
Flour
Honey
Ketchup
Lemon juice
Mayonnaise or salad dressing
Non-stick cooking spray
Nuts (almonds, pecans, walnuts)
Oatmeal
Oil (olive, vegetable)
Pancake baking mix
Pancake syrup
Peanut butter
Shortening
Sugar (granulated, brown, powdered)
Vinegar

PACKAGED/CANNED FOODS

Beans (canned, dry)
Broth (beef, chicken)
Cake mixes with frosting
Canned diced tomatoes
Canned fruit
Canned mushrooms
Canned soup
Canned tomato paste & sauce
Canned tuna & chicken
Cereal
Dried soup mix
Gelatin (flavored or plain)
Gravies
Jarred Salsa
Milk (evaporated, sweetened condensed)
Non-fat dry milk
Pastas
Rice (brown, white)
Spaghetti sauce

SPICES/SEASONINGS

Basil
Bay leaves
Black pepper
Bouillon cubes (beef, chicken)
Chives
Chili powder
Cinnamon
Mustard (dried, prepared)
Garlic powder or salt
Ginger
Nutmeg
Onion powder or salt
Oregano
Paprika
Parsley
Rosemary
Sage
Salt
Soy sauce
Tarragon
Thyme
Vanilla
Worcestershire sauce
Yeast

HERBS & SPICES

DRIED VS. FRESH. While dried herbs are convenient, they don't generally have the same purity of flavor as fresh herbs. Ensure dried herbs are still fresh by checking if they are green and not faded. Crush a few leaves to see if the aroma is still strong. Always store them in an air-tight container away from light and heat.

BASIL — Sweet, warm flavor with an aromatic odor. Use whole or ground. Good with lamb, fish, roast, stews, beef, vegetables, dressing and omelets.

BAY LEAVES — Pungent flavor. Use whole leaf but remove before serving. Good in vegetable dishes, seafood, stews and pickles.

CARAWAY — Spicy taste and aromatic smell. Use in cakes, breads, soups, cheese and sauerkraut.

CELERY SEED — Strong taste which resembles the vegetable. Can be used sparingly in pickles and chutney, meat and fish dishes, salads, bread, marinades, dressings and dips.

CHIVES — Sweet, mild flavor like that of onion. Excellent in salads, fish, soups and potatoes.

CILANTRO — Use fresh. Excellent in salads, fish, chicken, rice, beans and Mexican dishes.

CINNAMON — Sweet, pungent flavor. Widely used in many sweet baked goods, chocolate dishes, cheesecakes, pickles, chutneys and hot drinks.

CORIANDER — Mild, sweet, orangy flavor and available whole or ground. Common in curry powders and pickling spice and also used in chutney, meat dishes, casseroles, Greek-style dishes, apple pies and baked goods.

CURRY POWDER — Spices are combined to proper proportions to give a distinct flavor to meat, poultry, fish and vegetables.

DILL — Both seeds and leaves are flavorful. Leaves may be used as a garnish or cooked with fish, soup, dressings, potatoes and beans. Leaves or the whole plant may be used to flavor pickles.

FENNEL — Sweet, hot flavor. Both seeds and leaves are used. Use in small quantities in pies and baked goods. Leaves can be boiled with fish.

DILL
Seeds

HERBS & SPICES

GINGER
A pungent root, this aromatic spice is sold fresh, dried or ground. Use in pickles, preserves, cakes, cookies, soups and meat dishes.

MARJORAM
May be used both dried or green. Use to flavor fish, poultry, omelets, lamb, stew, stuffing and tomato juice.

MINT
Aromatic with a cool flavor. Excellent in beverages, fish, lamb, cheese, soup, peas, carrots and fruit desserts.

NUTMEG
Whole or ground. Used in chicken and cream soups, cheese dishes, fish cakes, and with chicken and veal. Excellent in custards, milk puddings, pies and cakes.

OREGANO
Strong, aromatic odor. Use whole or ground in tomato juice, fish, eggs, pizza, omelets, chili, stew, gravy, poultry and vegetables.

PAPRIKA
A bright red pepper, this spice is used in meat, vegetables and soups or as a garnish for potatoes, salads or eggs.

PARSLEY
Best when used fresh, but can be used dried as a garnish or as a seasoning. Try in fish, omelets, soup, meat, stuffing and mixed greens.

ROSEMARY
Very aromatic. Can be used fresh or dried. Season fish, stuffing, beef, lamb, poultry, onions, eggs, bread and potatoes. Great in dressings.

SAFFRON
Aromatic, slightly bitter taste. Only a pinch needed to flavor and color dishes such as bouillabaisse, chicken soup, rice, paella, fish sauces, buns and cakes. Very expensive, so where a touch of color is needed, use turmeric instead, but the flavor will not be the same.

SAGE
Use fresh or dried. The flowers are sometimes used in salads. May be used in tomato juice, fish, omelets, beef, poultry, stuffing, cheese spreads and breads.

TARRAGON
Leaves have a pungent, hot taste. Use to flavor sauces, salads, fish, poultry, tomatoes, eggs, green beans, carrots and dressings.

THYME
Sprinkle leaves on fish or poultry before broiling or baking. Throw a few sprigs directly on coals shortly before meat is finished grilling.

TURMERIC
Aromatic, slightly bitter flavor. Should be used sparingly in curry powder and relishes and to color cakes and rice dishes.

**Use 3 times more fresh herbs
if substituting fresh for dried.**

BAKING BREADS

HINTS FOR BAKING BREADS

• Kneading dough for 30 seconds after mixing improves the texture of baking powder biscuits.

• Instead of shortening, use cooking or salad oil in waffles and hot cakes.

• When bread is baking, a small dish of water in the oven will help keep the crust from hardening.

• Dip a spoon in hot water to measure shortening, butter, etc., and the fat will slip out more easily.

• Small amounts of leftover corn may be added to pancake batter for variety.

• To make bread crumbs, use the fine cutter of a food grinder and tie a large paper bag over the spout in order to prevent flying crumbs.

• When you are doing any sort of baking, you get better results if you remember to preheat your cookie sheet, muffin tins or cake pans.

3 RULES FOR USE OF LEAVENING AGENTS

1. In simple flour mixtures, use 2 teaspoons baking powder to leaven 1 cup flour. Reduce this amount 1/2 teaspoon for each egg used.

2. To 1 teaspoon soda, use 2 1/4 teaspoons cream of tartar, 2 cups freshly soured milk or 1 cup molasses.

3. To substitute soda and an acid for baking powder, divide the amount of baking powder by 4. Take that as your measure and add acid according to rule 2.

PROPORTIONS OF BAKING POWDER TO FLOUR

biscuits ....to 1 cup flour use 1 1/4 tsp. baking powder
cake with oil ....to 1 cup flour use 1 tsp. baking powder
muffins ....to 1 cup flour use 1 1/2 tsp. baking powder
popovers ....to 1 cup flour use 1 1/4 tsp. baking powder
waffles ....to 1 cup flour use 1 1/4 tsp. baking powder

PROPORTIONS OF LIQUID TO FLOUR

pour batter ....to 1 cup liquid use 1 cup flour
drop batter ....to 1 cup liquid use 2 to 2 1/2 cups flour
soft dough ....to 1 cup liquid use 3 to 3 1/2 cups flour
stiff dough ....to 1 cup liquid use 4 cups flour

TIME & TEMPERATURE CHART

Breads	Minutes	Temperature
biscuits	12 - 15	400° - 450°
cornbread	25 - 30	400° - 425°
gingerbread	40 - 50	350° - 370°
loaf	50 - 60	350° - 400°
nut bread	50 - 75	350°
popovers	30 - 40	425° - 450°
rolls	20 - 30	400° - 450°

PERFECT COOKIES

Cookie dough that must be rolled is much easier to handle after it has been refrigerated for 10 to 30 minutes. This keeps the dough from sticking, even though it may be soft. If not done, the soft dough may require more flour and too much flour makes cookies hard and brittle. Place on a floured board only as much dough as can be easily managed. Flour the rolling pin slightly and roll lightly to desired thickness. Cut shapes close together and add trimmings to dough that needs to be rolled. Place pans or sheets in upper third of oven. Watch cookies carefully while baking in order to avoid burned edges. When sprinkling sugar on cookies, try putting it into a salt shaker in order to save time.

PERFECT PIES

• Pie crust will be better and easier to make if all the ingredients are cool.

• The lower crust should be placed in the pan so that it covers the surface smoothly. Air pockets beneath the surface will push the crust out of shape while baking.

• Folding the top crust over the lower crust before crimping will keep juices in the pie.

• When making custard pie, bake at a high temperature for about 10 minutes to prevent a soggy crust. Then finish baking at a low temperature.

• When making cream pie, sprinkle crust with powdered sugar in order to prevent it from becoming soggy.

PERFECT CAKES

• Fill cake pans two-thirds full and spread batter into corners and sides, leaving a slight hollow in the center.

• Cake is done when it shrinks from the sides of the pan or if it springs back when touched lightly with the finger.

• After removing a cake from the oven, place it on a rack for about 5 minutes. Then, the sides should be loosened and the cake turned out on a rack in order to finish cooling.

• Do not frost cakes until thoroughly cool.

• Icing will remain where you put it if you sprinkle cake with powdered sugar first.

TIME & TEMPERATURE CHART

Dessert	Time	Temperature
butter cake, layer	20-40 min.	380° - 400°
butter cake, loaf	40-60 min.	360° - 400°
cake, angel	50-60 min.	300° - 360°
cake, fruit	3-4 hrs.	275° - 325°
cake, sponge	40-60 min.	300° - 350°
cookies, molasses	18-20 min.	350° - 375°
cookies, thin	10-12 min.	380° - 390°
cream puffs	45-60 min.	300° - 350°
meringue	40-60 min.	250° - 300°
pie crust	20-40 min.	400° - 500°

VEGETABLES & FRUITS

COOKING TIME TABLE

Vegetable	Cooking Method	Time
artichokes	boiled	40 min.
	steamed	45-60 min.
asparagus tips	boiled	10-15 min.
beans, lima	boiled	20-40 min.
	steamed	60 min.
beans, string	boiled	15-35 min.
	steamed	60 min.
beets, old	boiled or steamed	1-2 hours.
beets, young with skin	boiled	30 min.
	steamed	60 min.
	baked	70-90 min.
broccoli, flowerets	boiled	5-10 min.
broccoli, stems	boiled	20-30 min.
brussels sprouts	boiled	20-30 min.
cabbage, chopped	boiled	10-20 min.
	steamed	25 min.
carrots, cut across	boiled	8-10 min.
	steamed	40 min.
cauliflower, flowerets	boiled	8-10 min.
cauliflower, stem down	boiled	20-30 min.
corn, green, tender	boiled	5-10 min.
	steamed	15 min.
	baked	20 min.
corn on the cob	boiled	8-10 min.
	steamed	15 min.
eggplant, whole	boiled	30 min.
	steamed	40 min.
	baked	45 min.
parsnips	boiled	25-40 min.
	steamed	60 min.
	baked	60-75 min.
peas, green	boiled or steamed	5-15 min.
potatoes	boiled	20-40 min.
	steamed	60 min.
	baked	45-60 min.
pumpkin or squash	boiled	20-40 min.
	steamed	45 min.
	baked	60 min.
tomatoes	boiled	5-15 min.
turnips	boiled	25-40 min.

DRYING TIME TABLE

Fruit	Sugar or Honey	Cooking Time
apricots	1/4 c. for each cup of fruit	about 40 min.
figs	1 T. for each cup of fruit	about 30 min.
peaches	1/4 c. for each cup of fruit	about 45 min.
prunes	2 T. for each cup of fruit	about 45 min.

VEGETABLES & FRUITS

BUYING FRESH VEGETABLES

Artichokes: Look for compact, tightly closed heads with green, clean-looking leaves. Avoid those with leaves that are brown or separated.

Asparagus: Stalks should be tender and firm; tips should be close and compact. Choose the stalks with very little white; they are more tender. Use asparagus soon because it toughens quickly.

Beans, Snap: Those with small seeds inside the pods are best. Avoid beans with dry-looking pods.

Broccoli, Brussels Sprouts and Cauliflower: Flower clusters on broccoli and cauliflower should be tight and close together. Brussels sprouts should be firm and compact. Smudgy, dirty spots may indicate pests or disease.

Cabbage and Head Lettuce: Choose heads that are heavy for their size. Avoid cabbage with worm holes and lettuce with discoloration or soft rot.

Cucumbers: Choose long, slender cucumbers for best quality. May be dark or medium green, but yellow ones are undesirable.

Mushrooms: Caps should be closed around the stems. Avoid black or brown gills.

Peas and Lima Beans: Select pods that are well-filled but not bulging. Avoid dried, spotted, yellow or limp pods.

BUYING FRESH FRUITS

Bananas: Skin should be free of bruises and black or brown spots. Purchase them slightly green and allow them to ripen at room temperature.

Berries: Select plump, solid berries with good color. Avoid stained containers which indicate wet or leaky berries. Berries with clinging caps, such as blackberries and raspberries, may be unripe. Strawberries without caps may be overripe.

Melons: In cantaloupes, thick, close netting on the rind indicates best quality. Cantaloupes are ripe when the stem scar is smooth and the space between the netting is yellow or yellow-green. They are best when fully ripe with fruity odor.

Honeydews are ripe when rind has creamy to yellowish color and velvety texture. Immature honeydews are whitish-green.

Ripe watermelons have some yellow color on one side. If melons are white or pale green on one side, they are not ripe.

Oranges, Grapefruit and Lemons: Choose those heavy for their size. Smoother, thinner skins usually indicate more juice. Most skin markings do not affect quality. Oranges with a slight greenish tinge may be just as ripe as fully colored ones. Light or greenish-yellow lemons are more tart than deep yellow ones. Avoid citrus fruits showing withered, sunken or soft areas.

NAPKIN FOLDING

FOR BEST RESULTS, use well-starched linen napkins if possible. For more complicated folds, 24-inch napkins work best. Practice the folds with newspapers. Children will have fun decorating the table once they learn these attractive folds!

SHIELD

Easy fold. Elegant with monogram in corner.

Instructions:
1. Fold into quarter size. If monogrammed, ornate corner should face down.
2. Turn up folded corner three-quarters.
3. Overlap right side and left side points.
4. Turn over; adjust sides so they are even, single point in center.
5. Place point up or down on plate, or left of plate.

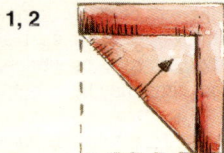

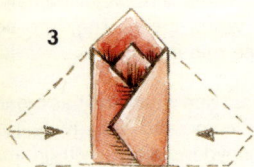

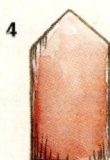

ROSETTE

Elegant on plate.

Instructions:
1. Fold left and right edges to center, leaving ½" opening along center.
2. Pleat firmly from top edge to bottom edge. Sharpen edges with hot iron.
3. Pinch center together. If necessary, use small piece of pipe cleaner to secure and top with single flower.
4. Spread out rosette.

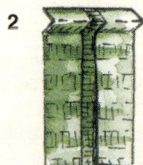

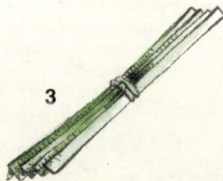

NAPKIN FOLDING

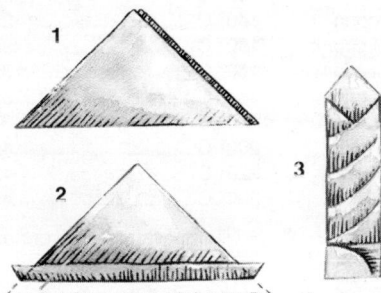

CANDLE

Easy to do; can be decorated.

Instructions:
1. Fold into triangle, point at top.
2. Turn lower edge up 1".
3. Turn over, folded edge down.
4. Roll tightly from left to right.
5. Tuck in corner. Stand upright.

FAN

Pretty in napkin ring or on plate.

Instructions:
1. Fold top and bottom edges to center.
2. Fold top and bottom edges to center a second time.
3. Pleat firmly from the left edge. Sharpen edges with hot iron.
4. Spread out fan. Balance flat folds of each side on table. Well-starched napkins will hold shape.

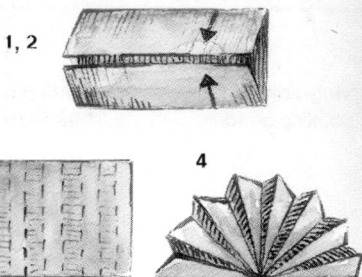

LILY

Effective and pretty on table.

Instructions:
1. Fold napkin into quarters.
2. Fold into triangle, closed corner to open points.
3. Turn two points over to other side. (Two points are on either side of closed point.)
4. Pleat.
5. Place closed end in glass. Pull down two points on each side and shape.

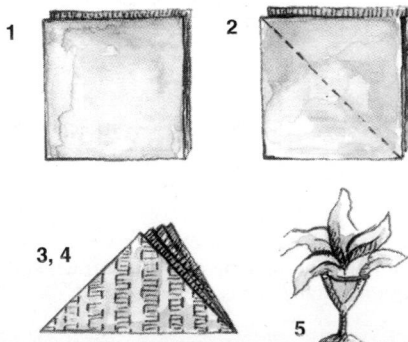

MEASUREMENTS & SUBSTITUTIONS

MEASUREMENTS

a pinch	1/8 teaspoon or less
3 teaspoons	1 tablespoon
4 tablespoons	1/4 cup
8 tablespoons	1/2 cup
12 tablespoons	3/4 cup
16 tablespoons	1 cup
2 cups	1 pint
4 cups	1 quart
4 quarts	1 gallon
8 quarts	1 peck
4 pecks	1 bushel
16 ounces	1 pound
32 ounces	1 quart
1 ounce liquid	2 tablespoons
8 ounces liquid	1 cup

Use standard measuring spoons and cups. All measurements are level.

C° TO F° CONVERSION

120° C	250° F
140° C	275° F
150° C	300° F
160° C	325° F
180° C	350° F
190° C	375° F
200° C	400° F
220° C	425° F
230° C	450° F

Temperature conversions are estimates.

SUBSTITUTIONS

Ingredient	Quantity	Substitute
baking powder	1 teaspoon	1/4 tsp. baking soda plus 1/2 tsp. cream of tartar
chocolate	1 square (1 oz.)	3 or 4 T. cocoa plus 1 T. butter
cornstarch	1 tablespoon	2 T. flour or 2 tsp. quick-cooking tapioca
cracker crumbs	3/4 cup	1 c. bread crumbs
dates	1 lb.	1 1/2 c. dates, pitted and cut
dry mustard	1 teaspoon	1 T. prepared mustard
flour, self-rising	1 cup	1 c. all-purpose flour, 1/2 tsp. salt, and 1 tsp. baking powder
herbs, fresh	1 tablespoon	1 tsp. dried herbs
ketchup or chili sauce	1 cup	1 c. tomato sauce plus 1/2 c. sugar and 2 T. vinegar (for use in cooking)
milk, sour	1 cup	1 T. lemon juice or vinegar plus sweet milk to make 1 c. (let stand 5 minutes)
whole	1 cup	1/2 c. evaporated milk plus 1/2 c. water
min. marshmallows	10	1 lg. marshmallow
onion, fresh	1 small	1 T. instant minced onion, rehydrated
sugar, brown	1/2 cup	2 T. molasses in 1/2 c. granulated sugar
powdered	1 cup	1 c. granulated sugar plus 1 tsp. cornstarch
tomato juice	1 cup	1/2 c. tomato sauce plus 1/2 c. water

When substituting cocoa for chocolate in cakes, the amount of flour must be reduced. Brown and white sugars usually can be interchanged.

SUGAR

EQUIVALENCY CHART

Food	Quantity	Yield
apple	1 medium	1 cup
banana, mashed	1 medium	1/3 cup
bread	1 1/2 slices	1 cup soft crumbs
bread	1 slice	1/4 cup fine, dry crumbs
butter	1 stick or 1/4 pound	1/2 cup
cheese, American, cubed	1 pound	2 2/3 cups
American, grated	1 pound	5 cups
cream cheese	3-ounce package	6 2/3 tablespoons
chocolate, bitter	1 square	1 ounce
cocoa	1 pound	4 cups
coconut	1 1/2 pound package	2 2/3 cups
coffee, ground	1 pound	5 cups
cornmeal	1 pound	3 cups
cornstarch	1 pound	3 cups
crackers, graham	14 squares	1 cup fine crumbs
saltine	28 crackers	1 cup fine crumbs
egg	4-5 whole	1 cup
whites	8-10	1 cup
yolks	10-12	1 cup
evaporated milk	1 cup	3 cups whipped
flour, cake, sifted	1 pound	4 1/2 cups
rye	1 pound	5 cups
white, sifted	1 pound	4 cups
white, unsifted	1 pound	3 3/4 cups
gelatin, flavored	3 1/4 ounces	1/2 cup
unflavored	1/4 ounce	1 tablespoon
lemon	1 medium	3 tablespoon juice
marshmallows	16	1/4 pound
noodles, cooked	8-ounce package	7 cups
uncooked	4 ounces (1 1/2 cups)	2-3 cups cooked
macaroni, cooked	8-ounce package	6 cups
macaroni, uncooked	4 ounces (1 1/4 cups)	2 1/4 cups cooked
spaghetti, uncooked	7 ounces	4 cups cooked
nuts, chopped	1/4 pound	1 cup
almonds	1 pound	3 1/2 cups
walnuts, broken	1 pound	3 cups
walnuts, unshelled	1 pound	1 1/2 to 1 3/4 cups
onion	1 medium	1/2 cup
orange	3-4 medium	1 cup juice
raisins	1 pound	3 1/2 cups
rice, brown	1 cup	4 cups cooked
converted	1 cup	3 1/2 cups cooked
regular	1 cup	3 cups cooked
wild	1 cup	4 cups cooked
sugar, brown	1 pound	2 1/2 cups
powdered	1 pound	3 1/2 cups
white	1 pound	2 cups
vanilla wafers	22	1 cup fine crumbs
zwieback, crumbled	4	1 cup

FOOD QUANTITIES

FOR LARGE SERVINGS

	25 Servings	50 Servings	100 Servings
Beverages:			
coffee	½ pound and 1 ½ gallons water	1 pound and 3 gallons water	2 pounds and 6 gallons water
lemonade	10-15 lemons and 1 ½ gallons water	20-30 lemons and 3 gallons water	40-60 lemons and 6 gallons water
tea	1/12 pound and 1 ½ gallons water	1/6 pound and 3 gallons water	1/3 pound and 6 gallons water
Desserts:			
layered cake	1 12" cake	3 10" cakes	6 10" cakes
sheet cake	1 10" x 12" cake	1 12" x 20" cake	2 12" x 20" cakes
watermelon	37 ½ pounds	75 pounds	150 pounds
whipping cream	¾ pint	1 ½ to 2 pints	3-4 pints
Ice cream:			
brick	3 ¼ quarts	6 ½ quarts	13 quarts
bulk	2 ¼ quarts	4 ½ quarts or 1 ¼ gallons	9 quarts or 2 ½ gallons
Meat, poultry or fish:			
fish	13 pounds	25 pounds	50 pounds
fish, fillets or steak	7 ½ pounds	15 pounds	30 pounds
hamburger	9 pounds	18 pounds	35 pounds
turkey or chicken	13 pounds	25 to 35 pounds	50 to 75 pounds
wieners (beef)	6 ½ pounds	13 pounds	25 pounds
Salads, casseroles:			
baked beans	¾ gallon	1 ¼ gallons	2 ½ gallons
jello salad	¾ gallon	1 ¼ gallons	2 ½ gallons
potato salad	4 ¼ quarts	2 ¼ gallons	4 ½ gallons
scalloped potatoes	4 ½ quarts or 1 12" x 20" pan	9 quarts or 2 ¼ gallons	18 quarts 4 ½ gallons
spaghetti	1 ¼ gallons	2 ½ gallons	5 gallons
Sandwiches:			
bread	50 slices or 3 1-pound loaves	100 slices or 6 1-pound loaves	200 slices or 12 1-pound loaves
butter	½ pound	1 pound	2 pounds
lettuce	1 ½ heads	3 heads	6 heads
mayonnaise	1 cup	2 cups	4 cups
mixed filling			
meat, eggs, fish	1 ½ quarts	3 quarts	6 quarts
jam, jelly	1 quart	2 quarts	4 quarts

QUICK FIXES

PRACTICALLY EVERYONE has experienced that dreadful moment in the kitchen when a recipe failed and dinner guests have arrived. Perhaps a failed timer, distraction or a missing or mismeasured ingredient is to blame. These handy tips can save the day!

Acidic foods – Sometimes a tomato-based sauce will become too acidic. Add baking soda, one teaspoon at a time, to the sauce. Use sugar as a sweeter alternative.

Burnt food on pots and pans – Allow the pan to cool on its own. Remove as much of the food as possible. Fill with hot water and add a capful of liquid fabric softener to the pot; let it stand for a few hours. You'll have an easier time removing the burnt food.

Chocolate seizes – Chocolate can seize (turn coarse and grainy) when it comes into contact with water. Place seized chocolate in a metal bowl over a large saucepan with an inch of simmering water in it. Over medium heat, slowly whisk in warm heavy cream. Use 1/4 cup cream to 4 ounces of chocolate. The chocolate will melt and become smooth.

Forgot to thaw whipped topping – Thaw in microwave for 1 minute on the defrost setting. Stir to blend well. Do not over thaw!

Hands smell like garlic or onion – Rinse hands under cold water while rubbing them with a large stainless steel spoon.

Hard brown sugar – Place in a paper bag and microwave for a few seconds, or place hard chunks in a food processor.

Jello too hard – Heat on a low microwave power setting for a very short time.

Lumpy gravy or sauce – Use a blender, food processor or simply strain.

No tomato juice – Mix 1/2 cup ketchup with 1/2 cup water.

Out of honey – Substitute 1 1/4 cups sugar dissolved in 1 cup water.

Overcooked sweet potatoes or carrots – Softened sweet potatoes and carrots make a wonderful soufflé with the addition of eggs and sugar. Consult your favorite cookbook for a good soufflé recipe. Overcooked sweet potatoes can also be used as pie filling.

Sandwich bread is stale – Toast or microwave bread briefly. Otherwise, turn it into breadcrumbs. Bread exposed to light and heat will hasten its demise, so consider using a bread box.

Soup, sauce, gravy too thin – Add 1 tablespoon of flour to hot soup, sauce or gravy. Whisk well (to avoid lumps) while the mixture is boiling. Repeat if necessary.

Sticky rice – Rinse rice with warm water.

Stew or soup is greasy – Refrigerate and remove grease once it congeals. Another trick is to lay cold lettuce leaves over the hot stew for about 10 seconds and then remove. Repeat as necessary.

Too salty – Add a little sugar and vinegar. For soups or sauces, add a raw peeled potato.

Too sweet – Add a little vinegar or lemon juice.

Undercooked cakes and cookies – Serve over vanilla ice cream. You can also layer pieces of cake or cookies with whipped cream and fresh fruit to form a dessert parfait. Crumbled cookies also make an excellent ice cream or cream pie topping.

COUNTING CALORIES

BEVERAGES

apple juice, 6 oz.	90
coffee (black)	0
cola, 12 oz.	115
cranberry juice, 6 oz.	115
ginger ale, 12 oz.	115
grape juice, (prepared from frozen concentrate), 6 oz.	142
lemonade, (prepared from frozen concentrate), 6 oz.	85
milk, protein fortified, 1 c.	105
skim, 1 c.	90
whole, 1 c.	160
orange juice, 6 oz.	85
pineapple juice, unsweetened, 6 oz.	95
root beer, 12 oz.	150
tonic (quinine water) 12 oz.	132

BREADS

cornbread, 1 sm. square	130
dumplings, 1 med.	70
French toast, 1 slice	135
melba toast, 1 slice	25
muffins, blueberry, 1 muffin	110
bran, 1 muffin	106
corn, 1 muffin	125
English, 1 muffin	280
pancakes, 1 (4-in.)	60
pumpernickel, 1 slice	75
rye, 1 slice	60
waffle, 1	216
white, 1 slice	60-70
whole wheat, 1 slice	55-65

CEREALS

cornflakes, 1 c.	105
cream of wheat, 1 c.	120
oatmeal, 1 c.	148
rice flakes, 1 c.	105
shredded wheat, 1 biscuit	100
sugar krisps, 3/4 c.	110

CRACKERS

graham, 1 cracker	15-30
rye crisp, 1 cracker	35
saltine, 1 cracker	17-20
wheat thins, 1 cracker	9

DAIRY PRODUCTS

butter or margarine, 1 T.	100
cheese, American, 1 oz.	100
camembert, 1 oz.	85
cheddar, 1 oz.	115
cottage cheese, 1 oz.	30
mozzarella, 1 oz.	90
parmesan, 1 oz.	130
ricotta, 1 oz.	50
roquefort, 1 oz.	105
Swiss, 1 oz.	105
cream, light, 1 T.	30
heavy, 1 T.	55
sour, 1 T.	45
hot chocolate, with milk, 1 c.	277
milk chocolate, 1 oz.	145-155
yogurt	
made w/ whole milk, 1 c.	150-165
made w/ skimmed milk, 1 c.	125

EGGS

fried, 1 lg.	100
poached or boiled, 1 lg.	75-80
scrambled or in omelet, 1 lg.	110-130

FISH AND SEAFOOD

bass, 4 oz.	105
salmon, broiled or baked, 3 oz.	155
sardines, canned in oil, 3 oz.	170
trout, fried, 3 1/2 oz.	220
tuna, in oil, 3 oz.	170
in water, 3 oz.	110

COUNTING CALORIES

FRUITS

apple, 1 med. 80-100
applesauce, sweetened, ½ c. 90-115
   unsweetened, ½ c. 50
banana, 1 med. 85
blueberries, ½ c. 45
cantaloupe, ½ c. 24
cherries (pitted), raw, ½ c. 40
grapefruit, ½ med. 55
grapes, ½ c. 35-55
honeydew, ½ c. 55
mango, 1 med. 90
orange, 1 med. 65-75
peach, 1 med. 35
pear, 1 med. 60-100
pineapple, fresh, ½ c. 40
   canned in syrup, ½ c. 95
plum, 1 med. 30
strawberries, fresh, ½ c. 30
   frozen and sweetened, ½ c. ..120-140
tangerine, 1 lg. 39
watermelon, ½ c. 42

MEAT AND POULTRY

beef, ground (lean), 3 oz. 185
   roast, 3 oz. 185
chicken, broiled, 3 oz. 115
lamb chop (lean), 3 oz. 175-200
steak, sirloin, 3 oz. 175
   tenderloin, 3 oz. 174
   top round, 3 oz. 162
turkey, dark meat, 3 oz. 175
   white meat, 3 oz. 150
veal, cutlet, 3 oz. 156
   roast, 3 oz. 76

NUTS

almonds, 2 T. 105
cashews, 2 T. 100
peanuts, 2 T. 105
peanut butter, 1 T. 95
pecans, 2 T. 95
pistachios, 2 T. 92
walnuts, 2 T. 80

PASTA

macaroni or spaghetti,
   cooked, ¾ c. 115

SALAD DRESSINGS

blue cheese, 1 T. 70
French, 1 T. 65
Italian, 1 T. 80
mayonnaise, 1 T. 100
olive oil, 1 T. 124
Russian, 1 T. 70
salad oil, 1 T. 120

SOUPS

bean, 1 c. 130-180
beef noodle, 1 c. 70
bouillon and consomme, 1 c. 30
chicken noodle, 1 c. 65
chicken with rice, 1 c. 50
minestrone, 1 c. 80-150
split pea, 1 c. 145-170
tomato with milk, 1 c. 170
vegetable, 1 c. 80-100

VEGETABLES

asparagus, 1 c. 35
broccoli, cooked, ½ c. 25
cabbage, cooked, ½ c. 15-20
carrots, cooked, ½ c. 25-30
cauliflower, ½ c. 10-15
corn (kernels), ½ c. 70
green beans, ½ c. 30
lettuce, shredded, ½ c. 5
mushrooms, canned, ½ c. 20
onions, cooked, ½ c. 30
peas, cooked, ½ c. 60
potato, baked, 1 med. 90
   chips, 8-10 100
   mashed, w/milk & butter, 1 c. ..200-300
spinach, 1 c. 40
tomato, raw, 1 med. 25
   cooked, ½ c. 30

COOKING TERMS

Au gratin: Topped with crumbs and/or cheese and browned in oven or under broiler.

Au jus: Served in its own juices.

Baste: To moisten foods during cooking with pan drippings or special sauce in order to add flavor and prevent drying.

Bisque: A thick cream soup.

Blanch: To immerse in rapidly boiling water and allow to cook slightly.

Cream: To soften a fat, especially butter, by beating it at room temperature. Butter and sugar are often creamed together, making a smooth, soft paste.

Crimp: To seal the edges of a two-crust pie either by pinching them at intervals with the fingers or by pressing them together with the tines of a fork.

Crudites: An assortment of raw vegetables (i.e. carrots, broccoli, celery, mushrooms) that is served as an hors d'oeuvre, often accompanied by a dip.

Degrease: To remove fat from the surface of stews, soups or stock. Usually cooled in the refrigerator so that fat hardens and is easily removed.

Dredge: To coat lightly with flour, cornmeal, etc.

Entree: The main course.

Fold: To incorporate a delicate substance, such as whipped cream or beaten egg whites, into another substance without releasing air bubbles. A spatula is used to gently bring part of the mixture from the bottom of the bowl to the top. The process is repeated, while slowly rotating the bowl, until the ingredients are thoroughly blended.

Glaze: To cover with a glossy coating, such as a melted and somewhat diluted jelly for fruit desserts.

Julienne: To cut or slice vegetables, fruits or cheeses into match-shaped slivers.

Marinate: To allow food to stand in a liquid in order to tenderize or to add flavor.

Meuniére: Dredged with flour and sautéed in butter.

Mince: To chop food into very small pieces.

Parboil: To boil until partially cooked; to blanch. Usually final cooking in a seasoned sauce follows this procedure.

Pare: To remove the outermost skin of a fruit or vegetable.

Poach: To cook gently in hot liquid kept just below the boiling point.

Purée: To mash foods by hand by rubbing through a sieve or food mill, or by whirling in a blender or food processor until perfectly smooth.

Refresh: To run cold water over food that has been parboiled in order to stop the cooking process quickly.

Sauté: To cook and/or brown food in a small quantity of hot shortening.

Scald: To heat to just below the boiling point, when tiny bubbles appear at the edge of the saucepan.

Simmer: To cook in liquid just below the boiling point. The surface of the liquid should be barely moving, broken from time to time by slowly rising bubbles.

Steep: To let food stand in hot liquid in order to extract or to enhance flavor, like tea in hot water or poached fruit in syrup.

Toss: To combine ingredients with a repeated lifting motion.

Whip: To beat rapidly in order to incorporate air and produce expansion, as in heavy cream or egg whites.